VOICES

UPPER INTERMEDIATE

DANIEL BARBER AND MAREK KICZKOWIAK

NATIONAL GEOGRAPHIC
LEARNING

Australia · Brazil · Canada · Mexico · Singapore · United Kingdom · United States

National Geographic Learning,
a Cengage Company

**Voices Upper Intermediate Student's Book,
1st Edition**
Daniel Barber and Marek Kiczkowiak

Publisher: Rachael Gibbon

Commissioning Editor: Kayleigh Buller

Development Editor: Laura Brant

Director of Global Marketing: Ian Martin

Product Marketing Manager: Caitlin Thomas

Heads of Regional Marketing:

  Charlotte Ellis (Europe, Middle East and Africa)

  Irina Pereyra (Latin America)

  Justin Kaley (Asia)

  Joy MacFarland (US and Canada)

Production Manager: Daisy Sosa

Media Researcher: Leila Hishmeh

Art Director: Brenda Carmichael

Operations Support: Hayley Chwazik-Gee

Manufacturing Manager: Eyvett Davis

Composition: Composure

Audio Producer: James Richardson

Contributing writer: Kelly Sanabria (Endmatter)

Advisors: Anna Blackmore, Bruna Caltabiano,
  Dale Coulter and Mike Sayer

For permission to use material from this text or product,
submit all requests online at **cengage.com/permissions**
Further permissions questions can be emailed to
permissionrequest@cengage.com

Student's Book with Online Practice and Student's eBook:
ISBN: 978-0-357-45871-6

Student's Book:
ISBN: 978-0-357-44337-8

National Geographic Learning
Cheriton House, North Way,
Andover, Hampshire, SP10 5BE
United Kingdom

Locate your local office at **international.cengage.com/region**

Visit National Geographic Learning online at **ELTNGL.com**
Visit our corporate website at **www.cengage.com**

Printed in Greece by Bakis SA
Print Number: 01 Print Year: 2021

Contents

Scope and sequence

		GRAMMAR AND 'FOCUS ON'	VOCABULARY	PRONUNCIATION
1 **Reactions** *Pages 10-21*		forming questions; adverbs of degree	emotions	using stress for emphasis (1); pronouncing short and long vowels
2 **Language and communication** *Pages 22-33*		present tenses; separable and inseparable phrasal verbs	phrasal verbs for communication	understanding weak forms of auxiliary verbs; saying the /r/ sound
3 **Unfamiliar places** *Pages 34-45*		narrative tenses; travel collocations with *go on*	travel verbs	pronouncing groups of two or more consonants
4 **Reconnecting** *Pages 46-57*		reported speech and reporting verbs; transitive and intransitive phrasal verbs	verbs for relationships	using stress for emphasis (2); pronouncing long and short 'i'
5 **Healthy body, healthy mind** *Pages 58-69*	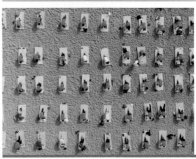	conditionals; *I wish ...* and *If only ...*	mental and physical health	understanding elision in connected speech; making vowels longer before voiced consonants

READING	LISTENING	WRITING	COMMUNICATION SKILL	CRITICAL THINKING	USEFUL LANGUAGE
an article about how sound affects us; identifying reasons	explorers talk about a memorable experience; inferring emotions	an informal email giving news; writing informal emails and messages	considering other people's emotions	evaluating evidence	expressing emotions; empathizing
an article about communication in the natural world; scanning and skimming	a podcast about English as a global language; identifying discourse markers	a formal email enquiry; organizing formal emails	building relationships using your first language identity	identifying the main message	talking about your first language identity; formal emails
a blog post about exploring your own city; active reading by annotating	an audiobook extract about Polynesian voyages; using visual information to help you listen	a blog post about travel; engaging the reader	fixing misunderstandings	ranking information	telling personal stories; fixing misunderstandings; making recommendations
an article about reconnecting with nature; summarizing	an interview about keeping in touch with friends and family; understanding accents	a story; making a story entertaining	adapting your turn-taking style	synthesizing information	taking turns
three success stories of projects tackling loneliness; identifying and understanding cause and effect	explorers talk about keeping mentally and physically fit; listening for keywords to understand the general meaning	a for and against essay; using discourse markers	adapting your English to be understood	distinguishing cause from correlation	essay introductions

Scope and sequence

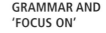

		GRAMMAR AND 'FOCUS ON'	VOCABULARY	PRONUNCIATION
6 Breaking news *Pages 70-81*		passive structures; *the ... the ...*	news and media	pronouncing consonant groups; pronouncing long vowels
7 Shared spaces *Pages 82-93*		causative verbs; useful structures for complaining	describing places	stressing multi-syllable verbs; pronouncing /b/, /v/, /w/
8 Incredible technology *Pages 94-105*		speculating about the past; forming nouns, verbs and adjectives	describing technology	understanding the weak form of *have*; pronouncing long and short 'o'
9 Against all odds *Pages 106-117*		talking about the future; verb-noun collocations	success and failure	pausing; saying /ʃ/, /ʒ/, /tʃ/ and /dʒ/
10 A world of cultures *Pages 118-129*		verb patterns with infinitive and *-ing*; *the* with groups of people and things	cultural identity	aspirating /p/, /k/ and /t/; saying *th*

READING	LISTENING	WRITING	COMMUNICATION SKILL	CRITICAL THINKING	USEFUL LANGUAGE
an article about fake images online; identifying unsupported claims	explorers talk about how they get their news; understanding connected speech: catenation	a news article; choosing your writing style	influencing styles	fact-checking online information	influencing people; being careful and objective
an article about an elephant programme in Mozambique; dealing with unknown words	an interview with a cave photographer; identifying figurative language	social media posts; using informal language in social media posts	dealing with difficult conversations	analysing solutions to problems	solving problems; softening the message
an article about science-fiction technology; recognizing synonyms and antonyms	a radio phone-in about a new app service; understanding prepositions in connected speech	a product review; multi-word adjectives	communicating online	examining writer assumptions behind texts	product reviews
four stories of people who have succeeded against the odds; making inferences about a writer's opinion	two anecdotes about learning from failures; understanding contrasts	a job application email; what to include in a job application email	adapting to direct and indirect communication styles	recognizing other perspectives	talking about the future; adapting to different communication styles; job application emails
a travel article about the music of Colombia; identifying figurative language in creative writing	an interview about cultural identity; understanding ellipsis in spoken language	a report about cultural attractions; expressing numbers approximately	dealing with assumptions	evaluating the relationship between text and supporting media	expressing numbers approximately

Meet the explorers

ABBY MCBRIDE

Lives: US
Job: I'm a sketch biologist – this means I study wildlife and draw pictures of it. I travel all over the world and write and illustrate stories about my adventures in ecology and conservation.
If you weren't doing this job what would you be doing? I might have focused on music professionally, and I might still do that in the future.
Find Abby: Unit 7

ANDREJ GAJIĆ

Lives: Bosnia
Job: I'm a shark research scientist – this means I work in the conservation of sharks and study the diseases caused by sea pollution in the Mediterranean and other marine environments. I'm also an author, underwater photographer, parachutist and pilot of remotely operated underwater vehicles.
Describe yourself in three words: Committed, enthusiastic, focused
Find Andrej: Unit 3

AFROZ SHAH

Lives: Brunei
Job: I'm a geologist – this means I am interested in everything that makes up the Earth. I am currently trying to improve the geological maps of India, Pakistan, Borneo and New Guinea and identify where there might be earthquakes.
What languages do you speak? English, Kashmiri, Hindi and Urdu
Find Afroz: Unit 6

ARIANNA SOLDATI

Lives: Germany
Job: I am a volcanologist – this means I study volcanoes. As a National Geographic Young Explorer, I studied a volcano on La Réunion, a tiny island in the Indian Ocean. I'm also very involved in teaching people about science.
Describe yourself in three words: Curious, excited, happy
Find Arianna: Unit 2

ALEC JACOBSON

Lives: Canada
Job: I'm a journalist, photographer and adventurer. My goal is to shine a light on important issues and give a voice to the people who experience them first hand. I do that by taking photos and telling human stories.
What would you be doing if you weren't doing this job? My parents keep asking me that question!
Find Alec: Unit 5

CAROLINA CHONG MONTENEGRO

Lives: Australia
Job: I am a fisheries ecologist – this means I study fish and their environment. I am also doing research for my PhD at the University of Queensland. I'm studying a kind of grouper fish from the Tropical Eastern Pacific, which has become rare because of too much fishing.
Describe yourself in three words: Adventurous, funny, thoughtful
Find Carolina: Unit 4

ALYEA PIERCE

Lives: US
Job: I'm a performance poet and educator. I work with young people to help them find their voice through creative writing and theatre. As a black female writer, I am also interested in telling the stories that are not being told.
Where is 'home'? Home for me is anywhere close to nature and art.
Find Alyea: Unit 10

ELLIE DE CASTRO

Lives: Philippines
Job: I'm an archaeologist – this means I am interested in what we can learn about our own history from what we find in the ground. I spend most of my time thinking of ways to get children interested in learning about their own heritage through my National Geographic Young Explorer project, the Dewil Valley Community Museum and Ecotourism plan.
Describe yourself in three words: Friendly, persistent, passionate
Find Ellie: Unit 3

FEDERICO FANTI

Lives: Italy
Job: I'm a palaeontologist and geologist – this means I study the history of life on Earth, looking at fossils and rocks. I'm also a professor at the University of Bologna in Italy. I am interested in who lives, who dies, and most importantly: why?
Describe yourself in three words: Curious, stubborn, scientist
Find Federico: Unit 4

FRANCISCO ESTRADA-BELLI

Lives: US
Job: I'm an archaeologist – I explore the history of an area by digging up what people left behind. I search for ancient Maya cities using aerial laser mapping in the Maya Biosphere Reserve of Guatemala. I have written about the Maya civilization and I'm also a research professor at Tulane University in New Orleans.
Describe yourself in three words: Archaeologist, explorer, father
Find Francisco: Unit 1 and Unit 8

IMOGEN NAPPER

Lives: UK
Job: I'm a marine scientist – I study what happens in the sea. I specialize in plastic pollution. My work recently helped stop the use of microbeads in cosmetics all over the world. With National Geographic, I'm working to identify technology that can catch the tiny microplastic fibers that enter the water when clothes are washed.
What do you do to relax? Play my guitar (badly)!
Find Imogen: Unit 6

LIA NAHOMI KAJIKI

Lives: Brazil
Job: I'm an ornithologist – this means I study everything to do with birds. I'm trying to learn more about the habits of one of the many birds that live only in Cerrado, an area of Central Brazil. I'm also a PhD student in Ecology at the University of Brasilia.
What advice would you give someone who wants to explore the world? Don't do too much planning and be ready for surprises!
Find Lia: Unit 10

MARIA FADIMAN

Lives: US
Job: I'm a conservationist – this means that I'm trying to protect places, peoples and plants. I study the relationship between people and plants and I work mostly in rural areas with a special interest in the rainforests of Latin America. I am also a professor at Florida Atlantic University.
What do you miss when you are away from home? My family and my cats. And pizza.
Find Maria: Unit 2; Unit 5

NORA SHAWKI

Lives: Egypt
Job: I'm an archaeologist – this means I study people and places from the past. I spend my time digging and doing research. Now, I'm working in the Nile Delta in Egypt to try to protect areas that are being taken over by the modern world.
Describe yourself in three words: Goofy, curious and fun
Find Nora: Unit 8

PAOLA RODRÍGUEZ

Lives: Mexico
Job: I'm a coral reef researcher and diver – this means I spend my time studying how coral reefs are affected by global climate change and looking for ways to protect them from changes in sea temperature and human activity.
Do you have any fears? I am very afraid of snakes (and a bit scared of heights)!
Find Paola: Unit 9

ROBBIE SHONE

Lives: Austria
Job: I'm a photographer with a special interest in caves. I travel to remote parts of the world to photograph the deepest, darkest, largest and longest systems under the earth. I also work as an expert on National Geographic Student Expeditions and for film and television crews.
Describe yourself in three words: Shy, focused, helpful
Find Robbie: Unit 7; Unit 9

TSIORY ANDRIANAVALONA

Lives: Madagascar
Job: I'm a palaeontologist with a special interest in shark fossils. I co-founded an organization to inspire young people to take an interest in science and encourage the next generation to make positive change in Madagascar.
What do you always take with you when you travel? I have a 'travelling book' that I always take on a long trip. I keep a souvenir of each place I go.
Find Tsiory: Unit 1

People queue to participate in
'Inside Out: The People's Art Project'
by artist JR in Paris, France.

10

1

Reactions

GOALS

- Identify reasons in an article
- Review and practise asking questions
- Talk about strong emotions
- Infer emotions when listening
- Demonstrate empathy in a conversation
- Write an informal email giving news

1 Work in pairs. Look at the photo and complete the tasks.

1 Take turns to describe people in the photo. Can you guess who your partner is describing?
2 What do you think the artist is trying to show through the portraits?
3 Would you like to participate in a project like this?

WATCH ▶

2 ▶ 1.1 Watch the video. Which person, Francisco (F) or Tsiory (T), talks about feeling …

a annoyed?   c happy?
b excited?   d impatient?

NATIONAL GEOGRAPHIC EXPLORERS

**FRANCISCO   TSIORY
ESTRADA-BELLI   ANDRIANAVALONA**

3 ▶ 1.1 Watch the video again. Make notes about the reasons for Francisco and Tsiory's feelings.

4 Make connections. When do you feel the emotions that Francisco and Tsiory mention?

Unlike Francisco, I don't mind waiting in traffic. But I get impatient when …

1A
I can't stand that noise!

LESSON GOALS
- Identify reasons in an article
- Evaluate evidence in an article
- Talk about pleasing and annoying noises

SPEAKING

1 🎧 **1.1** Listen to ten sounds. Match the sounds with the descriptions (a-j).

a	a dentist's drill	f	bicycle brakes squealing
b	a fire crackling	g	birds singing
c	someone eating with their mouth open	h	rain on a tent
d	a workmate humming	i	thunder
e	a baby crying	j	water flowing in a stream

2 Which of the sounds are the most and least annoying? Order them from 1 to 10 (10 = the most annoying).

3 Work in groups. Discuss the questions.
1 Which sounds in Exercise 1 are the most and least popular among the group?
2 Can you think of reasons why some sounds are pleasant and some are annoying?

READING

4 Read the article on page 13 quickly. Work in pairs and discuss the questions.
1 Which sounds from Exercise 1 are mentioned?
2 Which fact did you find the most interesting?

5 Read the article again. Choose from the sentences (1–5) the one that best fits each space in the text (a–e).
1 Because long-term stress can lead to illness, noise pollution is a real danger to your health.
2 Next, high-pitched tools such as drills were extremely unpopular, perhaps because they remind people of visits to the dentist.
3 That's why unpleasant noises can cause strong emotional reactions.
4 One theory is that birds may be anxious due to an inability to listen out for danger.
5 A simpler explanation is that these sounds can be physically painful at close range.

6 Look at the Reading skill box. Then underline words in Exercise 5 that signal reasons.

READING SKILL
Identifying reasons

Identifying reasons helps you better understand the connection between ideas. Look for words and phrases such as *because (of)*, *since*, and *due to* to help you identify reasons. They may appear before or after the action or effect.

7 Write why the three types of sound in the final paragraph of the article might be pleasant.

8 Read the sentences from the article (a–d). Discuss which give strong evidence and which weaker evidence. Then look at the Critical thinking skill box to check.
a According to a survey of two thousand people, bird calls came in as the fifth most popular sound.
b One theory suggests that alarm calls our ancestors might have heard were made at these frequencies.
c Noise pollution ... is likely to cause serious health issues too.
d And there is a great deal of scientific research to show that noise causes stress.

CRITICAL THINKING SKILL
Evaluating evidence

Articles might refer to scientific studies, but it's important to recognize how strong the evidence is. Verbs such as *may*, *might*, *suggest* and *seem to* or adverbs such as *likely* and *probably* tell you that scientists are not 100% certain. While phrases such as *a great deal of scientific research* tell you the evidence is based on research, you should always check the original sources and be suspicious if no sources are provided.

SPEAKING

9 Work in groups. What types of background noises or music would you choose for these places and activities? Why?
1 grammar study   3 driving long distances
2 getting to sleep   4 going for a run

I'd choose the sound of rain for grammar study. It's really relaxing and might help me concentrate.

The world's
MOST
(and least)
annoying sounds

1 When people are asked what annoys them, it isn't surprising that many of the most irritating things have noises associated with them: people slapping their lips while eating, humming or tapping their fingers. Scientists

5 have used MRI technology to see what happens in the brain when we hear noises like these. They played people different sounds and studied the brain's activity. They found that the most annoying sounds affected the part of the brain that deals with emotions – the

10 amygdala. **a** ____

More interesting perhaps, is that most of the 'worst' sounds were within a specific frequency range, from 2,000 to 5,000 Hertz. Why might we be more sensitive to these high-pitched noises? One

15 theory suggests that alarm calls our ancestors might have heard were made at these frequencies.

20 They would have needed to jump into action after hearing the squeal of a monkey, for example, as it was likely to warn about danger close by. **b** ____

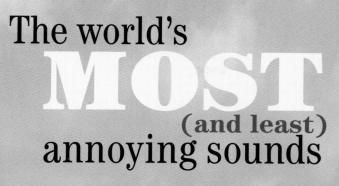

25 So what are the most annoying sounds? Well, according to the research, scraping sounds like nails on a blackboard or metal on glass were 'highly unpleasant'. **c** ____. Also in the top ten were two sounds that indicate pain and suffering of other people: a female scream and

30 a baby crying.

But some sounds aren't just unpleasant. Noise pollution, being exposed to loud sounds for long periods of time, is likely to cause serious health issues too. We often think of noise pollution as a problem of big cities.

35 Increasingly, however, it can also be found in suburban neighbourhoods, in the form of low-flying aircraft, barking dogs or garden machines, and within homes and workplaces – even your fridge makes a low hum. And there is a great deal of scientific research

40 to show that noise causes stress. **d** ____. It has been linked to heart disease, high blood pressure and poorer sleep quality.

Some people are more sensitive to noise than others.
45 People with autism sometimes find even normal noises unbearable and everyday sounds at home and in the street can cause pain and even panic. And it's not just humans that suffer. Birds living in areas with high levels of noise have been shown

50 to have increased levels of the stress hormone, corticosterone, resulting in smaller babies. **e** ____. Just the sound of human voices has been shown to result in greater stress levels of wild animals.

In contrast, one of the most pleasing noises to the
55 human ear is bird song. According to a survey of two thousand people, bird calls came in as the fifth most popular sound. The sounds of nature dominate the top fifty, especially water sounds, such as rain or waves crashing on rocks, and other weather sounds,

60 such as thunder. Also popular was food – the crunch of an apple, or popcorn popping, for example – and sounds like laughter and screams of delight on a roller coaster. The conclusion? If you're feeling stressed, the best

65 place to be is the countryside … or a theme park!

A low-flying plane over houses near Heathrow Airport, UK.

1B
Universal emotions?

LESSON GOALS
● Review and practise asking questions
● Use word stress to change the meaning of a sentence
● Design a questionnaire and report findings to the class

LISTENING AND GRAMMAR

1 Work in pairs. Discuss the questions.
1 Look at the infographic. What emotions do you think the different emoticons express?
2 Which parts of the face do you think express emotion most strongly: the eyes, nose or mouth?
3 Do you use emoticons and emojis? When? Which ones?

2 ∩ 1.2 Listen to a conversation between two friends. Are the sentences true (T) or false (F)?
1 Fatima doesn't think a smile has the same meaning for everyone on the planet.
2 Tomoya was surprised about how emoticons look in Europe.
3 People in different countries don't smile for different reasons.
4 Fatima sometimes smiles at strangers to be polite.

3 ∩ 1.2 Choose the correct option to complete the questions from the conversation. Then listen again to check.
1 Tomoya, you studied psychology, *did / didn't* you?
2 I'd like to know whether a smile *does mean / means* the same thing all over the world.
3 You've noticed, *you have / haven't you*?
4 *Don't / Do* you do it in the same way in Japan?
5 *At who do you smile / Who do you smile at*?

4 Look at the questions in Exercise 3 again and answer the questions (1–4). Then read the Grammar box on page 15 to check.
1 Which question is used to check the listener agrees?
2 Which question asks for confirmation of something the speaker already believes?
3 Which question shows surprise about some new information?
4 Which question asks for the information in an indirect way?

EMOTICONS AROUND THE WORLD

Emojis are here to stay 😃 👋, but good old emoticons still have their place in emails and texts. Do different styles of emoticons around the world tell us anything about the culture they come from? ¯_(ツ)_/¯

European style

eyes to the left, mouth to the right	nose optional	symbol repeated for emphasis (Russians often don't include eyes)	other variations
:-D	:O	)))))	>:(D:

Asian style

upright, brackets show face outline	emotion expressed through the eyes	mouth sometimes left off and brackets are also optional	use of extended characters e.g. Korean *jamo*
(-_-)	(T_T)	(^^) ^^	(ㄴ누_ㄴ누)

DID YOU KNOW?

The first use of an emoticon? A poet called Robert Herrick used a smiley emoticon :) in a 1648 poem. That's more than three hundred years before the first computer! :-0

GRAMMAR Forming questions

You can form questions with **question word +
auxiliary verb + subject + main verb**.
What do you think?

Negative questions often express surprise or
annoyance.
Don't you do it in the same way in Japan?

There are several other types of questions that you
form differently.

Short questions: do not have the main verb
and you often use them to express surprise or
interest
Wasn't it? Did you?

Subject questions: do not use an auxiliary verb
*Who **makes** you laugh?*

Indirect questions: use them to be more polite
or less direct; they follow **subject + verb** word order
*I'd like to know whether **a smile means** the same
thing all over the world.*

Question tags: use them to confirm what you
are saying or check that the listener agrees
*Tomoya, you studied psychology, **didn't you**?*

Go to page 140 for the Grammar reference.

5   🎧 **1.3** **Complete the conversation with one word
in each space. Then listen to check.**

A: Do you know what the difference
   ¹ _____ between emoticons and
   emojis?

B: Yes, emoticons are symbols used to represent faces
   and emojis are actual pictures.

A: Oh, OK!

B: You know you have to be careful with emojis,
   ² _____ you? What you see when you
   send it isn't necessarily what the other person sees.

A: ³ _____ it?!

B: No! A friend of mine texted his wife
   'Do you know how beautiful you
   ⁴ _____?' and sent the Spanish
   dancer emoji. Except the emoji on her
   phone was a fat yellow dancing blob!

A: Oh no! Who ⁵ _____ these emojis
   – the phone companies? By the way, why
   ⁶ _____ you send me a surprised face
   when I told you I got the tickets for the match
   yesterday?

B: What? ⁷ _____ I send you a smiley?

PRONUNCIATION

6   🎧 **1.4** **Listen to the question. Underline the
stressed word.**
   Were you surprised?

7   🎧 **1.5** **Look at the Clear voice box. Then listen
to the question from Exercise 6 said three
times, with different sentence stress. Match the
questions (1–3) with the meanings (a–c).**

CLEAR VOICE
Using stress for emphasis (1)

In English, content words (nouns, verbs,
adjectives, adverbs) are normally stressed.
Grammar words like prepositions, determiners
and auxiliary words are not stressed. However, this
can change if the speaker wants to emphasize a
particular meaning.

Question 1	a I wasn't surprised, but I'm
Question 2	curious to know if you were.
Question 3	b I want to know how you felt.
	c You said you were surprised, but I'm not sure I believe you.

8   **Work in pairs. Take turns to say the question
from Exercise 6, putting the stress on one of the
three words. Your partner should choose which
meaning from Exercise 7 (a, b or c) you were
thinking of.**

SPEAKING

9   **Work in pairs. Design a questionnaire to ask
your classmates about emotions, emojis and
emoticons. Follow the instructions.**

1 Write at least six questions. Use the Grammar box
   to help you.
   *What's your favourite emoticon or emoji? Why?
   Have you ever cried when watching a film?*

2 Individually, interview your classmates and write
   down their answers. Ask follow-up questions.

3 Share the answers with your partner. Which
   answers were the most interesting? Report these
   to the class.

EXPLORE MORE!

Search online for the 'app that knows how you feel
from the look on your face'. How does it work?

1C

I couldn't believe my eyes!

LESSON GOALS
- Talk about strong emotions using adverbs of degree
- Infer emotions when listening
- Practise short and long vowel sounds

VOCABULARY

1 Work in pairs. Look at the photo and discuss the questions.

1 Where are the people in the photo? What do you think might be happening?

2 How do you think the people might be feeling? Why?

3 Have you ever been in a similar situation? When?

2 Read the sentences. Underline the adjectives that describe emotions.

1 I saw a massive spider the other day. I was completely petrified!

2 I'm a bit concerned I might not pass the exam. Some of the questions were tricky.

3 The queue wasn't moving and I started to feel slightly impatient.

4 I'd been waiting for the book for months, so I was really thrilled when it finally came out.

5 I was tremendously relieved nobody noticed my mistake. I thought my boss would be angry.

6 I'm feeling relatively optimistic now that I know I will get to keep my job.

7 I was totally astonished when Germany beat Brazil 7-1. I really didn't see it coming!

8 I feel more motivated doing practical class projects than listening to a lecture.

9 The boss was absolutely furious with her. She'd missed the deadline again.

3 Match the adjectives from Exercise 2 (1–9) with their definition (a–i).

a very happy and excited

b no longer feeling worried

c positive

d very angry

e very scared

f very surprised

g wanting something to happen

h wanting to do the work

i worried

Go to page 135 for the Vocabulary reference.

4 Circle any adverbs used with the adjectives in Exercise 2. Which are used to make the emotion stronger? Which are used to make it weaker?

5 Read the Focus on box to check your answers to Exercise 4.

> **FOCUS ON** Adverbs of degree
>
> Many adverbs affect the strength of the word they modify, e.g. **very** happy, **a little** annoyed.
>
> **Adverbs that make the word stronger**
> absolutely, completely, really, totally, tremendously
>
> **Adverbs that make the word weaker**
> a bit, relatively, slightly

Go to page 141 for the Focus on reference.

6 Write three sentences about yourself using adjectives from Exercise 2. Use adverbs to make the emotion stronger or weaker.

PRONUNCIATION

7 Look at the adjectives, paying attention to the sound of the letters in red. Then complete the table.

astonished   delighted   impatient
optimistic   pleased   relieved   thrilled

/ɪ/	/iː/	/eɪ/	/aɪ/
exhausted	weak	afraid	excited

8 🎧 **1.6** Listen and check your answers to Exercise 7. Then practise saying the adjectives. Use the Clear voice box to help you.

CLEAR VOICE
Pronouncing short and long vowels

In English there is a difference between long and short vowel sounds that is important for clear pronunciation. The sounds /eɪ/, /aɪ/ and /iː/ are always long while /ɪ/ is always short.

LISTENING

NATIONAL GEOGRAPHIC EXPLORERS

9 🎧 **1.7** Look at the Listening skill box. Then listen to Francisco Estrada-Belli and Tsiory Andrianavalona. Try to infer which emotions they felt in each situation.

LISTENING SKILL
Inferring emotions

Sometimes people might not state how they feel directly and you will need to infer it from the description of the situation. For example, if your friend says 'I passed my driving test yesterday!', you can infer that they are probably feeling happy. To infer emotions, listen to the tone of voice, the type of situation described and for words or expressions that give you a clue.

10 🎧 **1.7** Listen again. Who, Francisco (F), Tsiory (T) or both explorers (B) …

1 couldn't see anyone else?
2 found it difficult to speak?
3 got help from other people?
4 is better prepared if the experience happens again?
5 was prepared for the experience?
6 was indoors when it happened?

SPEAKING

11 Look at the Useful language box. Then match the phrases in bold with the emotions (1–5).

Useful language   Expressing emotions

I **can't stand** waiting in queues.
It really **gets on my nerves** when people are late to meetings.
My dad really **lost his temper** when he found out I'd been skipping classes again.
I couldn't believe my eyes when I saw the exam results. I got 100%!
I never thought that my best friend could **let me down** so much.

1 annoyed
2 astonished
3 disappointed
4 angry
5 impatient

12 Work in pairs. Help each other memorize the expressions in the Useful language box. Take turns to read out a part of each expression. The other person must complete the expression without looking at their book.

A: I can't stand …
B: … waiting in queues!
A: Yes!

13 You are going to tell a story about a time when you experienced a strong emotion. Make notes to prepare. Use expressions from the Useful language box to help you.

14 Work in groups. Take turns to share your story. Don't say what emotions you felt. Can the rest of the group infer the emotions you felt?

1D
Empathizing with others

LESSON GOALS
• Discuss how to deal with difficult situations
• Demonstrate empathy in a conversation
• Consider other people's emotions and help others see the other side

SPEAKING

1 Read the situation. What would you do? Why? Discuss with a partner.

> Andrea is the new leader of a team working on a project. In a meeting, she is angry with you and tells you off in front of the rest of the team for not completing your work. You have explained that you needed more information to complete the job. You remember times in the past, before Andrea was leader, when she didn't finish her work on time. Do you …

  a think about why Andrea may be angry and talk to her about it after the meeting?
  b remind Andrea of the times in the past when she didn't finish her work?
  c decide that Andrea is a bad leader and complain about her to other team members?

MY VOICE ▶

2 ▶ 1.2 Watch the video. Complete the sentence in at least two ways. Then compare your sentences with your classmates.

Empathy is _____.

3 Work in pairs. How do you think empathy can help you manage situations like the one in Exercise 1? What might happen if you don't show empathy?

4 ▶ 1.2 Watch the video again. Make notes on …
1 why empathy is important.
2 ways of empathizing effectively.

5 Work in pairs. Read the four situations on page 19. Decide on the best way of dealing with each situation.

6 Look at the Communication skill box. Do the courses of action that you decided on in Exercise 5 follow its advice? What other advice could you add to the box?

COMMUNICATION SKILL
Considering other people's emotions

• Before reacting to a situation, consider how the other person might be feeling. Use this to decide on the most appropriate way to respond.

• Focus on similarities you share rather than differences. If you have trouble connecting with someone, try to think of three things you and the other person have in common.

• When talking to another person, try to listen more than you speak. Check you've understood by summarizing their point of view. This will also show them that you're listening.

• Try not to judge the other person. It's possible to disagree and still understand why the other person feels differently about a certain matter.

Exercise your empathy!

Consider the role of empathy in these four situations. In each, ask yourself:
What might the other person be thinking and feeling? How would you feel?

1 You are just about to sit down on a crowded bus when another passenger pushes in front of you and sits down herself. It is very clear that you were going to sit down. Even so, she doesn't say anything or look at you.

What do you do?

2 You are a student in class. Your friend makes an unkind comment about a classmate. Other people laugh. This classmate doesn't have any friends in the class and he sometimes disturbs the lesson, which you find annoying. He doesn't look unhappy, but this is probably because he is used to comments like this – it's not the first time.

What do you do?

3 You have just finished your exams and are celebrating at home. Quite early in the evening, your next-door neighbour complains about the noise and says he can't sleep. You and your friends have been looking forward to this party for a long time. You had warned the neighbours a few days before, but this neighbour is talking about calling the police if you don't stop the party immediately.

What do you do?

4 You cycle to work and find it difficult because the traffic is noisy and dirty. Your flatmate recently bought a car so that she could drive to work. However, the council has now banned cars from the city centre, which means her journey will now take an extra hour each day and cost her more money. She is annoyed and upset.

What do you do?

---

7 🎧 1.8 Listen to a conversation between two friends. How could each person deal with the situation better? Discuss with a partner, using the advice from Exercise 6.

8 Look at the Useful language box. Match the phrases in the box with the categories (1–4).

> **Useful language** Empathizing
>
> I'm sorry to hear that. It must be hard for you.
> I can see how that would be difficult.
> I'm glad you told me. Let me know if I can help.
> I want to make sure I understand. Are you saying that …?
> It sounds like you're feeling … Is that right?
> Have you thought about how they might feel?
> I imagine they're feeling quite …

1 Acknowledging difficulties
2 Helping others see the other side
3 Being there for others
4 Checking you've understood

SPEAKING

9 **OWN IT!** Work in pairs. Follow the instructions.

Student A: Choose to be either Gurpreet or Laurent from Exercise 7. You've just got back from the restaurant and you're angry/upset.

Student B: You are Student A's flatmate. Try to get your friend to calm down and help them see the situation from the other person's point of view.

Use the tips from the Communication skill box and the Useful language to help you.

B: Are you OK? You seem a bit down.

A: Yeah, well, I met up with Gurpreet / Laurent …

10 Work with another pair. Take turns to act out your conversations from Exercise 9. Did both pairs demonstrate empathy?

1E
Great news!

LESSON GOALS
- Use informal language to sound friendly
- Write an email giving news
- Respond to someone else's news

SPEAKING

1 Look at the photos. What news do you think each person has just received?

2 Work in pairs. Tell each other about a time you wrote to someone with good or bad news, or received news. How did it make you feel?

READING FOR WRITING

3 Read the email. Answer the questions.
1. What's the relationship between Erik and Ioana?
2. What's Erik's good news?
3. What do you think Ioana's response will say?

New Message

Hi Ioana!

How are things? Sorry I haven't been in touch for a while, but I've been really busy at work. Thought I'd drop you a line while I have a few minutes.

What have you been up to since we last chatted? Did you go to that university reunion party last week? I got the invitation, but I couldn't make it because I had to go to a family event. But I really wanted to see the old crowd and find out what everyone's up to these days. Who did you see? What's the latest? I'd love to know!

Do you remember that design job I told you about? Guess what? I went for it and I got it! 😌 I'm so thrilled. It's the perfect company for me. To be honest, I didn't think the interview had gone too well, so I couldn't believe my ears when I got the call today. It'll mean getting up early and commuting into town, but I'm sure I'll get used to it. By the way, don't mention it to anyone yet, will you? I don't want my boss getting wind of it just yet! I'll keep you posted.

I hear Aida's been in hospital. I had no idea she was ill. I hope she's better soon. Let's catch up properly soon. It's been ages. Just give me a ring when you're free and we can arrange to meet up.

Take care,

Erik

---

4 Read the email again and answer the questions. Then look at the Writing skill box to check.

1 How is the email organized?
2 What informal language can you find?

WRITING SKILL
Informal emails and messages

If emails and messages in informal contexts (e.g. to people you know personally) are too formal, they can sound unfriendly.

- Informal messages with good or bad news typically contain these elements: greeting and introductory phrase; details of the news; questions about the other person's current situation; invitation to meet/speak.
- Ask about the other person in the first paragraph – you don't have to say why you're writing straight away.
- Talk about the next time you might talk or see each other in the final paragraph.
- Use informal expressions for beginning and ending emails (*How're things?; Take care!*) and in the body of the email (*What have you been up to?; I'll keep you posted.*).

5 Find informal words and phrases in Erik's email that have the same meaning as these more formal phrases (1–10). They are in the same order as they appear in the email.

1 contacted you
2 write to you
3 doing
4 recent news
5 applied for
6 finding out about
7 inform you
8 didn't know
9 exchange news
10 a long time

6 Read Ioana's response to Erik. Answer the questions.

1 Does it include the points you predicted in Exercise 3?
2 Is the email organized into paragraphs appropriately?
3 Is the language suitably informal?
4 How would you feel if you were Erik and you received this from your friend? Why?

Dear Erik,

Thank you for your email yesterday. It was very good to hear from you.

I would like to offer my congratulations on your new position. I am extremely pleased for you. Please inform me about it once you have started work. I would be interested to learn all your news.

You enquired about the reunion party. I talked with Jenny for a long time. It was good to hear her news. She said she would like to exchange news with you as well, so I will inform you of our arrangements.

Thank you for your concern about Aida. She has fully recovered now and returned to college.

I look forward to seeing you in the near future.

Yours, with best regards,

Ioana

---

7 Rewrite Ioana's email so that it sounds less formal.

WRITING TASK

8 **WRITE** Write an informal email to a classmate giving your own good or bad news. Use one of these ideas or your own idea.

---

an exam you failed/passed   a job you got
something got stolen/broken
your team won/lost an important game

---

9 **CHECK** Use the checklist. I have ...
☐ included all the typical elements for this type of email (greetings, details of the news, etc.).
☐ organized the information appropriately.
☐ used informal language to sound friendly.

10 **REVIEW** Exchange emails with your partner. Did their email include everything from the checklist in Exercise 9? Take turns to give feedback.

11 Write a response to your partner's email. Remember to sound empathetic. Use the Useful language on page 19 to help you.

Go to page 130 for the Reflect and review.

EXPLORE MORE!

Write an email to someone you haven't spoken to for a while. Share your news and ask about theirs.

Two women from Nigeria braid a customer's hair at their salon in Como, Italy.

2

Language and communication

GOALS

- Skim and scan an article to identify the main ideas
- Discuss language learning experience and tips
- Talk about communication using phrasal verbs
- Use discourse markers to understand a podcast
- Understand how first language identity can be used in building relationships
- Write a formal email asking for information

1 Work in pairs. Look at the photo. How might knowing another language have helped the women?

WATCH

2 ▶ 2.1 Watch the video. Match the sentences with the explorer, Maria (M) or Arianna (A).

NATIONAL GEOGRAPHIC EXPLORERS

| MARIA FADIMAN | ARIANNA SOLDATI |

1 Learning French helped me professionally.
2 I always try to learn a few words of the language of the local people I'm working with.
3 I have worked as a Spanish to English translator for naturalist guides in Costa Rica.
4 I am currently learning German.

3 Make connections. How are Maria and Arianna's experiences similar to your own?

2A
Talking nature

LESSON GOALS
- Skim and scan an article to identify the main ideas
- Identify the main message in an article
- Summarize an article in a social media post

READING

1 Work in pairs. How do you think the animals and plants in the photos on page 25 communicate with each other? Match the photos (A–E) with the forms of communication (1–5).

1 sound
2 light
3 vibrations (small movements)
4 facial expression
5 colour

2 Look at the first part of the Reading skill box (Scanning). Then scan the article on page 25 to find which paragraph gives most of the answers to Exercise 1. Were your predictions correct?

READING SKILL
Scanning and skimming

Scanning: To find specific information quickly, look around the text to find relevant words and expressions.

Skimming: Skim to get the main idea of a text. Run your eyes quickly over the text, focusing only on the main content words: nouns, adjectives and verbs.

3 Look at the second part of the Reading skill box (Skimming). Then match the subheadings (a–g) with the paragraphs (1–7) in the article. Use these tips to help you:
- Scan the paragraphs for key words that match words and ideas in the headings.
- Skim the paragraphs to check your choice of heading was correct.

a Creating songs and music
b Achoo!
c The corn has ears
d Not just humans
e Many means of communication
f Tricks and lies
g Where's that accent from?

4 Find a word or phrase in the article for each definition.

1 ways of sharing information (l. 5)
2 parts of a subject (l. 7)
3 is different from each other (l. 16)
4 change to suit different situations (l. 19)
5 the form of a language spoken in an area (l. 19)
6 copies the way someone or something moves or speaks (l. 22)
7 an action that communicates a message (l. 38)
8 loudly blow air out of your nose and mouth in an uncontrolled way (l. 55)

5 Work in pairs. Look at the Critical thinking skill box. Then choose the main message (a–c) of the article. Where does the writer support the message?

CRITICAL THINKING SKILL
Identifying the main message

A text usually has one main message, or argument, that the writer wants to persuade the reader is true. Look for the same point being repeated in different ways throughout to identify the main argument. It may be mentioned near the beginning and end.

a Means of communication in the natural world are more complicated than human ones.
b We need to question the idea that human communication is special and unique.
c We know very little about how animals communicate and need to learn more.

SPEAKING AND WRITING

6 Imagine you want to post a link to the article on social media. Write a short summary to include with your post. Think about how you could persuade people to read the article (e.g. an image or surprising facts from the article).

I've just read an amazing article about animal communication. Did you know that … ?

7 Compare posts with your classmates. Which posts are the most persuasive?

EXPLORE MORE!

Search online for 'amazing animal communication' to find another strange means of communication in the natural world.

A chameleon

B treehopper

C corn

D horse

1 _____

It's often thought that only humans have the ability to use language. But animals do talk, of course, just not very often in words we'd understand. It turns out that, throughout the natural
5 world, there are means of communication that are just as innovative as any technology we can invent. Even more surprisingly, aspects of communication that we thought were limited to humans, such as accents, culture and lying, are known to feature in
10 the daily chitchat of many species.

2 _____

Take birdsong, for example. Did you know that many birds' calls change depending on where the bird comes from? A mockingbird from Kansas, US pronounces his chirps differently from another
15 mockingbird in Virginia, US. And birds aren't the only group in which accent varies from place to place; sperm whales recognize where strangers are from by their voice and monkeys have been shown to adapt to new places by learning the local dialect.

3 _____

20 Some birds can even use the language of other birds to deceive them. The fork-tailed drongo mimics the alarm calls of more than thirty species. It does so when it sees a bird with food in its mouth. The idea is that the other bird drops the food on
25 hearing the call, which is when the drongo steps in to collect the food. A human equivalent would be to shout 'Fire!' in a restaurant and then eat everyone's meals after they run out of the building.

4 _____

If you thought that humans are the only species to use
30 language creatively, think again. The humpback whale in the South Pacific invents new songs every year or two. Other groups living far away hear these songs and learn them if they like them. You might hear a song that started off the Australian coast near the island of Tahiti, six
35 thousand miles away!

5 _____

Many animals use sounds, but there are other strategies for getting your message across. The skin colour of chameleons constantly changes as a signal of their emotions and intentions. Treehoppers, tiny insects, shake their bodies
40 to send vibrations through plants to other treehoppers. Fireflies use light and can send signals between thousands of individuals. Remarkably, horses make facial expressions to show emotions.

6 _____

What about plants? We've known that they produce
45 chemicals to warn other plants of dangers, such as insects, but recent research shows that some plants even use sound. Corn roots, for example, make regular clicking noises that its neighbours respond to. And scientists have shown that when a plant 'hears' a neighbour is growing next
50 to it, it responds by growing faster.

7 _____

Finally, no article about communication in the animal kingdom would be complete without mentioning African wild dogs. These sociable creatures make decisions by sneezing! Yes, according to scientists, they get together
55 in groups and sneeze to decide whether to go on a hunt or not. If more than half sneezes, it's a yes. So it turns out even democracy wasn't invented by us!

E fireflies

I'm taking classes at the moment

LESSON GOALS
- Review present tenses
- Say auxiliary verbs clearly
- Discuss language learning experience and tips

LISTENING AND GRAMMAR

1 Work in pairs. Discuss the questions.
1. How many languages do you speak? How have you learned them?
2. Are there any other languages that you would like to learn?
3. Do you know anyone who speaks a lot of languages? How do they manage to learn so many?
4. What do you think is more important when learning a language: talent or hard work? Why?

NATIONAL GEOGRAPHIC EXPLORER

Arianna (centre right) with her German-speaking and French-speaking friends.

2 🎧 **2.1** Listen to Arianna Soldati talk about her language learning experiences. Answer the questions.
1. Which foreign languages does Arianna speak?
2. How long has she been using French?
3. Has she ever lived in a Spanish-speaking country?
4. Which language is she currently struggling with?

3 🎧 **2.2** Complete the sentences with the correct form of the verbs in brackets. Then listen to check.
1. I've _____ (study) English for a long time.
2. I also speak French and I've been _____ (use) it since I was 11.
3. I often _____ (speak) it with some French-speaking friends.
4. Our language has always _____ (be) French, so we speak in French.
5. Unfortunately, I've never _____ (have) the chance to live in a Spanish-speaking country.
6. It has _____ (not/be) that difficult to learn.
7. The last language I've been _____ (try) to pick up is German.
8. I'm _____ (take) classes at the moment, so hopefully I will improve soon.

4 Look at the sentences in Exercise 3 again. Answer the questions. Then read the Grammar box to check.
1. Which sentence refers to something that happens regularly?
2. Which sentences refer to an action that started in the past, continues into the present and is likely to continue in the future?
3. Which sentence describes an action in progress at the current moment?
4. Which sentence refers to Arianna's entire life?

GRAMMAR Present tenses

Present simple
Use to refer to present habits, actions that happen regularly and facts.
*I often **speak** it with some French-speaking friends.*

Present continuous
Use to refer to things happening at this moment or around the present moment (but not exactly right now).
*I**'m taking** classes at the moment.*

Present perfect simple
Use to describe present results of past actions when the time is not specified.
*Unfortunately, I**'ve never had** the chance to live in a Spanish-speaking country.*
Use to describe the results of actions that began in the past and continued into the present.
*I**'ve studied** English for a long time.*

Present perfect continuous
Use to refer to actions that began in the past, are still in progress and are likely to continue in the future.
*I**'ve been using** it since I was 11.*

Go to page 141 for the Grammar reference.

5 Find and correct the mistakes in the sentences.

1 She's studying languages since 2015.
2 I've been watching this film several times already.
3 Technology currently changes how people study languages.
4 She's read this book all day without stopping – it must be really fascinating.
5 I can't talk right now because I still write the report.
6 My parents have never been learning a foreign language.
7 I'm calling my parents every Saturday.

PRONUNCIATION

6 🎧 **2.3** Listen to two sentences said in two ways. In which version is the auxiliary verb easier to hear? Then look at the Clear voice box to learn more.

1 I am taking classes at the moment.
2 I have been using it since I was 11.

CLEAR VOICE
Understanding weak forms of auxiliary verbs

In fast speech, auxiliary verbs (e.g. *am, have been*) are typically reduced to weak forms (i.e. *'m* /əm/, *'ve* /əv/, *been* /bɪn/) and are unstressed. This can make them more difficult to hear. To be easy to understand, especially in international contexts, it can be better to pronounce the full forms of auxiliary verbs (/æm/, /hæv/, /biːn/).

SPEAKING AND LISTENING

7 Use the words to form questions. Then write two of your own questions about language learning. Ask and answer the questions with a partner.

1 English / you / how long / learn
2 study / another / language / you / currently / foreign
3 language / speak / ever / you / meet / someone / lots of
4 what / difficult / language / you / most / learn
5 study / most / you / what / enjoy / about / a foreign language

6 _____
7 _____

8 🎧 **2.4** Listen and write down the language learning tips Arianna gives. Which tip do you think is the best? Why?

9 Work in groups. Discuss the questions. Then decide on the three best tips for learning languages.

1 What do you find difficult when you are studying a language? What do you find easy?
2 What are you currently struggling with? Why?
3 How have you practised your English outside the class since this course started?
4 Which language learning tips have worked best for you?

EXPLORE MORE!

Search online for 'language learning tips'. Choose one tip and apply it to your language learning.

LISTENING

1 Work in pairs. Discuss the questions.

1 If you could study English anywhere in the world, where would it be? Why?
2 Are there a lot of English users where you're from? Do you think this number is growing?
3 Do you currently use your English more with people from English-speaking countries or people for whom English is a second language?

2 Look at the sentences from a podcast. Underline the words or phrases that introduce ideas.

1 Basically, whether you're from Ho Chi Minh City, New York, Warsaw, São Paolo or Nairobi doesn't matter.
2 On the other hand, when speaking Chinese, Spanish or Arabic, you're most likely to do it with first language users.
3 Interestingly, more than eighty per cent of them do not speak it as their mother tongue.
4 According to many experts, a foreign accent isn't usually a problem.
5 This brings me to my next point.

3 Match the words you underlined in Exercise 2 with the type of information that comes after them (a–e). Then look at the Listening skill box to check.

a contrast
b different subject
c explanation
d reference to sources
e surprising information

LISTENING SKILL
Identifying discourse markers

Listen out for the discourse markers a speaker uses. They will help you predict what type of information will come next.

New, surprising or interesting fact: *surprisingly, interestingly, funnily enough*
Contrast: *however, while, on the other hand*
Referring to sources: *according to*
Moving to a different subject: *this brings me to, moving on to*
Explaining: *basically*

4 🎧 2.5 Listen to the podcast. Write down three things the speaker says that you either agree with or disagree with. Then discuss in pairs.

5 🎧 2.5 Listen to the podcast again. Answer the questions.

1 How do English and languages such as Chinese or Arabic differ, according to the speaker?
2 What were the two things that the speaker believed about English?
3 How did travelling and working change her perspective?
4 What did she learn from research about communicating in English?
5 How did the speaker's identity as an English user evolve?

VOCABULARY AND PRONUNCIATION

6 Read Maria Fadiman's reaction to the podcast. 播客
Then discuss the questions (1–3) in pairs.

> One thing that came up in the podcast and surprised me was how many people speak English as second language users. It made me feel lucky that I get to speak English as my first language and that I can easily get my message across to so many people! But I also felt guilty that I get to do that so easily, simply because of where I was born.
>
> In terms of culture, it might be fun to read up on, *phrasal v. / study* but I wouldn't say there is a culture of English-speaking people, anyway. And I'm not sure this would help you use English better. ~~tend~~ *learn more by reading*
>
> It's worth pointing out there is no real American accent. When I lived in the South, I started to pick up a southern accent (of which there are many variations). In New York, as a child, I tried to pick up the accent there and my mum told me that my grandfather, originally from New York, had tried to *lose* his New York accent. It's similar in Spanish. I've kind of made up my own personal Spanish accent.

1 Were you surprised by how many people speak English as second language users?
2 Do you like to read up on the culture of a country when learning a new language? Why? / Why not?
3 Have you ever picked up a different accent?

7 Match the phrasal verbs (1–8) with the correct definition (a–h).

1 bring up   **3** a think of an idea
2 come up   **7** b draw someone's attention to
Come with 3 come up with   **8** c learn more by reading
4 get across   **1** d mention a topic
5 make up   **4** e explain (ideas)
6 pick up   **2** f be mentioned (topic)
7 point out   **6** g learn to do without much effort
8 read up on   **5** h invent

Go to page 135 for the Vocabulary reference.

8 🎧 **2.6** Look at the Clear voice box. Then listen and practise saying the words and phrases (1–4).

CLEAR VOICE
Saying the /r/ sound

Pronunciation of the /r/ sound can vary a lot among users of English. Be careful <u>not</u> to pronounce it as an /h/ or /l/. However, don't worry if your /r/ sounds different to how a first language user might pronounce it.

1 bring up   3 surprisingly
2 in contrast   4 read up on

9 Read the Focus on box. Then correct the mistakes in the sentences (1–3).

> **FOCUS ON** Separable and inseparable phrasal verbs
>
> Most phrasal verbs can be separated, e.g. **pick up** an accent <u>and</u> **pick** an accent **up**. You must always put the pronoun before the preposition (*pick up it* → *pick it up*).
>
> Phrasal verbs followed by an adverb and a preposition or two prepositions (e.g. *come up with*) can't be separated.
>
> There are a few phrasal verbs which must always be separated, e.g. **get** *my ideas* **across**.

Go to page 142 for the Focus on reference.

1 At first I believed her, but then it turned out she'd made up it.
2 When I'm nervous, I find it difficult to get across my meaning.
3 She's incredibly creative and comes up new ideas with all the time.

10 Work in pairs. Complete the questions with phrasal verbs from this lesson. Then choose three of the questions to discuss.

1 Have you ever been in a situation when you _____ an embarrassing conversation topic by mistake?
2 Do you know a person who is good at _____ stories?
3 Can you think of a time when you couldn't _____ your message _____ ?
4 Have you ever had to _____ a mistake to someone?
5 What's something you've _____ quite easily?

EXPLORE MORE!

Search online for 'a short history of the English language' to learn more about how English became the global language of communication.

Building relationships

LESSON GOALS
• Understand how first language identity can be used in building relationships
• Talk about similarities and differences between languages and cultures
• Practise sharing aspects of your first language identity

LISTENING

1 Imagine you are talking to someone from a different country who you don't know very well. Put the topics in order from the one you would most likely talk about to the least likely. Then compare with a partner. What other topics could you add to the list?
- your families
- food customs in your countries
- living and working conditions in your countries
- language similarities and differences
- current news stories from your countries
- the reason you are together that day
- sport teams and recent matches
- tourist attractions in each other's countries

2 🎧 2.7 Listen to two conversations. What things in common do the speakers use to build their relationships? What differences do they use for the same reason?

3 🎧 2.7 Listen again and answer the questions.
1 In the first conversation, what two ways of saying 'very hungry' are used? What do you say in your language?
2 In the second conversation, what does José Luis want to know about the UAE?

4 Work in pairs. Discuss the questions.
1 In which conversation …
a was a speaker's first language used?
b did the speakers find similar interests?
c did the speakers compare their first languages?
2 Do you sometimes switch between languages? When and why?
3 What aspects of people's first language identity do you find interesting?

MY VOICE ▶

5 ▶ 2.2 Watch the video. Write down …
1 at least one way your first language identity can help build relationships.
2 two pieces of advice that are given.

A group of friends talk in a coffee shop in Germany.

6 Work in pairs. Make a list of times when you have built a relationship with someone with a different first language identity to you, or when you may do so in the future. What advice in the Communication skill box do you think is the most useful to you? Why?

I'd like to work in a large international company, where I imagine I will work with people from different countries. It will be important for me not to feel embarrassed about my accent.

COMMUNICATION SKILL
Building relationships using your first language identity

Your language and cultural background are a great tool to help you build relationships with people from other countries.

- Be open about who you are and where you come from. Be proud of your culture, your first language and your accent!
- Ask open questions to find out about the other person's background.
- Look for things in common. Key moments in establishing friendships happen when you share similar experiences or realize that you aren't so different from one another.
- Celebrate the differences between you and show interest in understanding them.

7 🎧 **2.8** Listen to extracts from the conversations in Exercise 2. Complete the extracts with one word in each space.

1 Is capoeira _____ _____ in Turkey?

2 In my language, we _____ _____: 'I'm as hungry as a wolf'.

3 The _____ for us is: 'I could eat my arm'.

4 Do you have a word _____ _____ in Arabic?

5 I can't _____ _____ it!

8 Rewrite the sentences in Exercise 7 in a different way, using the expressions in the Useful language box.

Useful language Talking about your first language identity

Showing interest in others
How popular is [hip hop] where you live?
How does that compare with [the way you normally do that in your family]?
How do you say that in [Russian]?

Explaining your first language identity
I'd say we [give tips] in a slightly different way to how people do it here.
It sounds a bit like [a children's game in Kenya we call 'Escape the lions'].
We have a similar expression that translates as ['It's raining seas!']
I'm sure we have a phrase in [Urdu]. It's on the tip of my tongue!

SPEAKING

9 **OWN IT!** Think of three words, phrases or cultural concepts from your first language or another language. Explain them to a partner, using the Useful language.

My city is famous for this idea called cachondeo. *When we say someone has* cachondeo, *it means they're always joking and having fun.*

10 Work in groups. For each category, think of aspects of your culture and first language that you would like people from other countries to know. Make a list. What other categories can you think of?

- a word or expression that you think is special
- a festival, dance or celebration unique to your culture
- a type of humour that you would miss if you were away
- an important place that isn't well known abroad
- a grammatical structure that is different from other languages you know
- a well-loved TV show, film, song or book that represents your culture
- a dish that reflects the best food from home
- an aspect of the national character that you want people from other countries to know about

11 Share your ideas from Exercise 10 in new groups. Explain any cultural aspects that other members of the group do not know about.

EXPLORE MORE!

Listen to how you and the people around you talk about your language and culture. How often do you talk about different cultural concepts?

31

2E
LESSON GOALS
- Organize a formal email appropriately
- Use formal language and polite requests
- Write to ask for information about a course

2E
I am writing to enquire

SPEAKING

1 Work in pairs. Discuss the questions.

1 Do you speak any of the languages in the infographic? Which would it be useful to learn, e.g. for business, tourism, job opportunities? Why?

2 Why are you taking this English course? Is it for any of the reasons you mentioned for Question 1?

3 Which other types of courses (e.g. yoga, website design, creative writing) have you done, or would you like to do?

Languages with the highest number of first language speakers

Chinese – 1.3 billion
Spanish – 460 million
English – 379 million
Hindi – 342 million
Arabic – 315 million
Bengali – 228 million

*figures are approximate
Chinese and Hindi as macrolanguages include different languages and dialects

2 Read the advert. Imagine you are thinking of applying for the course. In pairs, think of three questions that you would want to ask about it.

> Learn Arabic in Marrakesh!
> Come and learn Arabic with us in the heart of this ancient city
>
> - Intensive courses
> - Four-week courses throughout the year
> - Small groups
> - Accommodation available close to the school and city centre
>
> **For more information, email**
> admisssions@olivebranch.mr
>
>

READING FOR WRITING

3 Read the email. Does Son ask the same questions that you thought of in Exercise 2?

New Message

Subject: Enquiry about Arabic course

Dear Sir or Madam,

[1] I saw your advertisement for Arabic courses in Marrakesh and I am interested in enrolling. I am writing to enquire about the next course.

[2] I do have a few questions. Firstly, please could you confirm the start date of the next course? The advertisement says the course is 'intensive', but I would be interested to know how many hours per week this is and what the course duration is. I would also like to know whether I will receive a formal certificate at the end of the course as I would like to use it in my application for jobs in my country. Would the certificate be recognized abroad?

[3] I would also be grateful for more information concerning course fees and accommodation. First, I am not entirely sure how I would need to pay and whether I would need to do this in advance. Second, since I am from Vietnam and currently live there, I was glad to see you offer accommodation. Could you give me some idea of the price? Finally, please also let me know whether a host family or hotel would be preferable for someone who is very keen to improve their Arabic quickly and whether you can arrange the accommodation for me.

[4] Regarding the level of the course, I was wondering whether you have courses for complete beginners. In addition, I would like to know whether you would recommend I study first to become slightly more proficient in Arabic before I sign up for your course.

[5] I look forward to hearing from you in the near future.

[6] Yours faithfully,

Son Ngo

---

4 Put the elements (a–e) in the order they appear in Son's email. Then look at the Writing skill box to learn more about the structure of formal emails.

a enquiry about course fees and accommodation

b enquiry about the course itself

c reason for writing

d asking for a reply

e question about the necessary language level

WRITING SKILL
Organizing formal emails

Formal emails are much more structured than informal ones. They typically begin with the reason for writing (*I am writing to enquire about …*). Then each paragraph focuses on one clear topic that is stated in the first sentence (*Regarding the course itself …*). Each paragraph is clearly structured (*First/Second/In addition*).
The email finishes with a polite request for a reply (*I look forward to hearing from you./I would appreciate a reply at your earliest convenience.*)

5 Find formal words and expressions in Son's email that have the same meaning as these more informal words and phrases (1–10).

1 Hi *Dear*

2 ad

3 ask about

4 price

5 at the moment

6 a place to stay

7 about (para 3 and 4)

8 if (para 2 and 4)

9 hoping to hear from you soon

10 Bye for now!

6 Read Son's email again and underline any examples of indirect questions or polite requests.

7 Rewrite Eugenio's email to make it more formal. Use the information in the Writing skill box and the Useful language to help you. Then compare with a partner.

~~Hi there!~~ *Dear Sir or Madam,*

A friend told me your driving school is really good, so just wanna ask how much it costs to do a driving course with you. No info about it on your site. Never driven before, so a total beginner. Also, when can we start?

Write back asap.

Bye for now,
Eugenio

Useful language   Formal emails

Formal forms of address
Dear Mr/Ms [last name] / Dear Sir or Madam

Reason for writing
I am writing with regard to/to enquire about …

Polite requests
Could you tell me …
I was wondering if you could …
I would appreciate a reply at your earliest convenience.
I look forward to hearing back from you.

Formal endings
Kind regards / Yours sincerely / Yours faithfully

WRITING TASK

8 Imagine you are interested in doing a course. You are going to write an email to make enquiries about it. Follow the instructions.

1 Work in pairs. Discuss what courses you are interested in (e.g. driving, dancing, art).

2 Individually, decide which questions you need to ask (e.g. course fees, start and end date).

3 Plan your email by deciding how many paragraphs you need and what to include in them.

9 **WRITE** Write your email. Use formal language and organize your email appropriately.

10 **CHECK** Use the checklist. I have …

☐ written a formal beginning and ending to the email.

☐ included a clear reason for writing.

☐ written well-organized paragraphs.

☐ used indirect questions.

☐ used suitable formal words and expressions.

11 **REVIEW** Exchange emails with a partner. Write down two things that you think they did better than you and one thing that they could improve. Share your feedback with each other.

Go to page 130 for the Reflect and review.

Campervan in Sequoia
National Park, US.

3

Unfamiliar places

GOALS

- Practise active reading by annotating
- Use narrative tenses to tell personal travel stories
- Talk about journeys
- Use visual information to help you listen
- Repair misunderstandings and confirm understanding
- Write a blog post

1 Work in pairs. Discuss the questions.

1 Look at the photo. What message(s) about travel does it send? Why?

a An unfamiliar place is anywhere that gets you away from your normal life.

b Everybody should travel – it broadens the mind.

c The best thing about travel is coming home at the end.

2 Do you agree with the ideas (a–c) about travel? Why? / Why not?

WATCH ▶

2 ▶ 3.1 Watch the video. Write the name of each place that Andrej and Ellie mention and the reason(s) they like it.

NATIONAL GEOGRAPHIC EXPLORERS

ANDREJ GAJIĆ   ELLIE DE CASTRO

3 Make connections. Discuss the questions.

1 Which of the places that Andrej and Ellie mention would you like to visit? Why?

2 What are your three favourite places? Why?

3A
No place like home

LESSON GOALS
- Practise active reading by annotating
- Rank ideas in order of usefulness
- Plan a trip in your own town/region

READING

1 Work in pairs. Discuss the questions.

1 How well would you say you know your own town, region and country? Why?

2 In Polish, there is an expression: *You praise the foreign, but don't know the local.* What do you think it means?

2 Read the title of the blog post on page 37. What do you think it will be about?

3 Read the blog post quickly to check whether your idea about the topic was correct. Does the writer persuade you to do more sightseeing in your town? Why? / Why not?

4 Read the blog post again. Are the sentences true (T) or false (F), according to the text?

1 The post is about something the writer has been doing for a while.

2 She's not happy about her normal travel habits.

3 Taking a tourist bus can teach you about a place's past.

4 Being a tourist is a lonely activity.

5 You can decide to be a tourist for the day that same morning.

6 It's easy to make small changes to your lifestyle to become a tourist in your own town.

5 Look at the Reading skill box and the example annotations in the blog post. Then annotate the rest of the blog post to prepare to give your opinion about it.

READING SKILL
Active reading by annotating

As you read a text, it can be useful to mark or annotate it. This helps you focus on important information to remember later. Ask questions about ideas and language in the text and notice new vocabulary.

- Use colours to highlight the main ideas.
- Add your own comments and reactions.
- Circle important information.
- Use symbols (e.g. ?, !, ★) next to things you don't understand, surprising information, etc.

6 Work in pairs. Use your annotations from Exercise 5 to discuss the questions.

1 Do you agree with the main idea of the blog post?

2 What information was the most interesting or surprising to you? Why?

3 Were there any words or expressions you didn't understand? Can you explain them to each other?

4 What words or expressions in the post would you like to learn?

7 Work in pairs. Look at the Critical thinking skill box. Then rank the five tips in the blog post from the most to the least useful. Give reasons for your choices.

CRITICAL THINKING SKILL
Ranking information

Ranking ideas from the most to the least useful can help you to organize your thoughts before you give your opinion. To do this effectively, …

- analyse the quality of each idea. What are the problems in doing it? (e.g. Is it expensive? Time-consuming?) What are the benefits of doing it?
- decide how relevant the ideas are to the specific situation e.g. Is it possible for everyone to do?

I think tip number 1 is the least useful. Bus tours are only available in big cities in certain countries. Lots of people, like me, don't have this option.

SPEAKING

8 Work in groups. Design a two-day holiday for yourselves in your town or region. Follow the instructions.

1 Find out what everyone in the group likes doing. Decide what places and activities in your area would appeal to everyone in the group.

2 Plan your two-day trip. Decide …
- what you will do in the morning, afternoon and evening of each day.
- where you will stay overnight.
- where you will eat.

The Center Island Ferry offers an exceptional view of the Toronto skyline, including the impressive CN Tower.

Destination...here

Text about simple trips, not going abroad

1 A trip that doesn't involve packing for two weeks or finding your passport may not seem like the highlight of your travel agenda, but it can be just as rewarding.

?? Meaning? Check later

I live in Toronto, Canada's largest city and one of its most popular tourist destinations. And yet, when I'm looking for a way to spend my time off, more often than not I head out of the city.

verb? = 'go'?

5 This year I'm determined to change that. Why is it I always feel the need to travel hundreds or thousands of miles to explore when I have so much to learn on my doorstep? ☺

Do you ...

Want to try it too? Here are five tips to set about seeing your city through new eyes.

= 'to start'

1 Take a historical tour.

Sure, you can tell a tourist the names of the buildings or tourist spots in your hometown, but do you know 10 their history? Those hop-on, hop-off bus tours might be meant for tourists, but they're a great way to improve your local history knowledge. Plus, taking note of what visitors find interesting can be fascinating, allowing you to see what might at first seem uninteresting in a whole new light. If there is no tourist bus, try joining a free walking tour. It's a great way of not only discovering things you didn't know about your city, but also meeting new people.

2 Get a room.

15 Waking up in a hotel or bed and breakfast is a tried-and-tested way to set the mood for exploring.

If you live in a suburb, head into the city. If you live in the city, consider spending a weekend getting to know the nearest town. The added excitement of being away from home for the night will only add to the day's fun.

3 Set a date.

20 There are places I pass on a regular basis in Toronto. Every time, I promise myself that one day I'll check them out. Take it from me: it will never happen without a plan. So pull out your calendar, set a date and keep it.

4 Act like a tourist.

I'm not suggesting you stand in the middle of the street taking selfies, while the locals angrily try to get past, but do pop into the tourist information centre, look out for upcoming events and follow local websites to find 25 out what's on.

5 Take something small and make it bigger.

Your daily wander around the block could turn into a walk around a new neighbourhood. Friday pizza night at home? Why not make it a mission to test out the newest pizzeria in town? You'll be surprised how simple adjustments to your everyday routines can broaden your experiences.

30 Discovering hidden places around you and being a tourist in your own city can not only be fun, but bearing in mind how much travelling can contribute to the climate emergency, it can also help save the planet. So, when planning your next holiday, start first by exploring your hometown!

EXPLORE MORE!

Search online for interesting things you can do in your town or region that you didn't know about or have never done.

3B
It's a long story!

LESSON GOALS
• Understand stories about memorable journeys
• Use narrative tenses to tell personal travel stories
• Pronounce groups of consonants correctly

Andrej Gajić with his friends in Hurghada, Egypt.

LISTENING AND GRAMMAR

1 Work in pairs. Look at the photo, which illustrates a travel story. Discuss the questions.

1 What kind of place does the photo show?
2 What do you think the story could be about?

NATIONAL GEOGRAPHIC EXPLORERS

2 🎧 3.1 Listen to Andrej Gajić talk about a memorable journey. Choose the best title for his story.

a A dangerous situation
b The tourist trap
c New friends
d Happy to be lost

3 🎧 3.1 Complete the sentences (1–5) with the correct form of the verbs in brackets, according to Andrej's account. Then listen again to check.

1 The story _____ (happen) eight years ago in Hurghada in Egypt.
2 Andrej _____ (study) sharks.
3 He _____ (walk) from the hotel when he _____ (see) a small souvenir shop.
4 He was frightened because the men _____ (close) the windows.
5 For the next two weeks, Andrej _____ (visit) them for some Egyptian tea.

4 Read the sentences in Exercise 3 again and answer the questions. Then read the Grammar box to check.

1 Which tense describes the main events in the story?
2 Which tenses are used to refer to events that were in progress?
3 Which tense is used to refer to longer actions that were in progress before the main events?
4 Which tense is used to emphasize that an action had finished before a main event?

GRAMMAR Narrative tenses

Past simple
Use for completed events in the past and the main events in stories.
*I **saw** a small souvenir shop selling papyrus.*

Past continuous
Use for events that were in progress at a specific moment in the past.
*I **was walking** from the hotel when …*

Past perfect simple
Use for events that happened before the main event and to emphasize the completion of activities.
*The salesman **had brought out** what looked like a wooden object.*

Past perfect continuous
Use for events that were in progress before the main event happened and to emphasize the continuation of activities.
*I'd **been studying** the sharks, skates and rays.*

Go to page 143 for the Grammar reference.

---

5 Complete Ellie de Castro's travel story with the correct form of the verbs in brackets. Sometimes more than one tense is possible.

Two years ago, my parents and I went on a road trip to Kiangan, Philippines. I ¹_____ (go) there for the last few years for a project I ²_____ (work on) and my parents ³_____ (want) to see the place I ⁴_____ (talk) about so much. While my dad was stuffing our bags with snacks and supplies, my mum and I ⁵_____ (race) to the car. In our family, the first person to sit down gets to choose the music on the radio! We had been expecting the journey to take about seven hours, but we ⁶_____ (forget) that it was the last weekend before Christmas. Everyone ⁷_____ (drive) out of the city back to their homes. We got there after sunset – the drive ⁸_____ (take) fourteen hours! The next day, we ⁹_____ (go) to the Education Centre where I work. But as it was the Christmas season, no one was around! My parents were disappointed that they hadn't been able to meet the people I work with. On our last day, we ¹⁰_____ (drop by) the centre again and, this time, the place was full of people! My parents were excitedly toured around by one of my teachers and closest friends. While I sat ¹¹_____ (watch) them, I was so happy to see my two homes – my parents and friends who mean so much to me – come together.

6 Work in pairs. Take turns to retell either Andrej or Ellie's stories from memory, paying careful attention to tenses.

PRONUNCIATION

7 ⌒ 3.2 Look at the Clear voice box. Underline the letters that make groups of consonants in the adverbs (1–6). Then listen to check. Practise saying the adverbs.

Some groups of consonants are more difficult to say than others, depending on …
- how many consonants are grouped.
- whether the consonant group exists in your language.
- how difficult it is for the mouth.

Practise saying the consonant groupings on their own as well as the whole words.

1 eve_nt_ually   4 unexpectedly
2 surprisingly   5 fortunately
3 interestingly   6 accidentally

SPEAKING

8 You are going to tell a story about a memorable journey. Choose one of these story titles or use your own idea. Then plan your story by thinking about the questions (1–3).

> A difficult choice   A frightening moment
> A helping hand   Lost in the city   Under the stars

1 What are the main events?
2 What background information would be useful for listeners to know?
3 What tenses will make the relationships between events clear?

9 Look at the Useful language box. Which of the expressions could you use to tell your story?

Useful language   Telling personal stories
This happened to me when I was …
I was … -ing when …
All of a sudden, …
I felt so …
Fortunately, …
I ended up …

10 Work in groups. Take turns to tell your stories. Whose story was the funniest? Whose was the most dangerous?

EXPLORE MORE!

Search online for the funniest, strangest or most incredible travel story.

3C
Out of sight of land

LESSON GOALS
- Use visual information to help you listen
- Learn travel collocations with *go on*
- Talk about journeys

Built in 1975, the *Hōkūle'a* is our best guess at what a Polynesian ocean-going canoe looked like.

HOW DID THE POLYNESIANS MAKE IT SO FAR?

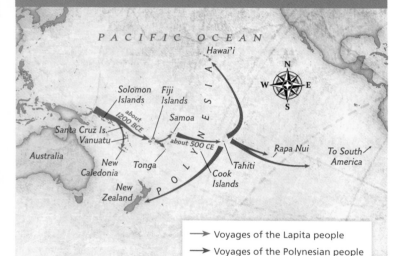

→ Voyages of the Lapita people
→ Voyages of the Polynesian people

- **twenty to thirty people on board**

- **no compasses or navigation tools – used the sun, moon and stars, and studied clouds, wave patterns, birds and fish to show them the way to land**

- **sang songs to help them remember the knowledge they needed**

- **took water and food with them and fished from canoes**

SPEAKING

1 Work in pairs. Look at the definition and discuss the questions.

voyage (n) a very long journey, often by ship

1 Why did people go on voyages in the past?
2 What were some of the dangers of long voyages?
3 Would you like to go on a voyage? Where to?

2 Look at the map and read the text. Why do you think the Polynesian voyages were impressive?

LISTENING

3 Look at the Listening skill box. Then read the map carefully. Familiarize yourself with the key places and dates and consider the direction of the journey.

LISTENING SKILL
Using visual information to help you listen

When listening, we often have visual aids such as maps, diagrams and photos. Here are some techniques to use visual information effectively.
- Familiarize yourself with the visual information before you listen.
- Listen for keywords and numbers that match names, places or other information you can see.
- As you listen, point to the parts of the image that the speaker is talking about. Follow a route with your finger, for example.
- Make notes on the image or while listening.

4 🎧 **3.3** Listen to an extract from an audiobook. Follow the tips from the Listening skill box. Add one additional piece of information you hear onto the map.

5 🎧 **3.3** Listen again. Number the questions about the Polynesians in the order that they are answered.

a How did they do it? ☐
b What did they take with them? ☐
c When did they travel? ☐
d Where did they come from? ☐
e What was the furthest they travelled? ☐
f Why are the journeys so amazing? ☐ 1

6 🎧 **3.3** Work in pairs. Divide the questions from Exercise 5 between you. Listen again and take notes on the answers.

VOCABULARY

7 Complete the summary with the correct form of these verbs.

---

end go head make reach set steer stop turn

It was the Polynesians who ¹_____ on the greatest voyages by sea when they ²_____ up on some of the remotest islands on the planet. These were sailors used to island hopping, ³_____ over for a while before carrying on. But around 1200 BCE, the Lapita ⁴_____ off on a journey east. Some settled down in the Santa Cruz Islands, but others ⁵_____ for new undiscovered islands. They ⁶_____ it as far as Tonga, where they stayed for a few hundred years. Eventually, the Polynesians ⁷_____ the Cook Islands; navigators used a combination of 'wayfinding' skills to ⁸_____ across the ocean. Much of the Pacific was within their reach in their fast canoes. If they needed to ⁹_____ back, they could just let the wind bring them home to safety.

Go to page 136 for the Vocabulary reference.

8 Read the Focus on box. Then discuss the difference in meaning, if any, between each pair of words and expressions in bold (1–5).

> **FOCUS ON** Travel collocations with *go on*
>
> *Go on* collocates with many expressions that describe: types of journey, e.g. *go on a cruise / bus tour*; travel for specific purposes, e.g. *go on a business trip / a language exchange / an expedition*; types of holiday, e.g. *a package holiday / a city break*.

Go to page 143 for the Focus on reference.

1 They're not here. They've gone on **holiday / vacation**.
2 When was the last time you went on a **journey / trip**?
3 When I was a student I went on several **exchanges / field trips** abroad.
4 Of those who went on the **expedition / voyage** to the South Pole, many lost their lives.
5 We're thinking of going on a **city break / package holiday** somewhere warm next month.

9 Work in pairs. Discuss at least three of the topics. The last time you …

- set off on a journey and realized you'd forgotten something important.
- went on a long journey.
- couldn't make it to an appointment or meeting.
- had to turn back.
- stopped over somewhere interesting.
- ended up somewhere you weren't expecting.
- headed home in the dark.

SPEAKING

10 Work in pairs. Imagine you're going on a very long journey. Discuss the questions.

1 Where are you going and how will you get there?
2 You can only take two people with you. Who will you take? Why?
3 You can only take five things with you. What will you take? Why?
4 How will you cope with being away from home?

11 Work in groups of four. Take turns to tell each other about your journey. Which did you enjoy listening to the most?

EXPLORE MORE!

Search online for 'the voyages of the Vikings', 'the Ming treasure voyages' or another voyage you'd like to learn about.

3D
Fixing misunderstandings

LESSON GOALS
- Identify misunderstandings in a conversation
- Learn three ways to fix misunderstandings
- Practise fixing misunderstandings and confirming understanding

SPEAKING

1 Work in pairs. Think of misunderstandings you have had with people, either in English, your first language or another language you know. What happened?

2 What were the reasons for the misunderstandings you described in Exercise 1? Choose from the list. What other reasons for misunderstandings can you think of?
- the message relied on cultural information that the listener didn't know
- the message used vocabulary that the listener didn't know
- the message was disorganized
- the speaker spoke too fast

LISTENING

3 ∩ 3.4 Listen to three conversations where a misunderstanding occurs. In which conversation is the person …
   a giving a recommendation?
   b giving instructions?
   c discussing accommodation arrangements?

4 ∩ 3.4 Listen to the conversations again. Choose the main reason(s) why the people in each conversation fail to understand each other from the list in Exercise 2.

MY VOICE ▶

5 ▶ 3.2 Watch the video about how misunderstandings occur. Complete each sentence with words from the video.
   1 Messages need to be _____, _____ and _____.
   2 If a message is long and complicated, you could ask the speaker to _____ it.
   3 Information that is specific to your _____ can cause misunderstanding if you don't explain it.
   4 If a message is disorganized, it might be necessary to _____ again.

6 ∩ 3.5 Look at the Communication skill box. Then listen to a continuation of one of the conversations from Exercise 3. Which strategies do the speakers use to fix the misunderstanding?

COMMUNICATION SKILL
Fixing misunderstandings

Simplify
- The speaker can: identify the key information and repeat; check the listener has understood.
- The listener can ask for a summary.

Clarify
- The speaker can: assume cultural knowledge will not be known; explain anything unique to their culture or language.
- The listener can ask the speaker to explain.

Organize
- The speaker can: signpost the order clearly; write or draw the instructions.
- The listener can ask the speaker to start again.

7 Look at the Useful language box. Then complete the sentences (1–4) with appropriate language.

Useful language   Fixing misunderstandings

Identifying misunderstandings
That isn't what I meant.
I'm getting mixed up.
That's the wrong way round.
I'm not following you.

Fixing misunderstandings
Let's start again from the beginning.
OK, to sum up, you need to …
So basically, you're saying …, right?
In other words, …
Shall I repeat it all back to you?

Confirming understanding
That makes sense.
Got it.
I see what you mean.

1 A: Let's meet at eight.
   B: Sorry, I'm getting _____ up. Are you _____ eight in the morning?

2 A: So in other _____, I think we should look at train prices before we book a flight.
   B: Yes, that makes _____.

3 A: OK, if I've been _____ you correctly, this should be right now.
   B: Let me see … No! You've got it the wrong way _____ still. This goes here, and that goes there.

4 A: Let me _____ it back to you. Out of the station, turn left. After 500 metres, second right into Broad Street.
   B: You've _____ it!

8 Work in pairs. Look at audio script 3.4 on page 161. Continue conversations 2 and 3 from Exercise 3 so that the speakers fix the misunderstandings.

9 Work with another pair. Take turns to act out one of your conversations from Exercise 8. Which strategies did the other pair use to fix the misunderstanding?

SPEAKING

10 **OWN IT!** Think of a situation in the past where you had a misunderstanding. You can use the misunderstandings you thought of in Exercise 1, or choose a different one. In pairs, explain what happened and discuss how you could have communicated more clearly to fix the problem.

Getting away from the crowd

LESSON GOALS
- Use descriptive language to make writing more engaging
- Make recommendations and give advice about a place
- Write a blog post

SPEAKING

1 Work in pairs. Discuss the questions.

1 Which type of holiday would you prefer? Why?
   a visiting friends or relatives in another city
   b a camping holiday in the mountains
   c a trip to the beach
   d backpacking on your own or with a friend

2 What other types of holiday can you think of?
3 What are the advantages of …
   a going on a package tour with a group of other people?
   b travelling alone without a schedule?

Arriving at the end of the earth

Finally reached Santiago (read about my journey up through Spain here). From the bus station I headed to the flat where I was staying. A friendly welcome and just a five-minute walk from the old town. You could stay in a *pensión*, a small hotel, but a homestay is the perfect way to practise the language and at a reasonable price. What's more, my host, Señora Vásquez, made delicious *tarta de Santiago* – a local speciality cake with wonderful almond flavours. Definitely try one if you visit!

The town is soaked in history and architecture but, with only three days, I had to prioritize. Señora Vásquez had predictable advice: 'You must go on a guided tour,' and 'Take an umbrella.' However, I didn't want to be slowed down so I went on a walking tour of my own. And thankfully, no need for that umbrella, though you should be aware that it can really pour down here.

The highlight of the city for me had to be the stunning *Parque de Alameda*, where buskers played their guitars while I enjoyed the view. I'd visited Santiago's huge cathedral that morning but, even by 11 a.m., it was crammed with tourists. As with all tourist spots, I highly recommend you make it there as early as possible. I steered through the crowds into the narrow streets of the old town. I was exhausted when I got to the park.

On my last day I took a bus to Finisterre, which means 'the end of the earth', the furthest point west in Spain. Dark clouds moved in from the ocean as I stared towards America. Finisterre was a dramatic spot to say *adiós* to the country and the perfect place to end up after an amazing trip.

I'd love to hear about your trips that have concluded in dramatic or special places. Please leave a comment!

READING FOR WRITING

2 Read the blog post on page 44. Where is 'the end of the earth' and why is it important in the blogger's trip?

3 Read the blog post again. Which of these three travellers, Piotr, Natsuki or Karinna, is the most likely to be interested in the trip the writer describes? Why?

Piotr is looking for a few days in the sun. He speaks Spanish fluently, so Spain is his preferred destination. He's never been to Santiago.

Natsuki enjoys meeting local people and getting to know a place informally. He wants to see as much of each place as he can, though he doesn't have much money.

Karinna wants to learn as much about Spanish culture and history as possible. She loves cooking and photography.

4 Look at the Writing skill box. Then follow the instructions (1–3).

WRITING SKILL
Engaging the reader in a blog post

- Personal blog posts may be about your life, but you should give readers a reason to read them. This may be to keep up to date with news, to get advice about something they are interested in doing or just for general interest.
- Use *you* to direct the message to the reader. Avoid formal language.
- Use descriptive language to make the writing more interesting. Use local words to give the reader a taste of the language and culture.
- End in an interesting way, e.g. by asking a question or inviting comments of a specific kind.

1 Find evidence in the blog post that the writer's intention is to give advice to readers who may want to go backpacking in Spain.
2 What Spanish words does the writer use to emphasize the culture of the place she's writing about?
3 What are readers invited to write about in the comments? Why does the writer ask for comments from readers?

5 Find descriptive words in the blog post that have the same meaning as these words.

1 full of
2 rain
3 beautiful
4 big
5 full
6 tired

WRITING TASK

6 You are going to write a blog post about a trip you have been on or a place you know well. Think about what kind of reader you want to interest and a reason they should read it. Share your ideas with a partner.

7 Look at the Useful language box. Write sentences using five of the expressions to include in your blog post.

Useful language Making recommendations

Recommending things to do
I'd highly recommend …
You really must visit …
… is the perfect way/place/spot to (relax)
… has so much to offer (travellers on a budget)
A highlight of the (city) for me was …

Warning and advising
You should be aware that …
Don't forget to …
It's important (not) to …

8 WRITE Write your blog post. Remember to follow the tips in the Writing skill box.

9 CHECK Use the checklist. I have …
- [ ] used descriptive language and local words to make my writing more interesting.
- [ ] used *you* to direct the message to the reader.
- [ ] used correct narrative tenses when describing events.
- [ ] used the Useful language to give advice and recommendations.
- [ ] ended the blog in an interesting way.

10 REVIEW Work in pairs. Read your partner's blog post. What was the most useful piece of advice? Which descriptive language engaged you in the post most?

Go to page 131 for the Reflect and review.

EXPLORE MORE!

Find a travel blog post about a place that interests you. Or start your own blog!

Eritrean sisters are reunited after more than two decades.

4

Reconnecting

GOALS

- Summarize and synthesize information from written and spoken sources
- Report what people say
- Discuss personal relationships
- Understand different accents
- Understand and adapt to different turn-taking styles
- Write a story

1 Work in pairs. Look at the photo and discuss the questions.

1 Why might the women have been apart?

2 How do you think they are feeling now?

WATCH ▶

2 ▶ 4.1 Watch the video and answer the questions. Write Federico (F), Carolina (C) or both (B).

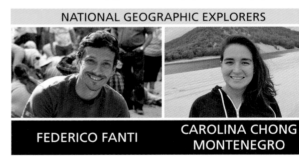

NATIONAL GEOGRAPHIC EXPLORERS

FEDERICO FANTI — CAROLINA CHONG MONTENEGRO

1 Who can't keep in touch with their family as much as they'd like to?

2 Who always surprises their children when they come home?

3 Who says they feel a strong connection to home?

3 Make connections. Discuss the questions.

1 How do you (or would you) feel about being away from your family or friends for a long time?

2 What do you normally do when you come back home after being away?

4A
In touch with nature

LESSON GOALS
* Summarize an article
* Synthesize information from written and spoken sources
* Talk about ways to connect with nature

READING

1 Work in groups. Rank the ways of staying in touch with nature from the most to the least enjoyable.

a going for walks

b watching nature documentaries

c living in a house in a forest with no electricity or running water

d visiting wildlife parks

e taking part in a conservation project, e.g. planting trees

f going camping

g looking at pictures of nature

2 Read the article on page 49 quickly, scanning it for key words. Which ways of staying in touch with nature from Exercise 1 are mentioned? What other ways are mentioned?

3 Read the article again. Are the sentences true (T), false (F) or not given (NG)?

1 John Benedict lives in his car because he doesn't have enough money to pay the rent.

2 Living close to nature isn't a completely new idea.

3 People who live in the countryside have a lower risk of fifteen diseases.

4 Walking in nature for at least five hours a month can lower your blood pressure.

5 Scientists also recommend that you stay at home and look at pictures of nature.

6 Most teenagers in the US spend time indoors rather than outdoors.

4 Look at the Reading skill box. Then summarize the article in a mind map using these two main topics: ways of connecting with nature and benefits.

READING SKILL
Summarizing

You may find it helpful to summarize a text …
* to remember the main ideas better.
* to use the notes in your own text later.
* to retell to a friend.

One way to do this is by using a mind map. Remember to focus on the main ideas only and use short phrases.

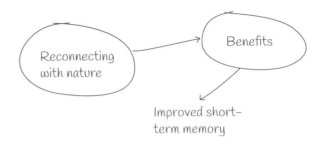

NATIONAL GEOGRAPHIC EXPLORER

5 🎧 **4.1** Listen to Carolina Chong Montenegro talk about connecting with nature. Note down the main ideas she mentions.

6 Work in pairs. Compare your notes from Exercise 5 and answer the questions.

1 Which ideas and topics from the article does Carolina also mention?

2 What new things did you learn?

7 Look at the Critical thinking skill box. Then combine your notes on the article and the listening into a 50–100 word summary.

CRITICAL THINKING SKILL
Synthesizing information

Sometimes you need to synthesize information from various sources, combining the main ideas from each one. It involves thinking critically about what the most important information is and how the sources differ or are similar.
* Remember to include information from each source.
* Don't focus on too many details.
* Only mention the most important points.
* Organize the text logically (e.g. write about the similarities first, then the differences).

SPEAKING

8 Work in pairs. Go to page 155. Roleplay the two situations.

People relax under the cherry blossoms in Sumida Park, Tokyo, Japan.

Stay healthy by reconnecting with nature

1 Can you imagine living a simple life close to nature? Can you imagine leaving most of what you own behind? It might seem impossible to many of us, but many people have done it and improved their mental and physical
5 health in the process.

People like John Benedict, for example. He's been living out of his van for the last 25 years. Reducing his possessions to a minimum and only turning on his phone to listen to voicemail, Benedict is able to lead a very
10 simple lifestyle that he says keeps him closer to nature and his community. And, as an added bonus, he's also saved a fair bit on the rent!

The idea of living a simple life in touch with nature might seem new to some, but many tribes around the
15 world have lived lives free of most modern possessions for thousands of years. They not only
20 live close to nature, but also feel a deep spiritual connection with it and the need to protect it.

> ... keeping in touch with nature can have enormous benefits for your body and mind.

25 According to scientists, keeping in touch with nature can have enormous benefits for your body and mind. If you're a city resident, the good news is you don't need to necessarily leave your house and start living in a forest. Here are some easy research-based tips that can have
30 big effects on your well-being.

1 Move closer to a park.
It seems that people who live within about half a mile of green space have a significantly lower risk of several diseases. Added bonus: you can easily go for a picnic or
35 do some sport.

2 Go for a walk.
Even a short walk in a park or the countryside can make you feel less stressed and reduce your blood pressure. And a longer walk in a green area improves your short-
40 term memory. Time to put those walking boots on!

3 Hang up a picture of nature at home.
Can't go for a walk every day? Don't panic! According to Korean scientists, just *looking* at nature images activates brain areas associated with caring for others.
45 On the other hand, looking at urban landscapes can make you feel more anxious.

4 Listen to nature.
Ideally, while walking in the park or a forest. But if that's not possible, listening to the sounds of nature, such as
50 bird calls or rain falling, while at home or work, can make you feel more relaxed. Something to consider when choosing the next playlist.

The scary thing is, though, that despite all these benefits that nature brings, it seems most of us are less and less
55 in touch with nature. For example, it turns out American adults spend less time outdoors than they do inside their cars! And, believe it or not, only ten per cent of American teenagers spend time outside on a daily basis.

There's an ancient Korean saying, *Shin to bul ee* – your
60 body and nature are one. It might be time we lived life with this in mind.

EXPLORE MORE!

Challenge yourself to reconnect with nature this month. Choose tips from the article or others you find online. Write a blog post or journal entry about your experience.

4B Reunited

LESSON GOALS
* Report what people say
* Use stress to highlight different information
* Resolve a conflict

READING AND GRAMMAR

1 Work in pairs. Discuss the questions.

1 Have you ever lost touch with an old friend or family member? Why?

2 Did you get back in touch with them? How?

2 Look at the headline and photo of the news article. With your partner, discuss what you think the story might be about. Then read the article to check.

3 Which person from the article might have said these sentences? Read the article again to check.

1 'We'd love it if you could come to the wedding.'
Maria and her partner or Maria's parents

2 'Come on, Samira, come to the wedding.'

3 'I have to say, I was very confused.'

4 'I think it was terrible you forgot me.'

5 'Of course I didn't forget you!'

6 'I *did* send you the invitation!'

7 'We'll definitely look into how the invitation got lost.'

8 'It's the postal service's fault we stopped talking to each other.'

4 Find the parts of the article that refer to the sentences in Exercise 3. Underline the reporting verbs.

When Maria's family <u>invited</u> her friends to attend her wedding ...

5 Match these verbs with the correct verb pattern in the Grammar box on page 51. Use the news article to help you.

admit	blame	claim	deny	invite	persuade	promise

Friends fall out over lost invitation

When Maria's family invited her friends to attend her wedding, Maria was sure she wouldn't need to persuade one of her closest friends, Samira, to come. After all, they had known each other for years. But the wedding came and went with no word from Samira. Meanwhile, Samira was waiting for her invitation. She admits being confused but said nothing, explaining that she didn't think it was correct to remind Maria to send her the invitation.

That was in 2015.

They met socially once afterwards and Samira accused Maria of forgetting her. Maria denied forgetting, of course, and claimed to have sent the invitation with all the others. But neither believed the other one and they gradually grew apart. Then, in August 2019, Maria got a message from Samira: 'Oh my goodness! You did send me an invite!' A photo showed the date of the letter: 10th January 2015. Somehow, it had got lost in the post. The postal service has promised to look into the situation. Maria and Samira blame the postal service for ending their relationship and say they can be friends again.

GRAMMAR Reported speech and reporting verbs

In reported speech, verb forms and reference words (e.g. time and place expressions) might change.

'Are you free **tomorrow?'** ➜ *Elyse asked her* **whether she was** *free* **the next day.**

Some reporting verbs follow a specific pattern.

verb + to + infinitive
*Maria **agreed to meet** Samira.*

verb + object + to + infinitive
*Maria **asked her friends to celebrate**.*

verb + -ing
*Samira **recommended using** online invitations.*

verb + preposition + -ing
*The post office **apologized for losing** it.*

verb + object + preposition + -ing
*Samira **accused Maria of forgetting**.*

Go to page 144 for the Grammar reference.

6 Report the conversations (1–2) using the verbs in the correct space. You might need to add extra words.

1 Man: You forgot to call me to say you were going to be late!

Woman: That's not true. I did call, but your phone was off.

Man: Oh, you're right! I'm so sorry! I'll make sure I charge my battery next time.

_____
accuse   apologize   deny   promise
_____

He _____ to call him.

He accused her of forgetting to call him.

The woman _____. The man
_____. He _____ he charges his battery next time.

2 Brother: Would you like to go for a coffee on Saturday?

Sister: Not really, after how you behaved last time!

Brother: I'm really sorry … I won't do it again.

Sister: OK, fine. Let's meet up then.

_____
agree   apologize   invite   promise   refuse
_____

The brother _____.
At first, the sister _____ because of his behaviour last time. But when he _____ and _____, she _____.

7 Work in groups. Follow the instructions.

1 Individually, choose one reporting verb from Exercise 5 or 6. Don't tell the rest of the group. Write a sentence that performs the verb's function.

accuse ➜ *'Sung-Hyun, you lost my pencil!'*

2 Take turns to say your sentence. The rest of the group writes it down as reported speech.

Eun accused Sung-Hyun of losing his pencil.

PRONUNCIATION

8 🎧 **4.2** Look at the Clear voice box. Then listen to the same sentence said three times. Which of the underlined words is stressed each time?

She <u>claimed</u> to understand what <u>I</u> had <u>said</u>.

CLEAR VOICE
Using stress for emphasis (2)

Stressed words carry the most important meaning, such as new information.
If the meaning changes, different words are stressed.
What did he do? ➜ *He **accused** me of lying.*
What did he accuse you of? ➜ *He accused me of **lying**!*
Who did he accuse of lying? ➜ *He accused **me** of lying!*

9 🎧 **4.2** Listen again. Pay attention to the stress to work out the meaning of the sentences. Which sentence (a–c) would follow each one?

a … But I don't think she actually understood me.
b … I don't think she understood you, though.
c … But she was still confused by what I wrote.

SPEAKING

10 Work in groups of three. Go to page 155. Read your role cards. Then try to reach an agreement.

EXPLORE MORE!

Find and read an unusual story online of a pet or possession that got lost and was reunited with its owners.

4C
Keeping in touch

LESSON GOALS
- Understand different accents
- Pronounce /iː/ and /ɪ/
- Discuss personal relationships
- Use phrasal verbs correctly

SPEAKING

1 Write the names of people in your life that match the descriptions (1–4). Exchange your list of names with a partner. Take turns to ask each other about the people on your list.

1 someone you have known for a long time
2 someone from your studies or work that you are glad to have met
3 someone you get along very well with
4 someone that you don't see often because they live far away

> A: How long have you known Petra?
> B: Only a few months, but she's someone I'm glad to know. She's a really close friend already.

LISTENING AND PRONUNCIATION

NATIONAL GEOGRAPHIC EXPLORER

2 🎧 **4.3** Look at the Listening skill box. Then listen to a sentence from an interview with Federico Fanti, an Italian speaker of English. Listen to how he pronounces the underlined words.

I <u>still</u> get together <u>with</u> a couple of them from time to time. I <u>mean</u>, it helps working still in the same <u>city</u> I grew up <u>in</u>.

LISTENING SKILL
Understanding accents

When you listen to people speaking English, you will hear a wide variety of accents. It's helpful to practise listening to as many different accents as you can. Accents you are used to hearing are easier to understand, wherever they are from.

Federico Fanti with friends and colleagues in the Dolomites, Italy.

3 Look at the Clear voice box. Practise saying the underlined words from Exercise 2, remembering the difference between long and short 'i'.

CLEAR VOICE
Pronouncing long and short 'i'

English has a long /iː/ as in *mean* and a short /ɪ/ as in *with*. Make sure that you make a difference in length between them. You may find it helpful to even exaggerate the long /iː/ slightly.

4 🎧 **4.4** Listen to the interview with Federico. Who does he talk about?

a family members

b old school friends

c people he works with at the university now

d people he has met when travelling for work

e people he has met when travelling on holiday

5 🎧 **4.4** Listen again. Choose the correct option to complete the sentences.

1 Federico *works / doesn't work* in the same city he grew up in.

2 He believes that the internet *has / hasn't* helped him keep in touch with friends.

3 Federico says it's important to have good relationships with people *at university / on a dig*.

4 He *keeps / doesn't keep* in touch with most of the people he meets on digs.

5 He met his best friend in *Japan / Canada*.

6 They last saw each other *two / ten* years ago.

VOCABULARY

6 Read the text. What relationships does the person mention?

I'm from Ghana, but now I'm part of a programme that helps migrants adapt to their lives in France. I've met a lot of fascinating people here. I ¹get along well with all of them, but with some you really ²hit it off instantly. We try not to ³lose touch with each other if they leave for another city, but it's difficult to ⁴keep in close contact. Fortunately, some of us stay in the city and we try to ⁵stick together, go out for a coffee once in a while to ⁶catch up. I miss my friends and family back in Ghana and try to ⁷keep in touch with them as much as possible. And whenever I go back, we ⁸reconnect immediately.

EXPLORE MORE!

Record yourself talking for one minute about someone special in your life or someone interesting that you have met.

7 Match the bold expressions in the questions (a–h) with the correct form of the underlined expressions in Exercise 6 (1–8).

a Which of your classmates do you **see, talk or write to outside class**?

b Which members of your family do you **see, talk or write to a lot**?

c Which people at work or at school do you **have a friendly relationship with**?

d Are you ever in situations where it's important to have friends so that you can **help and support each other**?

e Have you ever met someone and you **were very friendly with each other straight away**?

f Are there any friends that you have **stopped communicating with** who you'd like to see again?

g How often do you talk to your friends to **get their news and give them yours**?

h Who would you like to **meet and talk to again**?

Go to page 136 for the Vocabulary reference.

8 Read the Focus on box. Then write three other questions about relationships using expressions from Exercise 6. Make sure you use phrasal verbs correctly.

FOCUS ON Transitive and intransitive phrasal verbs

Some phrasal verbs can be both **transitive** (needing an object) or **intransitive** (not needing an object).

I need to finally **catch up with** *Rasman.* (Rasman is the object.)

Rasman and I need to finally **catch up**. (no object)

You can add *with* to many intransitive phrasal verbs to make them transitive.

Go to page 144 for the Focus on reference.

SPEAKING

9 Work in pairs. Use the questions from Exercises 7 and 8 to prepare a questionnaire about relationships. Follow the instructions.

1 Choose six questions to include.

2 Talk to as many people in the class as possible.

3 Prepare a two-minute presentation sharing the results with the class.

Understanding turn-taking styles

LESSON GOALS
- Understand the main turn-taking styles
- Adapt your style to communicate more effectively
- Participate and invite others to participate in a group discussion

SPEAKING

1 Work in pairs. Read the situations and discuss the questions (1–3).

a You're at a café with a friend you haven't seen for many years. There are pauses in between questions and answers from you and your friend.

b You're talking to your friends. You ask questions to invite each other to speak. You speak fairly fast but rarely interrupt each other.

c You're with some friends. They're speaking really fast. You're trying to participate, but they are interrupting each other and speaking loudly.

1 Who do you have similar styles of conversations with?

2 In which type of situations are you the most and the least comfortable? Why?

3 What kinds of people would find quieter conversations, like in the first scenario, more difficult? Who might find noisier conversations difficult?

LISTENING

2 🎧 4.5 Listen to three conversations. Match them with the situations in Exercise 1. Which group …

1 has the most similar conversation style to the one you normally use?

2 would you enjoy participating in the most?

3 🎧 4.5 Look at the infographic on page 55. Then listen again and match the conversations with the three turn-taking styles.

4 Work in pairs. Discuss the questions.

1 What do you know about the sports in the infographic?

2 How are the three turn-taking styles similar to bowling, basketball and rugby?

3 Which style is the most similar to your own?

4 Does your style sometimes change, depending on the situation?

Are you a bowling, basketball or rugby communicator?

Communication experts have identified three main styles of communication: bowling, basketball and rugby. Which one are you?

BOWLING
slow pace, pauses between turns, no interruptions

BASKETBALL
fast pace, quick turn-taking, rare interruptions

RUGBY
very fast pace, many interruptions, no pauses

MY VOICE

5 ▶ 4.2 Watch the video and think about the questions. Then discuss your answers in pairs.

1 In your opinion, which are the most important factors that influence your turn-taking style?

2 What's the most important piece of advice for you to remember when speaking? Why?

6 Look at the Communication skill box. What advice would you give to …

1 a rugby-style communicator talking to a bowling-style communicator?

2 a bowling-style communicator talking to a basketball-style communicator?

COMMUNICATION SKILL
Adapting your turn-taking style

Naturally, you probably have one dominant turn-taking style, but sometimes you might need to choose a different one to communicate effectively. There are several things you can change.

- You can increase / decrease your dominance by speaking more slowly and quietly, or more quickly and loudly.
- You can give others a greater or lesser chance to speak in your place, by changing how often you interrupt or pause.
- You can help create a more even participation by inviting others to participate, asking not to be interrupted and asking for more time to speak.

7 🎧 4.6 Listen to one of the conversations from Exercise 2 again. This time, the speakers adapt their turn-taking style. How do they do this?

8 🎧 4.6 Look at the Useful language box. Which expressions did the speakers use in Exercise 7? Listen again to check.

Useful language   Taking turns

Interrupting
I'd like to just add that …
I'm glad you brought that up because …
Can I just jump in there?

Dealing with interruptions
Sorry, can I just finish what I was saying?
As I was saying, …

Inviting others to participate
Tell me more about …
I've talked too much already. What did you want to say?

Buying yourself time to speak
So, let me see …
Where was I? Oh yes, …

SPEAKING

9 OWN IT! Work in groups of three. Go to page 155 and follow the instructions.

A chance encounter

LESSON GOALS
- Use short and long sentences to express a different mood in a narrative
- Make a narrative more interesting by describing actions
- Write a story

SPEAKING

1 Work in pairs. Discuss the questions.

1 Do you read or listen to stories? What type of story do you like?

2 Do you tell stories to other people or know anyone who does? What kind of stories?

3 Do you think telling and listening to stories is a good way to connect with others? Why? / Why not?

2 You are going to read a story. Look at the title and photo. What do you think the story will be about?

READING FOR WRITING

3 Read the story. How is it similar to your ideas from Exercise 2? How is it different?

I couldn't believe my eyes!

It was just another grey and rainy Monday morning with no signs anywhere that it would be any different from all the other Monday mornings, nor that anything extraordinary was supposed to take place.

I had been living in Utrecht for two months. I was walking to work holding an umbrella in one hand and my breakfast in the other, which I hadn't eaten at home because of lack of time. 'That's a poor excuse', I told myself off.

Completely lost in thought, I suddenly felt something hit my forehead. Then I was on the ground. Everything went black. The next thing I remember is someone's concerned face above mine. 'It's OK. I'm fine', I mumbled with difficulty.

And then I realized whose face it was. 'Carlotta, is that you?', I yelled in disbelief. I jumped to my feet at once as if I'd never fallen down. We gave each other a big hug.

'What a coincidence!', I shouted, still shaking her hand. We hadn't seen each other in years and the last I heard was that Carlotta was living in Argentina.

'I moved here last week', she said, smiling at me. 'You clearly haven't changed – as clumsy as ever! You walked right into that lamppost!', she laughed. She offered to drive me to work. We spent the next half an hour rapidly exchanging news and agreed to meet at the weekend to catch up properly.

I really couldn't believe my eyes when I saw her that day. The world can be such a small place.

4 Read the story again and answer the questions. Then look at the Writing skill box to check.

1 When is the present tense used?
2 The writer uses long and short sentences in different parts of the story. How does each sentence type affect the mood of the story?

WRITING SKILL
Making a story entertaining

In stories, longer sentences are often used for descriptions and to show a relaxed, slow mood. Short sentences, on the other hand, are used in action scenes to make them feel faster.

You can describe actions to make a story more interesting by using …
- adverbs, e.g. *happily, angrily, unexpectedly, silently.*
- prepositional phrases, e.g. *in anger, with effort.*
- gerunds, e.g. **shaking** his head, **running** *towards me.*

Stories use a variety of past tenses (see page 143 for reference), but present and future tenses are used to present characters' direct words and thoughts. This makes the story more immediate.

5 Look at the paragraphs (1–2). Which paragraph presents a relaxed (R) scene and which presents an action (A) scene? Change the length of the sentences to reflect what is happening.

1 It was a sunny afternoon. The birds were singing. The sun was slowly setting. I was jogging in the park. I tried to leave the busy day behind me.
2 While I was running, I held my phone in one hand trying to dial my son's number because I'd promised to pick him up from basketball practice and I knew I wouldn't make it on time; and with the other waving to stop a taxi, but they all seemed busy.

6 Rewrite the reported sentences as direct speech.

1 Alicia claimed she'd never seen that man before.
   'I've never seen this man before', Alicia claimed.
2 My dad offered to drive us to the airport.
3 Widya reminded me to invite Miguel to the party.

7 Read the story again. Underline examples of the three ways of describing action: adverbs, prepositional phrases and gerunds.

8 Make the descriptions more interesting by adding these expressions.

in anger   in surprise   not moving   silently
terribly   with difficulty

1 I got up _____. My back hurt me _____. Too much exercise yesterday.
2 I opened my eyes _____ and stood there _____. I'd won first prize in the story competition!
3 My mum looked at me _____ while I stared _____ at the floor. I'd broken her favourite vase.

WRITING TASK

9 **WRITE** Write a story based on either real or imaginary events. Follow the instructions.

1 Choose an option.
   a Work on your own. Write 200 to 250 words.
   b Work in pairs. Write 100 to 125 words each.
   c Work in groups of three. Take turns to begin, continue and end the story.
2 Choose a topic.
   a They thought they would never see each other again
   b A twin sister/brother I never knew I had
   c From enemy to best friend
   d Your own idea
3 Write your story. Use the Writing skill box to help you.

10 **CHECK** Use the checklist. I have …

☐ used longer sentences for descriptions of slow, relaxed events.
☐ used shorter sentences for action scenes.
☐ used adverbs, prepositional phrases and gerunds to describe actions.
☐ used present tenses for characters' thoughts and words.

11 **REVIEW** Exchange stories with another student or group. What's your favourite part of the story? Which sentences describe actions or a relaxed mood well?

Go to page 131 for the Reflect and review.

People practising yoga on the beach, Rizhao, China.

5

Healthy body, healthy mind

GOALS

- Identify and understand cause and effect in an article
- Talk about consequences using conditionals
- Discuss mental and physical health
- Listen for key words to understand general meaning
- Adapt language to be easier to understand
- Write a 'for and against' essay

1 **Work in pairs. Discuss the questions.**

1 Look at the photo. What are the people doing? Have you ever tried this type of exercise?
2 What do you do to stay healthy?
3 In what ways can physical exercise affect how you feel emotionally? Do you think how you feel emotionally can also affect your body? How?

WATCH ▶

2 ▶ 5.1 Watch the video. Answer the questions.

NATIONAL GEOGRAPHIC EXPLORERS

| MARIA FADIMAN | ALEC JACOBSON |

1 What does Maria do to help her relax?
2 What kinds of exercise does Alec enjoy?
3 In what ways are the body and the mind connected for Maria and Alec?

3 Make connections. Discuss the questions.

1 Do you enjoy the same activities as Maria and Alec?
2 What do you do when you feel stressed? How does it help?

LESSON GOALS
- Identify and understand cause and effect in an article
- Distinguish cause from correlation
- Discuss how to tackle loneliness

READING

1 Work in pairs. Discuss the questions.

1 What are some reasons why people might feel lonely?

2 What could people do to feel less lonely? Make a list of five things.

2 Read the article on page 61 quickly. Are any of your ideas from Exercise 1 mentioned? Which idea might be the most useful?

3 Complete the sentences with words from the article.

1 The article offers three _____ showing how people are finding _____ to the problem of loneliness.

2 Interacting with the animals brings _____ to the lives of residents in homes for the elderly and gives them a chance to _____ with others.

3 Polly and Audrey don't find the difference in _____ a problem because they have so much in _____.

4 Gamers don't just know each other _____; they get together _____ in gaming centres too.

4 Match the beginnings of the sentences (1–5) with the endings (a–e).

1 Loneliness has a negative impact …
2 It can also lead …
3 The positive effects might not be due …
4 Playing video games can result …
5 Thanks to gaming centres, …

a … on how people feel.
b … people can meet their online friends.
c … to poorer health.
d … in feeling more connected.
e … to the animals.

5 Read the sentences in Exercise 4 again. Underline the expressions that show cause and effect. Then look at the Reading skill box to check.

EXPLORE MORE!

Find out about projects that help tackle loneliness in your area and how you could take part.

Identifying and understanding cause and effect

There are a number of expressions that can help you identify and understand connections between effects and their causes.

To show effects: *have an impact/effect on, lead to, result in*

To show causes: *due to (the fact that), because (of), be caused by, one reason why is/was, thanks to*

6 Which part of the sentences in Exercise 4 is the cause (C)? Which is the effect (E)?

7 Work in pairs. Look at the Critical thinking skill box. Then read the article again and decide which sentences (1–3) show a correlation and which a probable cause.

CRITICAL THINKING SKILL
Distinguishing cause from correlation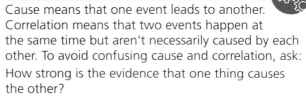

Cause means that one event leads to another. Correlation means that two events happen at the same time but aren't necessarily caused by each other. To avoid confusing cause and correlation, ask:
How strong is the evidence that one thing causes the other?
What other possible causes could there be?

1 Looking after hens can have a positive impact on physical and mental health.
There's not much evidence for it in the article. Other causes might be …
2 Playing video games helps people make friends.
3 Older people in big cities feel isolated because they don't know their neighbours.

SPEAKING

8 Work in groups. Discuss ways to build your school community and avoid loneliness among the students. Use the questions to help you.

1 What are possible causes of loneliness?
2 What ideas for social activities might work in your school (e.g. coffee mornings, a film club)?
3 When and where would the activities be?

Lonely people not so lonely any more

1 Loneliness can affect anyone and has a negative impact not only on how people feel, but it can also lead to poorer physical health. But it doesn't have to be that way! Organizations around the world are finding innovative ways to tackle the problem. Here are three success stories from around the world of people finding solutions for all ages.

5 (H)ENRICHING PEOPLE'S LIVES

Several projects in the UK, Australia and the Netherlands run by HenPower have been set up to tackle loneliness. Hens, female chickens, are brought to elderly homes, where the residents can feed them
10 and look after them.

The interesting thing is that the positive effects might not be due to the animals themselves but because the project gives the residents a sense of purpose and allows them to connect with people around them
15 while interacting with the animals.

Hen Roadshows bring the project into the community, with elderly volunteers, known as 'hensioners', sharing their knowledge with local schoolchildren and introducing them to their feathered friends.

20 One of the volunteers, 89-year-old Tommy Appleby, says: 'I wasn't sure about the hens at first, but when I think back now, I've never regretted it. I never miss a session. I've made some great friends through HenPower. What I like about it is that you're not
25 entertained, you're involved.'

WHO CARES? YOUR NEIGHBOURS

North London Cares is a charity that has built a sense of community by bringing together young professionals and their older neighbours at regular
30 social events and through one-to-one activities. They recognized that the rush and pace of the city can sometimes feel too much, and have helped many people who feel isolated. The group's founder, Alex Smith, says it's not just about befriending the older
35 people, as the benefits are two-way, with the younger volunteers getting as much out of the interactions as the older participants.

Volunteer Polly says: 'I love visiting Audrey every week. We have a great, easy-going friendship. Just because
40 there's an age gap doesn't mean we don't have lots in common. We both love the theatre and reading. We also listen to each other's problems (Audrey always has great advice) and most importantly we make each other laugh.'

45 REAL FRIENDS IN IMAGINARY WORLDS

Surprisingly, playing more video games can result in feeling more connected. So, if you're thinking 'Hold on, won't gaming in your bedroom make you even more lonely?', think again!

50 Playing more video games can actually result in feeling more connected. Some gamers don't feel accepted in the real world, so they look online where they can form friendships with like-minded people.

Thanks to gaming centres around the world, such as
55 Frikiplaza in Mexico City, people can also meet their online friends face-to-face. Here, the isolation caused by feeling different from others disappears and they are safe to be themselves and feel accepted. Video games are just the starting point towards a sense of
60 community and real-world relationships.

HenPower projects bring chickens to residents of homes for the elderly.

5B

The secrets of sleep

LESSON GOALS
- Read and understand an infographic about how to get a better night's sleep
- Talk about consequences using conditionals
- Understand elision in connected speech

READING AND GRAMMAR

1 Work in pairs. Discuss the questions.

1 How much sleep do you typically get each night? Do you think you get enough sleep?

2 What's the best night's sleep you've ever had?

2 Look at the infographic. Find …

1 three reasons we are not sleeping enough.

2 three tricks to help you get to sleep.

3 one piece of information that is important to you personally. Why?

3 Match the beginnings of the sentences (1–4) with the endings (a–d). Then look at the infographic again to check.

1 If we didn't have electric lights

2 If I'd read my book instead of my e-reader, …

3 It can be hard to get to sleep …

4 If you have a shower every night at the same time, …

a … unless you have enough melatonin.

b … you'll probably sleep better.

c … I would have been able to sleep.

d … we would have to go to bed earlier.

What makes us sleepy?

retina
Cells in the eye respond to blue light and set our body's internal clock, in time with day and night.

pineal gland
As blue light decreases, the brain releases melatonin, which tells the body to prepare for sleep.

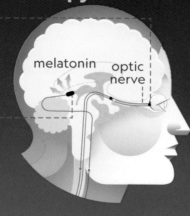

melatonin — optic nerve

Not getting enough sleep?

We are sleeping two hours fewer each night than people did one hundred years ago. Why?

- electric light artificially extends the day
- all-night television and other distractions
- LED and blue-light screens (mobile phones, tablets)

Sleeping tips and tricks

Take a warm bath or shower before bed

The change in temperature when you step back into the cooler air helps prepare your body for sleep more quickly.

The 4, 7, 8 breathing technique

- Breathe in through your nose while counting to four.
- Hold your breath for a count of seven.
- Breathe out through your mouth for a count of eight.
- Repeat four times.

Squeeze and relax your muscles

Starting from your head down to your toes, tighten each muscle for five seconds and then relax it.

Sleep delay at night

Tablet 96 min	Smartphone 67 min	E-reader 58 min	Electric lights 55 min	Candle 0 min
●●●●●●	●●●●	●●●●	●●●	●

← MORE BLUE — LIGHT SOURCE RANGE — LESS BLUE →

● = Brightness

4 Look at the sentences in Exercise 3 again and answer the questions (1–3). Then read the Grammar box to check your answers.

1 Which sentence describes a situation that is generally true? What verb form is used in each clause?

2 Which sentence describes a possible future situation? What verb forms are used?

3 Which sentences describe imaginary situations? Which of these is referring to the past?

GRAMMAR Conditionals

Present verb forms

Use **zero conditional** sentences to describe situations that are generally true.

If the eye doesn't receive enough blue light, the brain finds it difficult to wake up.

Use **first conditional** sentences to describe possible future situations.

You won't feel sleepy unless you turn off the light.

Past verb forms

Use **second conditional** sentences to describe imaginary present or future situations and their consequences.

Would we have more time if we didn't sleep?

Use **third conditional** sentences to describe imaginary situations in the past and their consequences.

He wouldn't have seen the sunrise if he hadn't woken up early.

Go to page 145 for the Grammar reference.

5 Choose the correct option to complete the sentences.

1 I'd be less grumpy if I *can / could* get more sleep!

2 I would *have stayed / stay* up late if I'd started watching that film.

3 I think if I *didn't try / hadn't tried* the 4, 7, 8 technique, I'd still be having sleep problems.

4 I'd never sleep on a long flight *if / unless* I didn't have my travel pillow.

5 You'll feel better if you *have / had* a nap.

6 It can be easy to feel stressed about not falling asleep *if / unless* you hide your clock!

7 If you *use / will use* a device with a lot of blue light at night, it *may / would* be harder to sleep.

8 If you *had / have* to look at your phone for long periods, you *can / will* use the 'Eye comfort' setting.

PRONUNCIATION

6 🎧 **5.1** Look at the Clear voice box and listen to the example sentence.

CLEAR VOICE
Understanding elision in connected speech

In fast speech, multiple words are often 'squeezed' together so that it is difficult to hear them.

I'd've seen him yesterday if he'd come to work.

In this example, it's difficult to hear the first three words. Notice how the past participle *seen* helps you understand.

7 🎧 **5.2** Listen and complete the sentences. Then practise saying the sentences fast like the speakers, then slowly and clearly. Which way do you prefer?

1 _____ fine if she'd managed to sleep on the train.

2 _____ a lot more comfortably last night if the bed _____ a bit bigger.

SPEAKING

8 Work in groups of three or four. Play 'Consequences'. Use these sentence beginnings and see how many sentences you can make. Each new sentence should follow on from the previous one.

1 If I hadn't forgotten to set my alarm, …

2 If I hadn't fallen asleep on the train, …

3 If it had been raining when I woke up this morning, …

A: If I hadn't forgotten to set my alarm last night, I wouldn't have got up so late.

B: If I hadn't got up so late, I …

9 Tell your 'consequences' as stories to the rest of the class. Which story is the longest? Which is the funniest?

I forgot to set my alarm, so I got up late and missed my train. That meant that I didn't get to the park on time and missed meeting my boyfriend …

EXPLORE MORE!

Search online for 'ways to improve your sleep'. Challenge yourself to get a better night's sleep by following some of the suggestions.

5C

Fit for the job

LESSON GOALS
- Discuss mental and physical health
- Listen for keywords to understand general meaning
- Talk about things you'd like to be true using *I wish* and *If only*

VOCABULARY

1 Work in pairs. Look at the photos. Which jobs …
1 can be physically exhausting?
2 are emotionally stressful?
3 involve working nights?
4 are dangerous?
5 have stressful working conditions?

2 Read the sentences. Are the problems described mainly physical (P) or mental (M)? What jobs do you think they might be talking about?
1 Those in competitive professions may find it hard to **cope with** the stress; many complain of **burn-out** at a young age.
2 My **symptoms** include feeling cold and a headache. I think I'm **coming down with** the flu. I probably got it from a customer.
3 Many workers suffer from **anxiety** and **depression**, just like their patients.
4 I have to **stay in shape**. If I wasn't, with all this physical work, I'd be **at risk** of serious injury.
5 This shift feels long. I haven't been able to **take a nap** yet. But there's no point **feeling sorry for yourself**. You just have to get on.
6 Normally it's me who covers classes when colleagues **call in sick**, but I'm off work at the moment. It's taking me ages to **get over** this cough.

3 Write five pieces of health advice using some of the phrases from Exercise 2. Then share your advice with a partner.

If you're coming down with a sore throat, you should drink hot water with honey and lemon.

Go to page 137 for the Vocabulary reference.

LISTENING AND GRAMMAR

4 🎧 **5.3** Look at the Listening skill box. Then listen to interviews with Alec Jacobson and Maria Fadiman. Answer the questions (1–3).

LISTENING SKILL
Listening for keywords to understand the general meaning

Listen for keywords related to the subject to help you work out the general meaning. Make sure you have heard at least two or three keywords to confirm your ideas. These might be …

- related by topic, e.g. *symptoms, sweaty, call in sick*.
- synonyms, e.g. *recover, get over it, get better*.

The keywords above suggest someone is ill and needs the day off to get better.

Be careful, you will hear some words that aren't important but could make you misunderstand.

A: *How are you feeling today?* B: *I'm* **coping**, *but I've been* **better**, *to be honest.*

In this example, Speaker B is saying that they feel ill, but Speaker A could misunderstand because they use positive words like *coping* and *better*.

1 Who discusses ways they look after their mental health at work?

2 Who talks about how they stay physically fit?

3 What words did you hear to help you decide the answers to questions 1 and 2?

5 🎧 **5.3** Listen to the interviews again. Complete the notes with one to three words in each space.

> Alec – likes running, cycling, ¹_____ and skiing. Says you should do exercise that ²_____ e.g. enjoys running in the ³_____ but not interested in running on ⁴_____. At work, Alec doesn't have much ⁵_____ to look after himself, but he's learned that if you're ⁶_____, you can't tell the story.

> Maria – finds not being able to express herself when she's abroad very ⁷_____. One way she copes is by ⁸_____, which helps her see the problem from ⁹_____. Writes letters to ¹⁰_____. Meditation is hard for her, but she enjoys ¹¹_____.

6 Work in pairs. Discuss the questions.

1 Alec talks about having to balance work and relaxation. What advice would you give him?

2 Maria talks about the stress of using a foreign language. Do you ever feel the same way? Do you think her tips could work for you?

7 Read the sentences and answer the questions (1–2). Then read the Focus on box to check.

Alec: *I just wish I was able to sleep.*

Maria: *If only I'd discovered yoga before.*

1 Is Alec talking about the past or present? Is he able to sleep?

2 Is Maria talking about the past or present? When did she discover yoga?

FOCUS ON   *I wish … and If only …*

Use *I wish …* or *If only …* to talk about something now or in the past that you want to be true.
I love my job, but **I wish** *it* **wasn't** *so stressful.*
If only I'd taken *a nap earlier.*
Use the past simple to talk about imaginary situations in the present. Use the past perfect to talk about imaginary situations in the past.

Go to page 146 for the Focus on reference.

8 Complete the second sentence in each pair to express disappointment about the information in the first sentence.

1 He went out in the rain and now he has a cold.
   He wishes he hadn't gone out in the rain.

2 I can't go to my gym anymore because my ex-girlfriend has joined! If only _____.

3 I want to lose weight, but I can't stop eating biscuits in the evenings! I wish _____.

9 Imagine you are the people in the photos in Exercise 1. Write sentences with *If only* and *I wish* about how they feel about their jobs.
'I wish there were fewer patients!'

SPEAKING

10 Imagine you can have any job (real or invented). What would you choose to ensure you were the healthiest and happiest you could be? Share your idea with a partner.
I'd be a writer and work on a private island. I'd walk along the beach to think of ideas!

5D

Being understood

LESSON GOALS
• Adapt language to be easier to understand
• Make vowel sounds longer before voiced consonants
• Help others be understood

LISTENING

1 Work in pairs. Discuss the questions.

1 Do you think you are easy to understand in English? What about when you speak your first language? Why?

2 Who do you find difficult to understand? Why?

3 How do you feel when you can't understand someone? What about when someone can't understand you?

4 What do you do, or could you do, in these situations?

2 ∩ 5.4 Listen to the conversation. Then answer the questions.

1 Who is speaking? What problem does the second speaker have?

2 Do the speakers understand each other? Why? / Why not?

3 Have you ever been in a similar situation? What happened?

3 Work in pairs. How could both speakers in Exercise 2 have made the communication easier to understand?

MY VOICE ▶

4 ▶ **5.2** Watch the video about adapting your English. Answer the questions.

1 Why is it sometimes necessary to adapt the way you speak English?

2 What are the main ways that you can adapt your English?

3 How can you help others to be better understood?

5 Look at the Communication skill box and check your answers to Exercise 4.

COMMUNICATION SKILL
Adapting your English to be understood

Simplify your language
- Avoid informal or complex vocabulary, complicated structures, long sentences.
- Speak slowly and clearly, using fewer words.

Listen to the listener!
Be patient and allow them to express themselves – if they are trying to tell you something, it is probably important!

Recognize problems of understanding between others
As a strong communicator, you are able to 'translate' complicated messages and simplify them for others.

Adapt to other languages
If you speak other languages, you may be able to switch to another language the other person knows to explain or to translate a word.

6 Work in pairs. Read the situations. Which expressions might be difficult for the listener to understand? Write a clearer version for them.

1 A passport control officer says to a visiting tourist: 'OK, so whereabouts in the US are you heading to?'

   She wants to know where …

2 In class the teacher says to a student: 'You sound like you're coming down with a cold. Do you want to leave early?'

3 After dinner, to the host: 'I'm exhausted after that meal! Need to take a nap if you don't mind.'

4 To a colleague in an office abroad: 'Something I've been meaning to ask you but, you know, just kind of wasn't sure whether you'd be up for it, is if there might be any chance you could potentially do this presentation instead of me.'

PRONUNCIATION

7 🎧 **5.5** Look at the Clear voice box. Then listen to the sentences (1–5). Underline the word you hear.

CLEAR VOICE
Making vowels longer before voiced consonants

Some words, such as *back* and *bag*, may sound very similar. To pronounce the difference between them clearly, make the vowel longer when it is followed by a voiced consonant (b, g, d, v). This also lets you pronounce the final consonant more easily and helps you avoid being misunderstood.

1 It's my *back / bag*!
2 Is that your *food / foot*?
3 He *hid / hit* it with his hat.
4 Do you have it *saved / safe*?
5 Take a *seed / seat*.

8 Work in pairs. Take turns to practise saying the sentences in Exercise 7. Decide which word your partner is saying.

LISTENING

9 🎧 **5.6** Listen to a continuation of the conversation from Exercise 2. How does the nurse help the patient understand what the doctor says?

10 🎧 **5.6** Listen to the conversation again. Write down what the nurse says to explain the doctor's words (1–5). What word from another language does he use?

1 elaborate on the type of pain
2 an acute pain
3 pinpoint whereabouts in the foot precisely
4 experiences the pain
5 get it X-rayed ASAP

SPEAKING

11 **OWN IT!** Work in groups of three. Look at the role cards on page 156. Act out the roleplay three times, changing roles each time.

5E
A matter of public health

LESSON GOALS
• Use discourse markers to organize your ideas
• Write an engaging essay introduction
• Write a 'for and against' essay

Students at the Rijksmuseum, Amsterdam.

SPEAKING

1 Work in pairs. Look at the photo and read the social media comments. Which comment do you agree with?

 Chris Itchingham
@ChrisItchingham

I'm not surprised this photo of #Rembrandt's #NightWatch has gone viral. It's the perfect image to explain the problems of our time.

 Marky Mark Maker
@MarkyMarkMaker

Replying to @ChrisItchingham

It's quite clear it's a school trip and these kids are all doing schoolwork, looking up info on their phones.

READING FOR WRITING

2 Read the essay title and discuss the questions.

> There should be a minimum age limit on mobile phones so that young people do not suffer the dangers of owning them.

1 What are the benefits of owning a mobile phone?
2 What are the dangers?
3 Do you think young people are particularly at risk from these dangers? Why? / Why not?
4 Do you agree that there should be a minimum age limit on mobile phones? Why? / Why not?

3 Read the essay on page 69. Answer the questions.

1 Are any of your ideas from Exercise 2 mentioned?
2 What is the writer's overall opinion: are they for or against the statement in the essay title?

4 Look at the Writing skill box. Then underline all the discourse markers you can find in the essay. Match them with the categories in the Writing skill box.

WRITING SKILL
Using discourse markers

In an essay, make sure you guide the reader through your arguments with discourse markers …

- to introduce more supporting ideas. *In addition, … , Furthermore, … , as well as, … , Secondly, …*
- to introduce reasons. *because … , due to …*
- to indicate opposing ideas. *However, … , On the other hand, …*
- to conclude. *In conclusion … , On the whole … , Personally, I believe that …*

WRITING TASK

5 Choose one of the essay titles (1–3). Make a list of reasons for and against the statement and decide which side you agree with. Then discuss with a partner. Can you add any other reasons?

1 Schools should teach students how to look after their mental health.
2 Vegetarianism is a healthier diet, so governments should tax meat.
3 Employers should provide space for workers to do exercise.

6 Look at the Useful language box. Match the expressions for essay introductions with the categories (1–4). Which expression could you use in your introduction?

Useful language Essay introductions

Many people think that …
It is commonly believed that …
There is no doubt that …
It is certainly true that …
Recently, there has been greater awareness of …
Is it the case that …?

1 State a fact about the topic.
2 State a common opinion about the topic.
3 Ask a question about the topic.
4 Describe changes that make the topic relevant.

7 WRITE Write your essay. Use the Writing skill box and Useful language to help you.

8 CHECK Use the checklist. I have …

☐ divided the essay into at least four paragraphs.

☐ begun the essay in an engaging way.

☐ used discourse markers to help the reader follow the argument.

☐ clearly stated my opinion in the conclusion.

9 REVIEW Exchange essays with a partner. Use the checklist in Exercise 8 to review their writing. What other arguments for and against the statement could they have mentioned?

Go to page 132 for the Reflect and review.

Mobile phones have become an essential tool for people of all ages. Over the last fifteen years, however, we have become more aware of the dangers of mobile phones. These include time wasting, addiction and poor sleep quality because of using phones too much. The question is whether people are right to be worried that young people are at risk.

On the one hand, it's true that some young people are suffering more than ever from anxiety and depression. Problems like loneliness and lack of sleep are also increasing amongst teenagers. What is more, young people are undoubtedly spending less time keeping fit outdoors if they are on their devices. Although it is true mobile phones distract us all from essential routines such as work, sleep and exercise, it may be that young people are simply less able to control their behaviour.

If this is the case, it could be argued that they are at greater risk from the dangers of mobile phones.

On the other hand, we must recognize the usefulness of these devices for teenagers, who use them for study purposes. Moreover, it is not clear whether problems such as anxiety are due to mobile phone use or other reasons. In addition, since teenagers are not the only group suffering from mental disorders, we might, in fact, need to limit everyone from using these devices.

To sum up, stopping young people from owning mobile phones may not be the answer. Instead, we need to educate everyone – young people and adults – about the harm that mobile technology can cause, as well as teach people how to cope with mental health problems. Nevertheless, decisions about letting each teenager use a mobile phone should remain with their parents.

Astronauts Christina Koch and Jessica Meir replace a broken machine during a seven-hour spacewalk, 18th October 2019.

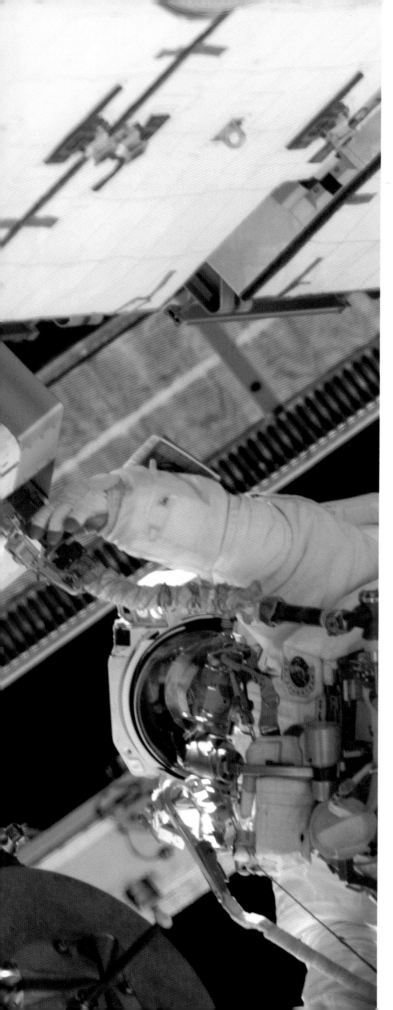

6

Breaking news

GOALS

- Identify unsupported claims in an article
- Report news using passive structures
- Understand catenation in connected speech
- Talk about the news
- Practise influencing others
- Write a news article

1 Work in pairs. Discuss the questions.

1 Look at the photo. What news story do you think it shows?
2 What have been some of the biggest news stories for you personally? Why were they important?
3 If you could interview one of the people in these stories, what would you ask them?

WATCH

2 ▶ 6.1 Watch the video. Answer the questions.

NATIONAL GEOGRAPHIC EXPLORERS

| AFROZ SHAH | IMOGEN NAPPER |

1 What sort of news do Afroz and Imogen normally find the most interesting?
2 Which two stories does Afroz mention? How did they make him feel?
3 Why did Imogen enjoy following the London Summer Olympic Games in 2012?

3 Make connections. What sort of news do you find the most interesting? What sort do you dislike? Why?

6A
The camera never lies

LESSON GOALS
- Identify unsupported claims in an article
- Learn how to fact-check online information
- Discuss how reliable online media is

READING

1 Work in pairs. Look at the title of the article and the photos on page 73. Discuss the questions.
1 What do you think the article is about?
2 How might the photos show things that aren't true or real?

2 Read the article quickly to check if your answers to Exercise 1 were correct.

3 Read the article again. Answer the questions.
1 Why is the advice 'You can't trust everything you read' not enough these days?
2 In what ways is the 'deep fake' of Dalí different from a video of him from when he was alive?
3 Why are beautiful fake images on social media especially dangerous to young people?
4 Why can't 'the truth compete with lies'?
5 What's wrong with some food 'hacks'?
6 What is the main aim of the article: to describe, entertain or teach? How do you know?

4 Look at the Reading skill box. Then read the article again and identify any claims the writer makes without supporting evidence.

READING SKILL
Identifying unsupported claims

In articles where writers report facts, they should support any claims with evidence. A common way of providing this online is to include links to other websites that provide the relevant evidence, such as scientific papers and studies.

To identify unsupported claims, look for clear statements of fact that are not accompanied by facts and figures.

5 For each unsupported claim you identified in Exercise 4, think about what sort of information you could include a hyperlink to.

6 Work in pairs. Discuss the questions.
1 Do you think you would normally be able to notice faked images or videos?
2 Do you think it's OK to edit photos to make your life seem better than it is? Why? / Why not?

7 Work in pairs. Look at the Critical thinking skill box. Discuss how you might fact-check the story of the shark mentioned in the article. Then do the same for the headlines (a–c).

CRITICAL THINKING SKILL
Fact-checking online information

Here are some strategies to avoid being tricked by fake news!
- **Check that the source is reliable.** Do other articles on the website look suspicious? Do fact-checking websites tell you that you can trust this website?
- **Check that the information is supported by evidence.** Does it have a list of references? Does it have hyperlinks and do they link to reliable sources?
- **Check to see if anyone else has investigated the story.** What hits do I get when I search the keywords + *fake*?

a **By 2050 there will be more plastic in the oceans than fish**
b **30-year old man ordered to move out of his parents' house**
c **Chicago the most dangerous city in the US**

SPEAKING

8 You are going to spread news around the class. Follow the steps.
1 Think of two pieces of news (one true, one fake) about yourself or something you did.
   I scored three goals in a football match on Sunday.
2 Talk to three other students in the class and share your news. Ask each other questions to work out how reliable the information might be.
   What football team do you play for?
3 Work in pairs. Share the news you heard. Decide which is true and which is fake.
4 Share your ideas with the class and see if you were right.

EXPLORE MORE!

Search online for 'how to spot fake images with reverse image search' to learn how to fact-check images for yourself.

The camera NEVER lies
(except when it does)

A · B · C

1 'You can't trust everything you read.' Well, now it seems we can't trust anything we *see*, either. A lot of online content has been shown not to be genuine, from <u>product reviews</u> on shopping websites to incorrect science. And images, in particular, can have
5 a powerful effect on what we believe.

Deep fakes

At The Dalí, a museum dedicated to the artist's life and work, visitors watch an on-screen Salvador Dalí telling them about his life, even though he died more than thirty years ago. He even
10 takes a selfie of himself with his visitors on his phone!

The creators used artificial intelligence to 'learn' how he moved and talked. This isn't an old video; it's Dalí recreated – his face skilfully controlled for a lifelike result. While 'deep fake' videos like this can be used to teach and entertain, the technology
15 opens the doors to less honest uses. For example, damaging the reputation of celebrities by making it look like they've done or said things that they haven't.

Photoshopped fakes

It's easier to alter still images. We do it every time we add filters
20 to photos on social media. But fake photos can distort people's view of reality in serious ways. According to a study by YMCA, almost two thirds of the surveyed teenagers felt pressure to look a certain way because of the images on social media. That study also revealed that Instagram influencers with their 'perfect'
25 lifestyles had the biggest impact on teenagers' self-esteem.

What's more, fakes often go viral more often than photos that haven't been altered and may get shared millions of times. A faked photo of a shark swimming up a flooded road goes viral every time there is a hurricane in the US. Online, the truth just
30 can't compete with lies.

Fake bakes

A popular type of YouTube video is food 'hacks', videos of people making attractive-looking food in a few quick and
35 easy steps. These clips get millions of hits, generating big money for the makers. But are these recipes too good to be true? It turns out many of them are. When people try to recreate the dishes, they end up
40 inedible. This may not seem serious but, when videos suggest using dangerous chemicals on strawberries to make them white, we have to worry about the spread of misinformation. So why make a video
45 showing a recipe that doesn't work? The simple answer is money; 'clickbait' videos like these generate millions by grabbing our attention.

So what can we do to protect ourselves
50 from believing misleading images? We can use fact-checking websites, such as Snopes.com, to find out how reliable a news source is. We can also fact-check photos using 'reverse image searches'.
55 These let you see where else the image exists on the web. If it's being used in a variety of stories, there's a good chance it's being misused here. The more you ask yourself about the truth of information
60 you meet, the better you will be at spotting it.

73

6B
In the headlines

LESSON GOALS
- Understand a news bulletin
- Report news using passive structures
- Pronounce consonant groups in past participles clearly

LISTENING AND GRAMMAR

1 Work in pairs. Discuss the questions.

1 How often do you listen to news bulletins on the radio or on TV?
2 What other ways do you use to keep in touch with what's going on?

2 🎧 6.1 Listen to a news bulletin. Match the stories (1–3) with the topics (a–c). Which story would you most like to learn more about?

Story 1	a entertainment
Story 2	b sport
Story 3	c environment

3 🎧 6.1 Listen to the news bulletin again. Complete the sentences with these verbs in the correct form.

believe   hope   reveal   say   suggest   think   understand

1 The plan to become carbon neutral within two years _____ today by the Costa Rican government.
2 …, as it _____ it will lead other nations to take similar action.
3 The plan _____ to be an important step in the global fight against climate change.
4 … which _____ to have made 2.79 billion dollars from cinema ticket sales.
5 Marvel _____ to be close to bankruptcy.
6 However, it _____ that the shoes he was wearing gave him an unfair advantage.
7 It _____ that the World Athletics committee might ban their use in the Olympics.

In 2019, Eliud Kipchoge became the first athlete to run a marathon in under two hours.

4 Look at the sentences in Exercise 3. Answer the questions. Then read the Grammar box to check.

1 How are passive structures typically formed?
2 What structure follows the passive in sentences 2, 6 and 7? What about sentences 3, 4 and 5?
3 When are these two different structures used?

GRAMMAR Passive structures

News reports often use passive structures to emphasize the action, when the person or thing that did the action is unknown, unimportant or obvious. In general, you form the passive voice using *be + past participle*.
*This decision **was praised** by environmentalists.* **(passive)** vs *Environmentalists **praised** the decision.* **(active)**
News reports often use …

• **subject + *be* + past participle + *to* + infinitive**.
*The plan **is thought/said/reported/understood/ believed to be** an important step …*

• **it + *be* + past participle + (*that*) + clause.**
*… but **it is understood/thought/hoped/said (that)** the World Athletics committee might ban their use in the Olympics.*

Go to page 146 for the Grammar reference.

5 Complete the sentences with the correct form of the words in brackets. In pairs, discuss if you've seen these news items.

1 Single-use plastic bags _____ recently by several countries, including France, China and Botswana. (ban)
2 It _____ that thousands of social media accounts were hacked in a cyberattack. (think)
3 Belgian singer Stromae _____ to be planning a return to the stage after several years of 'retirement'. (rumour)
4 Commercial flights to the Moon _____ before 2030, say the experts. (launch)
5 Meat grown in a lab _____ to become part of our daily diet in the next decade. (expect)
6 It _____ that, in some countries, sales of electric vehicles will soon overtake those of traditional cars. (say)
7 Olga Tokarczuk _____ the Nobel Prize in Literature, becoming the fifth Polish person to win. (award)
8 It _____ earlier this week that the economic growth in the EU is slowing down. (report)

6 🎧 6.2 Read the news report. Replace the phrases in bold with passive structures. Then listen to check.

Crowds gathered to welcome Peter Tabichi as he returned from Dubai, where [1]**they had chosen him** for the 'best teacher in the world' award. [2]**People think the prize is** one of the most important in the world. [3]**They award it** for exceptional teaching achievements. [4]**The judges congratulated Mr Tabichi** on his passion and for inspiring girls to study science. [5]**People say his students' scores** have improved dramatically since he started working at the school, and some have won international awards. [6]**People also admire Mr Tabichi** for his charity. He gives away almost all of his salary every year to help children from poorer families. [7]**There are reports that he is also planning to** donate the one-million-dollar prize he received.

PRONUNCIATION

7 🎧 6.3 Listen to the words. Underline any consonant groups (two or more consonant sounds together, e.g. *sugge_st_ed*) you hear.
a expected   d observed
b believed   e hoped
c praised   f introduced

8 Look at the Clear voice box. Then practise saying the words from Exercise 7.

CLEAR VOICE
Pronouncing consonant groups

Many past participles have consonant groups at the end (ho_ped_), some also at the beginning (_pr_aised) or in the middle (e_xp_e_ct_ed). To be easy to understand, it is important to pronounce all consonants in the group.

SPEAKING

9 Work in pairs. Follow the instructions to prepare a two-minute radio news bulletin.
1 Find at least three news stories that interest you.
2 Take notes on the important facts of the stories.
3 Use your notes to write a news bulletin. Remember to use passive structures.
4 Practise giving the news in pairs.
5 Work with another pair. Present your news bulletins.

EXPLORE MORE!

Search online for one of the news stories mentioned in this lesson. What extra information did you learn?

6C

Have you heard the news?

LESSON GOALS
- Understand catenation in connected speech
- Talk about the news
- Pronounce long vowels clearly
- Talk about effects using *the … the …*

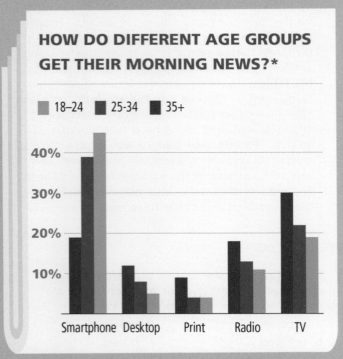

HOW DO DIFFERENT AGE GROUPS GET THEIR MORNING NEWS?*

■ 18–24 ■ 25-34 ■ 35+

*Data from US, UK, France, Italy, Spain, Ireland, Norway, Finland, Netherlands, Japan.

IN OTHER NEWS …

50% of Malaysians and Brazilians use WhatsApp to share and discuss news.

33% of people in Turkey use Instagram for news.

32% of people worldwide avoid the news.

59% of Greeks think the media is too negative.

SPEAKING

1 Work in pairs. Look at the infographic and discuss the questions.

1 Which information in the infographic matches your own news habits and those of people you know?
2 Which of these topics do you think are the most important to people of different age groups?

---

celebrities and entertainment   economics
environment   health and fitness
local news   politics   science   sport

LISTENING

NATIONAL GEOGRAPHIC EXPLORERS

2 🎧 **6.4** You are going to hear Imogen Napper and Afroz Shah talk about how they get their news. First, listen to the extracts and write down what you hear.

1 I _____ my news from social media.
2 The five-minute news bulletins give me _____ what today's top stories are.
3 For example, I often _____ newspapers and magazines.

3 🎧 **6.5** Listen to the phrases from Exercise 2 said fast and then more slowly. How does the pronunciation change? Look at the Listening skill box to check.

LISTENING SKILL
Understanding connected speech: catenation

In connected speech, words often come together and sound like one word. When one word ends with a consonant sound (e.g. /z/, /t/, /p/) and the next word starts with a vowel (e.g. /ɒ/, /ɪ/, /ə/), the final consonant attaches to the vowel of the next word, e.g. *an idea* → *a nidea* /naɪˈdɪə/. This is called catenation.

---

4 🎧 **6.6** Listen to Imogen and Afroz. What are their main sources of news? Whose habits and opinions are most similar to your own?

5 🔊 **6.6** Listen again. Are the sentences true (T), false (F) or not mentioned (NM)?

1 Imogen listens to podcasts when driving.
2 Imogen doesn't read newspapers.
3 Afroz tends to read more serious articles.
4 Imogen says some stories are reported many times to provide an in-depth analysis.
5 Afroz has a negative opinion of some news sources because they don't report news accurately.
6 Afroz's work on earthquakes was not presented accurately by the media.

VOCABULARY

6 Complete the collocations with these words. Some words may be used twice.

foreign   in-depth   make   objective   sensational
skim over   tabloid   the news   top

1 report _____
2 today's _____ story
3 _____ / _____ the headlines
4 _____ headlines
5 a(n) _____ / _____ journalist
6 the _____ press
7 a(n) _____ / _____ article

7 Complete the sentences with words from Exercise 6.

1 I only watch the first few minutes of the news, just to get the _____ stories.
2 Can a newspaper owned by a billionaire be _____ about taxes on the rich?
3 I didn't read it properly, I just _____ it.
4 The _____ press spend too long on silly stories about the private lives of celebrities.
5 When scientific research is reported, they often distort the information to make it more _____.
6 Because podcasts are longer, they can offer _____ interviews with interesting guests.

Go to page 137 for the Vocabulary reference.

PRONUNCIATION

8 🔊 **6.7** Listen to the words. Which ones have a long vowel?

argument   journalist   misleading   news
objective   report   skim   story

9 Look at the Clear voice box to check your answers to Exercise 8. Then practise saying the words, making sure the vowel is long.

Pronouncing long vowels

English has five long vowels. It's important to pronounce these as long. This will help the listener hear the difference with short vowels (e.g. reach vs rich).

/ɜː/ journalist, world   /ɑː/ argument, article
/iː/ misleading, piece   /ɔː/ report, story
/uː/ news, choose

GRAMMAR

10 Read the Focus on box. Then put the words in order to make sentences (1–4). You will need to add *the*.

> **FOCUS ON**   *the ... the ...*
>
> Use ***the* + comparative ..., *the* + comparative ...** to show that one thing depends on another.
> **Comparative adjectives: *The longer*** the article is, ***the fewer*** readers it will have.
> **Adverbs: *The more*** you get your information from different sources, ***the more*** objectively you'll see the news.

Go to page 147 for the Focus on reference.

1 include / more / on the website / our audience / videos / we / will be / younger
   The more we include videos on the website, the younger our audience will be.
2 to get / less likely / older / you are / your news online / you are
3 became / he / interesting / less / more / spoke / the interview
4 become / better / can / more / practise / you / you

SPEAKING

11 Work in groups. You're in charge of editing a news site. Follow the instructions.

1 Decide who your main readers are (e.g. people under 35, businesspeople).
2 Which news topics (e.g. politics, celebrities, sports) do you think you would need to report most in order to interest your readers? Why? Give examples of recent stories.

EXPLORE MORE!

Find an English language news source that you like. Challenge yourself to read an article every day for a week.

Influencing styles

LESSON GOALS
- Understand three different influencing styles
- Practise influencing others
- Propose an idea for a class project

SPEAKING AND LISTENING

1 Read the story. What lesson does it teach? How does it relate to the topic of influencing styles?

The North Wind and the Sun

The North Wind and the Sun were arguing about which of them was the strongest, when a traveller came along wrapped in a warm coat. They agreed that the one who succeeded in making the traveller take his coat off would be considered the strongest. First, the North Wind blew as hard as he could, but the more he blew, the more tightly the traveller pulled his coat around him. Then the Sun shone warmly. Immediately, the traveller took off his coat. So, the North Wind had to admit that the Sun was the stronger of the two.

2 🎧 6.8 Listen to three friends talking about a trip they're planning. Then answer the questions in pairs.
1 Which of the speakers sounds more like the North Wind from the story?
2 Which speaker's influencing style would work best on you? Why?
3 Which speaker's style do you think is most like your own?

MY VOICE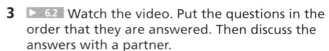

3 ▶ 6.2 Watch the video. Put the questions in the order that they are answered. Then discuss the answers with a partner.
a Should you use more than one influencing style?
b What three influencing styles are mentioned?
c When are influencing skills useful?

4 ▶ 6.2 Watch the video again. Take notes about each influencing style. Then look at the Communication skill box to check.

COMMUNICATION SKILL
Influencing styles

Here are three approaches you can use to influence people. You may use more than one approach at once, or different approaches in different situations.

Inspiring style
Communicate your idea with enthusiasm and confidence so that others feel it too. Make it clear how your idea will benefit them.

Negotiating style
Develop relationships with others by listening carefully to their opinions and taking their feelings and opinions into account.

Convincing style
Use evidence, reasoning and common sense to convince people that your idea is a good one.

5 Work in pairs. Imagine you are part of a team working on a project. You want to persuade other people about an idea of yours. Which influencing style(s) might work best in the situations (1–4)? Why?

1 You need a decision quickly. You only need them to agree to this one idea, not to show long-term commitment. They are normally open to ideas.

2 Your idea is quite unusual, so it would be good to have another person's opinion.

3 You've only spoken to the other people a few times. You're not sure how much they like you.

4 Your idea is not fully developed and you're not 100% convinced yourself yet.

6 Look at audioscript 6.8 on page 165. Underline the expressions the speakers use to influence each other. Then match them with the three styles. Look at the Useful language box to check.

Useful language Influencing people

Inspiring
Just imagine/picture this …
Wouldn't it be amazing if …
I know how much you love …

Negotiating
I can see where you're coming from.
Would you be willing to consider …?
How about this?

Convincing
According to …
I've read/heard that …
The reason I say that is because …

SPEAKING

7 **OWN IT!** Imagine you are going to do a class project in groups to produce a five-minute audio or video programme for other learners of English. It should both entertain them and help them improve their English.

Individually, look at the ideas in the table and decide which you think your group should produce.

Media type	Programme type
• radio show • podcast • TV programme • online vlog • Facebook/Instagram stories	• news programme • entertainment news • mini drama • a guide to a place • documentary • chat show • your own idea

I think a podcast that tells other English learners about the local area is the best idea. Podcasts are really popular these days and you can listen to them everywhere …

8 Plan how you are going to persuade the other members of your group to make the programme you want. You can choose one influencing style or a mix of styles. Use these questions and the Useful language to help you.

Convincing style:
What information, such as facts and statistics, could you mention to support your idea? For example, check how many daily listeners a radio show has.

Negotiating style:
What do you think the other people in your group might suggest? What reasons might they give? Consider their opinions and show curiosity by asking questions.

Inspiring style:
How can you show others your enthusiasm for your idea (e.g. by sounding enthusiastic, using emotional language)? How will your idea benefit the rest of the group?

9 Work in groups. Take turns to make your proposal. Use influencing skills to 'sell' your idea and listen to other team members. As a group, decide which idea you will use.

EXPLORE MORE!

Observe how others around you try to influence each other. Which styles do they use? How successful are they?

6E
Same news, different style

LESSON GOALS
- Recognize formal and informal article styles
- Use sensational or objective language as appropriate
- Write a news article

SPEAKING

1 Work in pairs. Discuss the questions.

1 Do you ever read news articles? Do you prefer a more formal or informal style? Why?
2 Which headline do you think comes from a more formal article and which from a more informal article? Which would you be more likely to read?
   a Airlines slash fares as passenger demand plummets
   b Airlines reduce fares due to lower passenger demand

READING FOR WRITING

2 Read the two articles. Do you believe El Dorado has been found? Why? / Why not?

A woman reading a newspaper at a kiosk in Kathmandu, Nepal.

A

'City Of Gold' El Dorado Finally Found

The golden city, or El Dorado, was first described by Spanish and Portuguese conquistadores. This mysterious city was widely thought to be only the stuff of legends. But it looks like it's finally been found.

Recent satellite images reveal huge man-made buildings right in the middle of the Brazilian Amazon. 'When I saw them, I knew this has got to be El Dorado', we were told by Joao Felix, a local enthusiast.

This discovery promises mountains of gold for those adventurous enough to get it. But to reach the golden city, you'll have to battle mosquitos, survive 40°C heat and avoid deadly animals such as jaguars.

Not that it scares people like Joao. He's determined to get there, no matter the cost, and despite repeated warnings from authorities that it's too dangerous. 'The government and the scientists don't want us to find the gold, but we will!'

B

Ancient City Found In The Amazon

For decades, archaeologists have said that no great civilizations existed in the Amazon. However, a recent discovery is putting this view into question, suggesting large cities connected by a vast network of roads and canals did exist.

According to the researchers who found it, the newly discovered city was likely home to approximately sixty thousand people. Even more impressively, it seems to have been part of a vast 250-kilometre-wide network of cities, possibly built by the same civilization.

Since such enormous size and advanced engineering was thought to be impossible in the Amazon, the archaeologists were surprised by their findings. Nevertheless, it is rather unlikely to be the famous city of gold, El Dorado, which adventurers have been looking for since the 1500s but that researchers now agree is a myth.

3 Read the articles again. Which article (A or B) …
1 focuses more on facts?
2 presents personal stories?
3 uses longer sentences?
4 uses more formal language?
5 is more careful and objective?
6 uses more sensational language?

4 Look at the Writing skill box to check your answers to Exercise 3. Which article style do you prefer? Why?

WRITING SKILL
Choosing your writing style

The style and tone that you choose when writing will affect the story being told and the way the reader reacts to it.

Some articles follow a more informal style. They use shorter sentences and paragraphs. Vocabulary is more sensational. They focus more on personal stories and opinions and are often more subjective.

Other articles are more formal. The sentences and paragraphs are longer. Vocabulary is more formal. They focus more on objective facts and research.

5 Look at the sentence below. Which words make it sound more sensational? Find other examples of sensational language in article A.

This discovery promises mountains of gold for those adventurous enough to get it.

6 Make the sentences (1–4) more sensational by replacing the words in bold with the correct form of the words in the box.

chase   incredible   smash   thugs

1 He **kicked** the ball into the net.
2 The **criminals** were finally caught by police.
3 She will continue to **go after** her dream.
4 Her **unusual** story might inspire many others.

7 Which sentence (1 or 2) sounds more objective?
1 According to researchers, it is rather unlikely to be the famous city of gold, El Dorado.
2 Local enthusiasts are certain they have finally found the long-lost city of gold, El Dorado.

8 Look at the Useful language box. Rewrite the sentences (1–4) so that they sound more objective. Use at least two 'careful' expressions in each sentence.

Useful language Being careful and objective

Verbs
About sixty thousand people **seem to** have lived there. The findings **suggest that** …

Modal verbs
Scientists **might/could/may** soon discover …

Adverbs
This city was **probably/possibly** built by …;
Practically/Virtually all scientists agree …;
We still know **relatively** little …

Adjectives
It is **likely/possible/probable** that …

1 Everyone is able to learn a foreign language to a high level.
2 No one owns an electric car these days.
3 This shows stories about an ancient city in the Amazon were true.
4 Climate change is the cause of the recent heatwaves.

WRITING TASK

9 **WRITE** Write a news article of at least 200 words.

Decide whether you will write in a formal or informal style. Then choose a news topic that interests you. You can choose a current story or choose one of the headlines (1–3) to write about.
1 City plans to be carbon neutral by 2050.
2 Fans devastated as singer cancels tour.
3 Tourists left stranded after airline goes bankrupt.

10 **CHECK** Use the checklist. I have …
☐ included a headline.
☐ used passive structures.
☐ used careful and objective language (formal).
☐ used sensational language (informal).
☐ used long or short sentences as appropriate for the style I chose.

11 **REVIEW** Exchange articles with a partner. Answer the questions.
1 Which style did your partner choose? How do you know?
2 What is the most interesting part of the article?

Go to page 132 for the Reflect and review.

A fish market on the Galápagos Islands is popular with the local human and sea lion population.

82

7

Shared spaces

GOALS

- Deal with unknown words in an article
- Use causative verbs to talk about solutions to problems
- Identify figurative language when listening
- Describe places
- Explain a problem without offending others
- Write and respond to social media posts

1 Work in pairs. Look at the photo and discuss the questions.

1 What is happening in the photo?
2 Why do you think the people tolerate the animals in this place? Why do you think the animals tolerate the people?
3 What animals do you share space with in your home, your neighbourhood or your country?

WATCH ▶

2 ▶ 7.1 Watch the video. Match the sentences with the correct explorer, Abby (A) or Robbie (R).

NATIONAL GEOGRAPHIC EXPLORERS

ABBY MCBRIDE   **ROBBIE SHONE**

1 Sharing space with other people can be difficult.
2 Sharing space with a big animal can be dangerous.
3 What seemed like a mistake was actually a very good idea.
4 Sharing space means being aware of how much we need, and how much we can harm, each other.

3 Make connections. Do you remember any funny or interesting stories about when you've shared spaces with other people or animals?

Sharing space with animals

LESSON GOALS
* Deal with unknown words in an article
* Analyse solutions to problems
* Discuss spaces shared between humans and animals

READING

1 Work in pairs. What problems might happen when elephants and people live close to one another?

Elephants don't have enough space. They might destroy people's homes.

2 Read the article on page 85. What problem caused by people and elephants sharing space is mentioned? What solution to this problem has been used?

3 Look at the Reading skill box and discuss the questions (1–2).

READING SKILL
Dealing with unknown words

When reading a text, you will find words you don't know. Looking them up in a dictionary can sometimes be impractical and slow down your reading. So, instead, you can also …

* **check the context:** e.g. after *rebounded* in paragraph 1, it says *from one hundred to over seven hundred*, so *rebound* probably means *go up again*.
* **compare the new word with words from your first language:** e.g. *voracious* in paragraph 2 has similar words in French (*vorace*), Spanish and Portuguese (*voraz*), Romanian (*vorace*).
* **look at how the word is formed:** e.g. you may not know *protection* in paragraph 2, but you understand *to protect* and know that *-ion* is used to make nouns.
* **use the visuals:** e.g. in paragraph 7, *suspend the beehives from poles* might be difficult to understand, but the photo can help you.

1 Which tips in the Reading skill box have you used before? How effective were they?
2 Which tips would you like to try?

4 Find at least five words in the article that you don't know. Use the tips in the Reading skill box to work out their meaning. Then share with a partner.

5 Read the article again. Which of the ideas are mentioned?

1 Increasing elephant populations have caused difficulties for the local people.
2 Farmers used to shoot the elephants that destroyed their fields.
3 Bees are small but strong fighters.
4 The best place for a bee to sting an elephant is on its ears.
5 *Piri-piri* is a chilli that can be used to scare elephants away.
6 The bee and chilli fence has more than one benefit for local communities.

6 Work in pairs. Look at the Critical thinking skill box. Then analyse the bee and chilli fence solution from the article by discussing the questions in the box.

CRITICAL THINKING SKILL
Analysing solutions to problems

When analysing proposed solutions to a problem, ask yourself questions to evaluate how effective the solution might be. For example:
* What effects (positive and negative) can it have on those involved?
* How practical is it?
* How much will it cost (e.g. materials, staff)?
* What training or skills might be needed?

7 Analyse two different solutions to the problem in the article, using the questions from Exercise 6. Do they seem more or less effective than the bee and chilli fence solution?

Solution 1: Moving the elephants to a new region.
Solution 2: Compensating (paying) farmers for the loss of money caused by elephants eating their corn.

SPEAKING

8 Work in pairs. Do you know of any problems caused by people and animals sharing space in your country? Discuss the questions.

1 Are the problems in cities or the countryside?
2 What problems do the animals cause humans? What problems do humans cause the animals?
3 Have you heard about any possible solutions?

EXPLORE MORE!

Search online for other unusual ways animals and humans interact. You can use these key words to help you: 'wild boars + Rome'; 'butterfly wings + waterproof raincoats'.

'BEE' ware of the fence!

Over the last two decades, elephant numbers in Gorongosa National Park in Mozambique have rebounded, from just one hundred to over seven hundred. While this has been a great success story from an environmental point of view, it has also created challenges for the local communities living around the park. It's a challenge that the Elephant Ecology team at Gorongosa have been trying to tackle.

Elephants are voracious eaters. They spend over half the day eating and an adult will easily eat four hundred kilograms of food a day. So, a field full of corn is quite a tasty temptation. For the local farmers then, the elephants are not animals in need of protection, but pests that destroy their only means of making money. It's important to protect both the elephants and the people's livelihood by considering and balancing their separate needs.

How? By building a natural fence to block the elephants' path. A fence made of bees.

Three hundred times smaller than the African elephant, the bee seems a rather unlikely candidate to stop a hungry elephant from having a farmer's crops for lunch. But don't let its size fool you. Bees can be fierce fighters.

While elephants have quite a thick skin, the bees know where to sting to force an elephant to move away. They'll attack the skin around the eyes, for example. You might be a big elephant, but you certainly don't want to make these bees angry.

The Gorongosa team added another ingredient to make their fence elephant-proof: the chilli pepper, or *piri-piri* as it's called in Mozambique. While typically used to give a spicy kick to local food, chillies can also be a fantastic defence system against elephants. Apparently, these giants don't like spicy food.

So how do you create a *piri-piri* bee fence? The recipe is simple. Take a few beehives and link them with a rope covered in chilli powder. Then suspend the beehives from poles.

The first thing that happens when an elephant tries to enter a field is that they smell the *piri-piri*. They'll very likely leave the fence, and the field on the other side of it, alone. If they don't, the bees buzz into action. When an elephant touches the rope, it shakes the beehive and the bees fly out in their hundreds, stinging the elephants and scaring them away.

These natural fences not only help the locals keep their farms safe from elephants, they also provide them with an additional income. Farmers can now collect and sell the honey that the bees produce. It's a win-win situation. This helps encourage the locals to protect rather than harm the elephants.

This is just one example of how cooperation between humans and nature can help solve the key challenges of sharing the same environment. People need employment, schools, food. Elephants, on the other hand, need an enormous amount of space and food to be able to survive. But these needs do not have to be in opposition. By learning how to share space together in a smart way, both humans and animals can thrive.

Fences with beehives and chilli powder keep elephants away from farms.

7B
It helps you save space

LESSON GOALS
* Read about and discuss space-saving solutions in cities
* Use causative verbs to talk about solutions to problems
* Stress the correct syllable in verbs

READING AND GRAMMAR

1 Work in pairs. Look at the text and photos and discuss the questions.

1 What are the advantages and disadvantages to each space-saving solution?
2 Could any of the solutions work in your town or city? Why?
3 Which of the solutions would you be happy to use or experience?

2 Read the Grammar box. Find verbs in the text that match each pattern in the box.

> **GRAMMAR** Causative verbs
>
> Causative verbs describe different ways to affect the actions of someone or something.
>
> **verb + object + *to* + infinitive**
> *House prices **forced us to move** away even though we loved the area.*
>
> **verb + object + infinitive (without *to*)**
> *There are a number of great ideas to **help you save** space if you have a small apartment.*
>
> **verb + object + *from* + –ing**
> *We have a really small apartment, but that doesn't **stop us from having** visitors because we have a sofa bed in the living room.*

Go to page 148 for the Grammar reference.

3 Which of the verbs from the text describe ways of …

1 forcing someone to do something?
force, _____, _____
2 allowing someone to do something?
allow, _____, _____
3 stopping someone from doing something?
stop, _____, _____

NATIONAL GEOGRAPHIC EXPLORERS

4 🎧 **7.1** Listen to Robbie Shone and Abby McBride talk about the spaces they live in. Which topics does each person talk about?

1 city living
2 their home
3 unusual spaces they've lived in
4 getting around town
5 space-saving possessions

5 🎧 **7.1** Complete the sentences (1–8) with the correct form of these verbs. Sometimes more than one answer is possible. Then listen to Robbie and Abby again to check.

advise   allow   enable   encourage   force   help
let   make   permit   prevent   require   save   stop

SAVING SPACE
IN CITIES

In this Bangkok food market, stall owners are required to move out of the way to let trains get through! Shoppers must stand to one side to let the train pass.

1 A: I don't spend much time in cities because they always _____ me feel crowded.

2 R: Tunnels _____ us from having to make long journeys around the mountains.

3 A: There is usually some sort of space limitation that _____ me to make adjustments …

4 A: The lack of personal space _____ me to spend time outdoors by myself.

5 R: Gina's office is at the university, so that _____ me use the home office.

6 A: Travelling so much _____ me from having too many possessions.

7 A: It _____ me to keep everything I needed with me all the time!

8 R: It _____ us to store all our pots and pans without taking up much space.

6 Complete the sentences so that they are true for you. Then share them with a partner.

1 My [parents/partner/friend] encouraged me …

2 My [parents/teacher/job] sometimes stopped me from …

3 [My/My sister's/My friend's teacher] helped …

4 I'd like a job where the boss lets me …

PRONUNCIATION

7 [🔊 7.2] Listen to the verbs from Exercise 5 that have more than one syllable. Where is the stress in all of them?

8 Look at the Clear voice box to check your answer to Exercise 7. Then practise saying the verbs.

SPEAKING

9 Work in groups. Choose one of the situations below. Suggest solutions using the Useful language box. Look for ideas online to help you.

A Your school is planning to convert one of the classrooms into a library. However, it is a very small room. Suggest ways to fit everything in the room, while giving students enough space to study in.
You could build shelves into the walls. This would save you from having big bookcases.

B Your friend has just bought a studio apartment. It is only 25 m². Help them decide how to fit all their belongings into such a small space, while at the same time making it practical and comfortable.
A foldable sofa bed would help you save space.

Useful language Solving problems

It deals with the problem/issue of …
It stops/saves you from having to …
It means you don't have to …
It allows more people to …

In various cities, including Glasgow, Amsterdam and Johannesburg, architects have converted shipping containers into university housing. This has saved universities from having to buy big areas of land. This ingenious solution enables hundreds of students to live close to university.

Paris has one of the largest urban farms in Europe … on a roof! The increasing demand for fresh food in cities will only encourage more people to farm on their rooftops.

Where do you fit a football pitch among the skyscrapers? People in Bangkok found a perfect solution allowing them to do just that. Strange-shaped pitches permit footballers to play their favourite game.

A public system of cable cars above Caracas prevents commuters from getting stuck in traffic. A journey to the office makes you feel as if you're on a skiing trip!

7C
Confined spaces

LESSON GOALS
• Identify figurative language when listening
• Describe places
• Pronounce /b/, /v/ and /w/ clearly

Robbie's team begin their journey into the lowest levels of Veryovkina, Georgia.

LISTENING

1 Work in pairs. Discuss the questions.

1 How would you feel about exploring a cave like the one in the photo?

2 Are you claustrophobic? (Do you have a fear of small spaces?) Do you know anyone who is?

NATIONAL GEOGRAPHIC EXPLORER

2 🎧 **7.3** Listen to an interview with Robbie Shone. Make notes about the topics (1–4). Then work in pairs and summarize what Robbie said.

1 Robbie's work

2 the 'Veryovkina' cave system

3 his home life

4 how he 'gets away from it all'

3 🎧 **7.3** Listen again. Choose the correct option to complete the sentences.

1 Robbie is a …
a writer.
b painter.
c photographer.

2 The interviewer …
a enjoys caving.
b thinks the caves are amazing.
c has visited Veryovkina.

3 The water …
a was black.
b came from above them.
c hit them hard.

4 They had to …
a climb through the waterfall.
b leave their equipment.
c swim to safety.

5 Robbie …
a thinks about home a lot when he's away.
b likes Italian coffee.
c lives in a busy city.

4 🎧 **7.3** Look at the Listening skill box. Then listen to the first part of the interview again. Complete the figurative language (1–4) with one word.

LISTENING SKILL
Identifying figurative language

Figurative language is language used, not with its basic meaning, but with a more imaginative meaning. For example, *to see the light* can mean *to understand*, which has nothing to do with actual seeing or light.

• If you hear a word that seems unlikely in the context, don't focus too much on specific words. Try to guess what the speaker probably means in the context.

• Imagine the pictures that figurative language creates. If someone tells you they were *on the edge of their seat* when they watched a film, the image should help you understand that they were nervous and excited.

• Learn commonly used figurative language. This includes idioms, phrasal verbs and metaphors.

Meaning	Figurative language
1 describe	_____ a picture
2 scares me a lot	frightens the _____ out of me
3 not everyone likes it	it's not everybody's _____
4 it's never easy	it's never a _____ in the park

5 🎧 **7.3** Work in pairs. Listen to the last part of the interview again. What do you think the figurative language means?

1 You've got to **get back on the horse**.
2 Don't you ever feel the need for your **creature comforts**?
3 When the end is **in sight**, I start to think about home.
4 The mountains are **my escape**.

6 Work in pairs. How comfortable would you feel in each of these confined or busy spaces?

- a busy train carriage or bus
- a concert or football match
- a famous tourist site with crowds of sightseers
- a small tent
- a lift full of people

VOCABULARY

7 What words and expressions can describe caves, like the one shown in the photo? Use a dictionary to help you.

absolutely stunning   breathtaking   cold and damp
cramped   densely crowded   elegantly decorated
light and airy   narrow   sheltered
spacious   vast   warm and cosy

8 Complete each sentence with two nouns. Notice the common adjective-noun collocations.

car   cave   flat   rooms   sight   spot   streets
tent   tourists   view   weather   windows

1 I can't wait to get inside, out of this **cold, damp** _____ and back to my **cosy** _____.
2 The charming **narrow** _____ of the old town are **densely crowded** with _____.
3 On the first night we slept in the _____, which was **a bit cramped**, so we bought a four-man _____, which was more **spacious**.

4 Look! The _____ from the top is **absolutely stunning**! But it's so windy. Let's find a **sheltered** _____ to eat our sandwiches.
5 Suddenly, the passage opened out into a bigger space. Their torches revealed a **vast** _____. The _____ was **breathtaking**.
6 The _____ are **elegantly decorated**, with large _____ that give them a **light and airy** feel.

9 🎧 **7.4** Listen and check your answers to Exercise 8.

Go to page 138 for the Vocabulary reference.

PRONUNCIATION

10 🎧 **7.5** Look at the Clear voice box and listen to the words (1–4). Then practise saying the sounds in pairs. Take turns to say one of the words. Your partner decides what word you have said.

CLEAR VOICE
Pronouncing /b/, /v/ and /w/

To pronounce the /b/ sound (e.g. Ro*bb*ie), use both of your lips. For /v/ (e.g. *v*ast), put your lower lip on your upper teeth. To say /w/ (e.g. *w*arm), keep your lips slightly apart and rounded. It's important to pronounce these three sounds correctly to be easily understood.

1	best	vest	west
2	bee	V	we
3	bet	vet	wet
4	bent	vent	went

SPEAKING

11 Work in pairs. Take turns to describe some of these places.

- your favourite room
- a great view near you
- a good place for a picnic
- a popular area in your town
- the cosiest place you can think of

EXPLORE MORE!

Find out more about Robbie Shone online, and choose a photo of his that you like.

7D
Difficult conversations

LESSON GOALS
- Practise complaining
- Explain a problem without offending others
- Use language that softens the message

SPEAKING

1 Work in groups. Discuss the questions.

1 Have you ever lived with someone in the same house or flat? What did you like and dislike about it?

2 Rank how annoying these habits would be in a flatmate. Give reasons.

  a Insists on thoroughly cleaning the flat twice a week.

  b Leaves a pile of dirty dishes in the sink.

  c Listens to very loud music until late in the evening.

  d Often invites friends round and has parties.

  e Spends most of the time in their room and rarely talks to you.

LISTENING AND GRAMMAR

2 🎧 **7.6** Listen to someone complaining about a flatmate. Do you agree that the person they're talking about is a nightmare flatmate? Why? / Why not?

3 🎧 **7.6** Listen to the conversation again. Complete the complaints with one or two words. Then read the Focus on box to learn about useful structures for complaining.

1 He's just _____ messy.

2 For example, he's _____ dirty dishes in the sink for days!

3 I wish he _____ them at least once a day.

4 He's also _____ a party animal.

5 _____ he had people over once a week, but it's like three or four nights a week!

FOCUS ON Useful structures for complaining

Use **so + adjective** and **such a + noun** to complain about things that annoy or upset you.
*He's **so messy**.*
*His room is **such a mess**.*

Use the **present continuous with *always*** to emphasize that something happens all the time.
*She**'s always listening** to loud music in the middle of the night.*

Use **I wish/If only + past simple** and **I wish/If only + would + infinitive** to say that you want something to be different.
***If only he looked after** his money better!*
***I wish he would wash** the dishes!*

Go to page 148 for the Focus on reference.

4 Look at the first sentence in each pair. Complete the second sentence so it has the same meaning. Use four words, including the word in bold and the structures from the Focus on box.

1 It's annoying that they don't throw their litter away.
I _____ their litter away. **would**

2 Those exam questions were so difficult.
Those were _____. **such**

3 My brother makes such a mess.
I _____ make such a mess in our room. **wouldn't**

4 She's such a lazy flatmate.
My _____. **flatmate**

5 He never switches lights off.
He _____ on. **leaving**

5 Think about people who have habits that annoy you. Write five sentences complaining about them. You do not need to mention who they are.

I have a friend who's always looking at his phone when we're together. It's so rude!

6 Work in pairs. Share your sentences from Exercise 5 and answer the questions.

1 Which habits are the most annoying? Why?
2 Do you usually talk about problems with the people who are upsetting you?
3 What can happen if you don't talk to them?

MY VOICE

7 ▶ 7.2 Watch the video. How can the person from Exercise 2 encourage their flatmate to change their behaviour? Write at least two pieces of advice, using tips from the video. Look at audioscript 7.6 on page 167 if you need to.

8 Work in pairs. Look at the Communication skill box. How easy is this advice for you to follow?

COMMUNICATION SKILL
Dealing with difficult conversations

If you are trying to encourage someone to change their behaviour, try to …

1 describe the problem from your point of view as an observation, not an emotion, e.g. *I notice that …* Don't exaggerate, e.g. *You never …*

2 explain why the issue is important to you, e.g. *It means that I can't …*

3 describe your feelings without acting them out, e.g. *It upsets me when …*

4 request a change, e.g. *Would you be willing to …*

9 🎧 7.7 Listen and complete the words in each sentence. Then match the phrases with similar expressions in the Useful language box.

1 Could I m_____ a s_____? Why d_____ we write a 'to do' list together?

2 I u_____ that you want to relax in the evening, but so do I.

3 I'm s_____ you won't m_____ me a_____ this, but do you have some headphones you could use?

4 It's just that if you were a_____ to avoid messaging me when I'm at work, I could reply sooner.

Useful language   Softening the message

I hope you don't mind me saying this, but …
I appreciate that you want to … but I …
I'd really appreciate it if you could …
It's just that if you could … that would allow me to …
Can I suggest something? How about …?

10 Work in pairs. Think about the people you complained about in Exercise 5. How could you explain the problem without offending them? Use the tips in the Communication skill box and the Useful language to help you.

SPEAKING

11 **OWN IT!** Work in pairs. Imagine you are flatmates or neighbours. Follow the instructions.

1 In pairs, decide on two annoying behaviours each of you has that makes living together or next to one another difficult.

2 Individually, use the tips in the Communication skill box to decide how to explain the problems to your partner without offending them.

3 Discuss the annoying behaviours together. Try to find a solution.

12 Act out the conversation in front of another pair. How well did the other pair give feedback? What could they have done better?

7E Social media sharing

LESSON GOALS
- Omit pronouns and auxiliaries to make writing more informal
- Use informal quantifiers, expressions and phrasal verbs
- Write and respond to social media posts

SPEAKING

1 Work in pairs. Look at the infographic and discuss the questions.

1 Which social media platforms do you use? If you don't use any, why not?
2 What content would you be most and least likely to share on social media? Why?
3 Which type of social media person are you? Are you sometimes a different type depending on what and why you share? Why?

READING FOR WRITING

2 Read the three social media posts on page 93. Match them with a type of content and a personality type from the infographic. Explain your choices to your partner.

3 Work in a group. Discuss the questions.

1 Which of the social media posts would you be most likely to read in real life?
2 What comment would you leave below each post?

4 Look at the Writing skill box. Find two examples of each type of informal language in the social media posts and comments.

WRITING SKILL
Informal language in social media posts

When writing on social media, we tend to be more informal. Some common examples are …

Omitting pronouns and auxiliary verbs
~~Have you~~ Ever seen a bear doing yoga?

Informal quantifiers
after **a bit of** a nap
got **a ton of** comments

Phrasal verbs
She**'s** quite **into** yoga
What have you **been up to**?

Informal expressions
I might **give it a shot** myself!
You'd love it! It's **right up your street**.

SOCIAL MEDIA SHARING

WHAT PEOPLE SHARE

photos and videos **60%**

opinions **26%**

news items **22%**

status update of what they are doing **45%**

links to articles and websites **47%**

SOCIAL MEDIA PERSONALITY TYPES

THE COMIC
This sharer likes to share funny posts, memes and updates with their connections to make them laugh.

THE PROFESSIONAL
This person uses social media for professional networking and to share work-related posts. They might have an online business.

THE DEBATER
This sharer often posts controversial opinions and links. They enjoy getting a reaction and debating controversial ideas.

THE SHARE-IT-ALL
They share nearly every moment of their life on social media, posting photos, stories and videos of their daily life.

THE THINKER
They share serious and useful links and information. Their posts are likely to make you stop and think.

THE SILENT ONE
This sharer uses social media only occasionally to post important things. They also rarely comment on others' posts.

Dani
2 hrs ago

Ever seen a bear doing yoga? Pretty cool, right?! Santra is a bear in Ahtari Zoo, Finland and she's quite into yoga. Apparently, she'll get down to her fifteen-minute yoga routine every day after a bit of a nap. I might give it a shot myself!

Anya That's class! Love it!

Juana
1 hr ago

I don't normally talk behind people's backs on social media, but I've seriously had it! My flatmate is so messy! He never tidies up. There's a ton of dirty dishes piled up in his bedroom. 😫 I really don't know how to deal with it. I've told him a million times to clean up. He's always promising he will but then just puts it off and off forever! Any advice? What should I do?

Jacob Why don't you just talk to him? It means you don't have to live in a messy flat!

Kaish
4 hrs ago

Just got back from a fab weekend trip to Berlin, and the city is full of moss! They've been putting up benches with a wall of moss behind them all over the city. There are loads of them everywhere. But wait for this – apparently one bench like that cleans as much air as a small forest. Could we get something like this in our city too? What do you all think?

Amit Wow! That's so cool. Would be great to have some moss benches here! How about we come up with an online petition and share it on social media?

5 Change the expressions in bold to make them more informal. Use the Writing skill box and social media posts to help you.
   1 **I've just** got back from the city. There's **a large amount of** air pollution there.
   2 I think I'll **try yoga. I've never** done it, but it looks fun.
   3 The benches can be **installed** in **many** different places.
   4 **Have you got** any thoughts on this? **I would** love to hear your opinion.
   5 **I really** hate people who always **postpone** things.

WRITING TASK

6 WRITE Write three social media posts. Use your own ideas or choose from the table. Write about 200 words in total and leave room for comments underneath. Find or describe any photos or links you would like to include with your post.

Things you've read about	Personal stories	Recommendations
• interesting articles • funny stories • important news	• places you've visited or things you've done • frustrations and complaints	• a film / book / video game you'd recommend • a product you bought and liked

7 CHECK Use the checklist. I have ...
   ☐ written posts that are engaging and/or useful to other people
   ☐ used informal quantifiers.
   ☐ replaced formal verbs with phrasal verbs.
   ☐ omitted unnecessary pronouns and auxiliary verbs.

8 REVIEW Stick your posts up around the classroom. Walk around the room and read your classmates' posts. Leave a comment below at least two of the posts.

SPEAKING

9 Discuss the questions as a class.
   1 Which post did you find the most interesting?
   2 What new information about your classmates did you learn from their posts?
   3 Based on the posts, what sort of social media personality from the infographic are your classmates?

Go to page 133 for the Reflect and review.

Go to page 133 for the Reflect and review.

EXPLORE MORE!

Find examples of social media posts that sparked your attention recently. Which could you reshare on your social media?

A family share a birthday celebration via live stream in Barcelona, Spain.

Incredible technology

GOALS

- Recognize synonyms and antonyms in an article
- Speculate about the past using modal verbs
- Talk about gadgets and technology
- Understand prepositions in connected speech
- Understand and discuss online etiquette
- Write a product review

1 **Work in pairs. Discuss the questions.**

1 Look at the photo. How are the people using technology?
2 The photo shows a positive side to technology; what photos would you suggest to show the negative sides to technology?

WATCH

2 ▶ 8.1 **Watch the video. Make notes about …**

1 whether Nora and Francisco think of themselves as 'techie' people and why.
2 one important piece of technology in their lives and why they like it.
3 any worries that they have about technology.

NATIONAL GEOGRAPHIC EXPLORERS

| NORA SHAWKI | FRANCISCO ESTRADA-BELLI |

3 **Make connections. Discuss the questions.**

1 Are you a 'techie' (someone who likes tech) or a technophobe (someone who dislikes tech)?
2 What piece of technology are you particularly glad you have? Why?

8A
Impossible tech

LESSON GOALS
* Recognize synonyms and antonyms in an article
* Examine the writer's assumptions behind an article
* Talk about science fiction and technology

SPEAKING AND LISTENING

1 Work in pairs. Have you ever watched science-fiction films or read science-fiction books?

NATIONAL GEOGRAPHIC EXPLORERS

2 🎧 **8.1** Listen to Nora Shawki and Francisco Estrada-Belli. Answer the questions.
1 What is one aspect of sci fi that each explorer likes? What annoys Francisco?
2 Do you agree with their opinions? Why? / Why not?

READING

3 Work in pairs. Which sci-fi technology in the box have you heard of? Which do you think are impossible? Which might be possible ...
1 in the next few decades?
2 within a hundred years?
3 in several hundred years?
4 in thousands of years from now?

---

faster than light travel   invisibility   lightsabers
teleportation (instant transport across space and distance)

---

4 Read the article on page 97. Were your predictions in Exercise 3 right?

5 Look at the Reading skill box. Then scan the article to find a close synonym or an antonym of the words (a–h) in the same paragraph.

READING SKILL
Recognizing synonyms and antonyms

Writers often use synonyms (words/phrases with the same meaning) and antonyms (words/phrases with opposite meanings) to avoid repeating words. Recognizing them can help you guess the meaning of unknown words. Understanding one word can help you understand its synonym or antonym.

Synonyms:	Antonyms:
a change [l. 9]	f possible [l. 22]
b hot gas [l. 23]	g appear [l. 42]
c power source [l. 31]	h stretch [l. 53]
d breaks the rules [l. 49]	
e make a hole [l. 56]	

6 Read the article again. Answer the questions.
1 Why would flying an invisible spaceship be difficult?
2 Why shouldn't we get too excited about lightsabers yet?
3 When does teleportation happen naturally?
4 How might we be able to travel faster than light?

7 Look at the Critical thinking skill box. Then decide which of the assumptions (a–c) you think the writer is making in the article. Find sentences that support your ideas.

CRITICAL THINKING SKILL
Examining writer assumptions behind texts

Assumptions are ideas you accept as true without evidence. Texts contain unwritten assumptions based on what writers think they know about their readers, such as: 'This will be interesting to readers', and 'Readers will know what I'm talking about'. There are often assumptions about specific topics too, even if there is no evidence.

Thinking about the assumptions a writer has made can help you understand why they've chosen to write the text, and to consider how useful, relevant and interesting it is to its readers.

---

a Readers enjoy thinking about sci-fi inventions.
b It is the responsibility of science to try to make fictional inventions become reality.
c Technological advances mean that everything we think of as impossible now will become reality in the future.

8 What other assumptions can you identify? Do you think the assumptions the writer has made are fair and correct? Why? / Why not?

SPEAKING

9 Work in groups. What do you think are the three most needed and the three most exciting tech inventions of the future? Use the suggestions below or your own ideas.

---

alternatives to plastics   clean energy sources
cure for cancer   intelligent robots   self-driving cars
space travel   teleportation   time travel

EXPLORE MORE!

Search online for 'da Vinci's inventions'. Watch one of the suggested videos. Are they similar to any current technology?

The SCIENCE of the IMPOSSIBLE

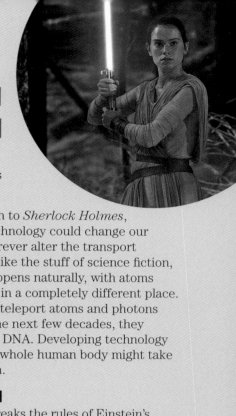

Can you make a spaceship invisible? What about building a *Star Wars* lightsaber? In his book, *Physics of the Impossible*, physicist Michio Kaku uses the latest advances in science to explain how sci-fi technology could actually work in the near future.

Invisibility

There are spaceships in *Star Trek* that can disappear. This sci-fi technology is slowly becoming reality. In 2007, scientists managed to create flat materials that became invisible in red and blue light by manipulating their structures to change how they reflected light waves. The next challenge is to make 3D objects disappear, but this should be possible in the next ten to twenty years. However, some scientists point to an obvious issue with travelling in an invisible spaceship: because all visible light from the outside would be reflected without ever getting inside the ship, the crew wouldn't be able to see what's outside the spaceship without making it visible first!

Lightsabers

Star Wars' iconic lightsabers have become part of pop culture. Although initially experts were quick to laugh them off as unrealistic, new advances in physics show that they are technically possible. What you need is some plasma, or an incredibly hot gas (25,000°C), and an empty tube with small holes along it. The plasma flows into the lightsaber and then out through the holes, creating a current of hot gas that can cut through steel. If you're already getting excited at the possibility of becoming a Jedi, there's a bit of a problem, unfortunately. To create plasma, you'd need a very powerful energy supply. So, unless you'd want to stay constantly plugged in to a power source, running around with a lightsaber isn't possible yet. Still, it might be within a hundred years.

Teleportation

Teleportation, or instantly sending objects or people across vast distances, has fascinated humans from *Arabian Nights*, through to *Sherlock Holmes*, to modern sci fi. This technology could change our civilization and would forever alter the transport system. While it sounds like the stuff of science fiction, teleportation already happens naturally, with atoms vanishing and appearing in a completely different place. Currently, scientists can teleport atoms and photons (units of light). Within the next few decades, they might be able to teleport DNA. Developing technology that allows teleporting a whole human body might take several centuries, though.

Faster than light travel

Faster than light travel breaks the rules of Einstein's theory of relativity. So how does the Millennium Falcon from *Star Wars* do this? There are two possibilities that do not violate Einstein's theory. Option one: bend spacetime. If you could stretch the space behind you and contract the space in front of you, you could get to even the most distant stars almost instantly. Option two: rip spacetime to make a hole that connects two distant parts of the universe (often referred to as a *wormhole*). The problem is you would need an almost unimaginable amount of energy to do either of the two. So faster than light travel is possible, but it might only become reality thousands of years from now.

Just a hundred years ago your smartphone would have been considered an impossible sci-fi technology. Similarly, the potential day-to-day tech from 2120 might seem like impossible sci-fi gadgets to us.

8B
It must have been invented by ...

LESSON GOALS
- Speculate about the past
- Understand the weak pronunciation of *have*
- Talk about inventions from the past

READING AND GRAMMAR

1 Work in pairs. When and where do you think these innovations might have been invented?

brain surgery   concrete   eye make-up
water sanitation systems

✤✦ Ancient inventions ✤✦

Thousands of years ago people invented many things that we now think of as 'modern'. Here are some of the most surprising ancient inventions.

Make-up We all know ancient Egyptians for their incredible architecture, but they also may have been the first to use make-up, more than 6,000 years ago. Their art also shows it must have been worn both by men and women.

Brain surgery Brain surgery has been practised for more than 8,000 years, and some of the earliest evidence comes from France. Even though our ancestors couldn't have known about bacteria, and perhaps shouldn't have performed these surgeries, many patients did survive and get better.

Concrete Over 2,000 years ago the Romans invented concrete. While scientists say it can't have been as good as modern concrete, it must have still been very strong as two thousand years later it still supports one of the largest domes in the world: the Pantheon.

Water system The first system for managing and cleaning dirty water in a city was invented 4,000 years ago in the Indus valley. It might have kept the city and the population safe from dangerous diseases.

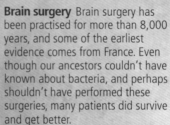

2 Read the text about ancient inventions. How close were your predictions in Exercise 1? Which information did you find the most surprising?

3 Read the text again. How certain is it that the sentences are true? Write certainly true (CT), possibly true (PT) or certainly <u>not</u> true (NT).

1 Egyptians invented make-up.
2 Both men and women in ancient Egypt wore make-up.
3 Our ancestors knew about bacteria.
4 It was a bad idea to perform brain surgery.
5 Roman concrete was as good as modern concrete.
6 Roman concrete was very strong.
7 The people in the Indus valley were safe from dangerous diseases.

4 Find the sentences in the text that told you the answers to Exercise 3. Match the modal structures with their meaning (1–4). Then read the Grammar box to check.

1 It's very probable or certain that something happened.
2 It's quite possible that something happened.
3 It's impossible that something happened.
4 It was wrong to do something.

GRAMMAR Speculating about the past

You can talk about possibility and certainty in the past using the structure: **modal verb + *have* + past participle**.

- Use **must have** if it's very probable or certain that something happened.

*Some of these operations **must have been** successful.*

- Use **may have** or **might have** if it's possible that something happened.

*Egyptians **may/might have been** the first to use make-up.*

- Use **can't/couldn't have** if it's impossible that something happened.

*Roman concrete **can't have been** as strong as modern concrete.*

- Use **should/shouldn't have** to talk about mistakes or express criticism.

*They **shouldn't have been** doing surgery then.*

Go to page 149 for the Grammar reference.

---

5 Choose the correct option to complete the sentences.

1 A million years ago, pottery and metal didn't exist, so people *can't / may* have boiled water in pots.

2 Archaeologists found rocks that have been heated up many times in fires. They aren't certain, but some claim these rocks *might / must* have been used to boil water.

3 Wild sheep are less aggressive than cows or pigs. They *may / can't* have been the first animals to be domesticated for farming.

4 Trepanning, a type of brain surgery, was a dangerous operation. It *can't / must* have killed more people than it saved.

5 In the 1970s, Joey Mellen made a hole in his own head and ended up in hospital. He *shouldn't / can't* have tried to trepan himself!

6 The ancient Maya *might / couldn't* have been the first to invent chocolate, although Aztec and Toltec civilizations are also likely candidates.

NATIONAL GEOGRAPHIC EXPLORER

6 🎧 8.2 Listen to Nora Shawki talking about important innovations in ancient Egypt. Complete the sentences using an appropriate modal verb and the verb in brackets.

1 The Egyptians _____ (use) papyrus for many other things we don't know about.

2 It _____ (be) very exciting to read hieroglyphics for the first time in centuries.

3 They _____ (speak) without vowel sounds even though they only wrote the consonants.

4 They _____ (make) bread in a similar way to how we make it today.

5 This type of pottery _____ (be) very important to ancient Egyptians.

PRONUNCIATION

7 🎧 8.3 Listen and check your answers to Exercise 6. How does the speaker pronounce *have*? Look at the Clear voice box to check.

CLEAR VOICE
Understanding the weak form of *have*

In past modal structures *have* is usually unstressed, and some speakers reduce it to its weak form /əv/, making it harder to hear. To be easily understood, it can be better to pronounce the full form /hæv/.

8 🎧 8.4 Listen and write the sentences you hear.

SPEAKING

9 Work in groups. Look at the photos of inventions from the past. For each invention, discuss the questions.

1 What might it have been used for?

2 When and where might it have been invented?

3 How do you think it might have worked?

It can't have been invented in Europe. I think it could have been somewhere in China, because …

Two sides to tech

- Talk about gadgets and technology
- Form nouns, verbs and adjectives in word families
- Understand prepositions in connected speech
- Pronounce long and short 'o' sounds clearly

Francisco Estrada-Belli and his team use technology called LIDAR to find Maya ruins in the Guatemalan jungle.

VOCABULARY AND LISTENING

1 Work in pairs. Look at the technology in the box and discuss the questions.

driverless vehicles   electric scooters
self-service checkouts   sharing apps (e.g. Uber, Airbnb)
video conferencing

1 What are the advantages of each technology: to the company? to workers? to customers?
2 What disadvantages can you think of?
3 Which technology have you used or experienced yourself? Why did you use it?

NATIONAL GEOGRAPHIC EXPLORER

2 🎧 8.5 Listen to Francisco Estrada-Belli talk about technology in his work. What advantages and disadvantages does he mention about ...
1 LIDAR?
2 his smartphone?

3 🎧 8.5 Listen again. Complete each sentence with one word.
1 Remote sensing uses a number of _____ to find ancient remains.
2 LIDAR is really _____ but it's not very _____. You need a lot of training because it's so _____.

3 Francisco couldn't work without his smartphone because it is so _____. It's a _____ collection of _____: G.P.S., compass, flashlight, camera and notepad.
4 But on the flip side, it's not _____, so it might get wet and damaged.

4 Match the words (1–10) with the definitions (a–j).

1 gadget	6 pocket-sized
2 handy	7 recharge
3 innovative	8 sophisticated
4 outdated	9 user-friendly
5 perform	10 waterproof

a a small machine with a particular purpose
b advanced in design so it can do complex things
c small enough to carry in your pocket
d fill something with electricity so it keeps working
e complete an action or job, especially a difficult one
f using new and different ideas and methods
g not allowing water to enter it
h old and no longer as good as more modern things
i useful
j simple for people to use

5 Write sentences using the words from Exercise 4 to describe …

1 the technology you often use.
2 the technology in Exercise 1.

Go to page 138 for the Vocabulary reference.

6 Which words from Exercise 4 (1–10) are in the same word families as the bold words (a–c)? Are they nouns, verbs or adjectives? Read the Focus on box to check.

a a computer with high **performance**
b the latest **innovations**
c **rechargeable** batteries

FOCUS ON Forming nouns, verbs and adjectives

You can expand your vocabulary by exploring the word families of words you are learning.
Notice some common suffixes that are typically added to words to create different parts of speech.
Nouns: -ion, -ment, -ity, -e/ance, -ness
complicated ➜ complicat**ion**,
achieve ➜ achieve**ment**, complex – complex**ity**,
silent ➜ sil**ence**, happy ➜ happi**ness**
Adjectives: -al, -ical, -able, -ous, -ive
universe ➜ univers**al**, technology ➜ technolog**ical**,
afford ➜ afford**able**, danger ➜ danger**ous**,
act ➜ act**ive**
Verbs: -ate, -ize, -ify, -en
active ➜ activ**ate**, memory ➜ memor**ize**,
simple ➜ simpl**ify**, strength ➜ strength**en**

Go to page 149 for the Focus on reference.

---

7 Complete the sentences, using suffixes to change the words in the box to the correct part of speech. Then use a dictionary to check.

---

invent   memory   sense

---

1 The Chinese are typically credited with the _____ of paper.
2 This app saves you from having to _____ all your passwords.
3 The alarm is _____ to movement and beeps as soon as someone enters the room.

LISTENING

8 🎧 **8.6** You are going to listen to a radio phone-in about a new sharing app. First, look at the Listening skill box. Then listen to three extracts and complete the sentences (1–3).

LISTENING SKILL
Understanding prepositions in connected speech

In connected speech, prepositions might not be heard clearly. They will often be connected to the words next to them, so *for example* might sound like /frəˈzɑːmpl/. Note that speaking like this might make you *less* easy to understand.

---

1 We've had them _____.
2 MyCarYourCar is revolutionizing _____.
3 That way they share the cost _____.

9 🎧 **8.7** Listen to the phone-in. Match the statements (1–5) with the person who said them: the host, Marsha, Yuki or Jens.

1 One benefit of carpooling is the interesting conversations you can have.
2 Carpooling is cheaper than the alternatives.
3 Carpooling isn't the most environmentally-friendly way of travelling.
4 Personal safety is an issue when carpooling.
5 There is an important difference between carpooling and hitchhiking.

PRONUNCIATION

10 🎧 **8.8** Look at the Clear voice box and listen to the words (1–6). Do they have a short or long 'o' sound? Practise saying the words.

CLEAR VOICE
Pronouncing long and short 'o'

In English there are two different 'o' sounds: a short one /ɒ/ (usually spelled 'o') and a long one /ɔː/. (often spelled as 'au' or 'or').

1 <u>au</u>tomatic   3 lapt<u>o</u>p   5 p<u>o</u>cket-sized
2 c<u>o</u>mplex   4 perf<u>o</u>rmance   6 w<u>a</u>terproof

SPEAKING

11 Work in groups of three. Read the statement and discuss whether you agree or not, and why.

The internet has damaged our personal and professional lives more than it has helped them.

8D
Communicating online

LESSON GOALS
- Discuss online communication habits
- Understand and discuss online etiquette
- Create a poster about online etiquette

SPEAKING

1 Work in pairs. Discuss the questions.

1 How often do you communicate with others online? Who do you typically chat with?
2 Which do you prefer: messaging, calling or video calling? Why?
3 Do you think we will soon communicate with others more online than face-to-face? Would this be something positive or negative? Why?
4 What problems can occur when people communicate online? Why?

2 Look at the definition. What examples of 'netiquette' rules can you think of?

> ## netiquette /'netɪket/
> rules about acceptable behaviour on the internet
> *It's considered bad netiquette to use all capital letters in emails.*

3 Do the quiz on page 103. Then go to page 156 to see the answers. Share your answers in groups. Who is the most and least relaxed about 'netiquette'?

4 Work in pairs. Do you think any of the behaviours in the quiz can help to build a relationship with the other person? Could any of the behaviours damage the relationship?

MY VOICE ▶

5 ▶ 8.2 Watch the video about online etiquette. Answer the questions.

1 Are any of the rules you listed in Exercise 2 mentioned?
2 Which behaviours from the quiz are discussed?
3 Which other behaviours are discussed?

6 ▶ 8.2 Watch the video again. Answer the questions.

1 Why can emotions be interpreted differently in online communication?
2 How can emojis be helpful?
3 Why can abbreviations cause problems in online communication?
4 Why should you be careful when posting photos on social media?

7 Look at the Communication skill box and discuss the questions (1–2).

COMMUNICATION SKILL
Communicating online

- Consider how the emotions behind your words or emojis can be interpreted differently. It's important to make sure that your meaning is clear. Ask the other person for clarification if you're not sure how to interpret their message.
- Avoid using too many abbreviations; not everyone will be familiar with them.
- Be careful what you share and who with – you don't want to offend or upset others.
- Try to read other people's messages with an open mind rather than assuming they're being rude or unfriendly.

1 Do you think these rules are universal or do they depend on the person and context? Why?
2 Have you ever had any misunderstandings when talking to someone online? What happened? How could the misunderstanding have been avoided?

8 Look at the messages and situations. How appropriate is each message? Why? Rewrite any that you think aren't appropriate.

1 WhatsApp message to a good friend: I was wondering if you had time to meet later today.
2 First message to someone you have only just met: It was 😄😄😄 meeting you yesterday 😬
3 Email to your teacher: Thx 4 checkin my homework 😜
4 Post on your professional social media profile: I wanted to share with you some of the BIGGEST lessons in marketing I've learned.

SPEAKING

9 **OWN IT!** Work in groups. Create a poster about online etiquette. Follow the instructions.

1 Include the online etiquette rules that are the most important to you. They can be rules from the Communication skill box or your own ideas.
2 Add specific examples, stories or pictures that illustrate the rules.
3 Present your poster to another group. Did you choose similar rules?

QUIZ

How seriously do you take netiquette? Take this quiz to find out.

How often do you do each of the following?

1 Reply to an email a week later.

Never   Rarely   Sometimes   Often   Always

2 Use abbreviations such as LOL or BTW.

Never   Rarely   Sometimes   Often   Always

3 Write using capital letters only.

Never   Rarely   Sometimes   Often   Always

4 Use emoticons in work emails.

Never   Rarely   Sometimes   Often   Always

5 Post an embarrassing photo of someone you know.

Never   Rarely   Sometimes   Often   Always

6 Write as you speak, e.g. *coz, gonna*.

Never   Rarely   Sometimes   Often   Always

7 Send emails with no subject line.

Never   Rarely   Sometimes   Often   Always

8 Add people you've never met or don't know as friends on Facebook.

Never   Rarely   Sometimes   Often   Always

Score

Never – 1 point, Rarely – 2 points, Sometimes – 3 points, Often – 4 points, Always – 5 points

8E
Five-star gadgets

LESSON GOALS
- Use multi-word adjectives to describe gadgets
- Give opinions about gadgets and other products
- Write a product review

a waterproof speaker

b sports video camera

c instant camera

d solar-powered power pack

SPEAKING

1 Work in pairs. Look at the photos. Why might someone buy each product?

2 When you buy a new gadget, what helps you decide which one to choose? Put the criteria (a–h) in order from 1 (the most important) to 8 (the least important). What other criteria might you take into account?

a appearance and size
b availability near you
c brand
d impact on the environment
e other people's opinions
f performance and special features
g user-friendliness
h value for money

READING FOR WRITING

3 Read the three reviews. What kind of gadget is each one reviewing? How many stars out of five do you think each reviewer gave the product?

 Shavi

Misleading info but decent sound

This would be the ideal choice if you're looking for a small but powerful device to travel with. The design is clean and simple, but the fact that it's waterproof makes it the perfect companion for outdoor activities like camping. Plus it doubles up as a power charger for other devices, which saves space. On the flip side, another review claimed it has a long-lasting, 24-hour battery life, but they must have been talking about a different model because the most it's lasted for me was about 10 hours. Luckily, the recharge time is surprisingly quick. The only other downside is that there's no volume button. All in all, not bad.

 Petra

OK for kids, not so much for adults

Needed a cheap and cheerful one quickly for a friend's wedding but couldn't find anything locally so had to buy online. Fortunately, it arrived in good time. Clear and easy-to-use on-screen buttons makes editing straightforward. That, and the fun choice of colours (comes in blue, pink, or red) makes me think it's really for kids. Picture quality OK in good light, but the flash isn't strong enough for indoor photography. Also, the print quality is a lot worse than I expected, though I got some acceptable results in black and white. The other major drawback is the poor Bluetooth connection - you need to be very close to your phone to send photos. They should have included a USB cable.

 Otto

Great value for money

This make is well-known as high-end (they say the camera is a must if you enjoy photography) so I thought the C14 was out of my price range until I looked at second-hand offers. What a great deal! Plus it's better for the planet. Just a few minor scratches on the screen and the battery is perhaps not as long-lasting as it was when new. Really, I couldn't have got a better phone for the price.

4 Read the reviews again. Which of the criteria listed in Exercise 2 does each one mention?

5 Look at the Writing skill box. Then find at least five compound adjectives and three adjective pairs in the reviews.

WRITING SKILL
Multi-word adjectives

Compound adjectives allow you to write more economically. They are made of more than one word and are usually joined by a hyphen.

This handy feature saves space. It combines two functions in one. → *This handy, **space-saving** feature combines two functions in one.*

It comes with a guarantee of two years. → *It comes with a **two-year** guarantee.*

Some adjectives are often seen together in **adjective pairs**, joined by *and*.

*The app is free and, though it's quite **rough and ready**, it works well.*

The order of the adjectives in these expressions is fixed, i.e. not ~~ready and rough~~.

6 Put the words in order to complete the sentences. You may need to add hyphens.
1 This operating system starts very quickly and … a / and / clean / has / interface / simple.
2 No other model can compete … its / minute / recharge / thirty / time / with.
3 I recommend this running machine if you're looking for … and / cheap / cheerful / something.
4 Talkback was the only … and / easy / free / to / use … video conferencing platform that we found.
5 You can sing along to each song … by / lyrics / on / reading / screen / the.
6 The controls are multi-coloured, but the problem is that the manual … and / black / in / is / printed / white.
7 It's known as … a / brand / end / high …, but you can find bargains if you search online.
8 The plastic cover provides … and / lasting / long / protection / strength … for the watch screen.

7 Look at the expressions in the Useful language box. Are you more likely to hear positive or negative comments with each expression? Which could be used with both positive <u>and</u> negative comments?

Useful language   Product reviews
This is the ideal option if you're looking for …
… makes the perfect choice for …
On the flip side, …
Another downside is that …
All in all, …
A minor drawback is …
You could do a lot worse than …
… is a must.
… within your price range.

WRITING TASK

8 You are going to write a review for a gadget or other tech product that you own or have used. Write five sentences to include in your review, using expressions from the Useful language box.

9 **WRITE** Decide how many stars out of five you will give the product. Then write the review.

10 **CHECK** Use the checklist. I have …
☐ included several criteria from the list in Exercise 2.
☐ said what type of person would enjoy or benefit from the product.
☐ described both the positive and negative aspects of the product.
☐ used multi-word adjectives to make my writing economical.

11 **REVIEW** Exchange reviews with a partner. Did they include everything in the checklist in Exercise 10? Does their review reflect the number of stars they have given their product?

Go to page 133 for the Reflect and review.

EXPLORE MORE!

Find out what percentage of online reviews are fake, i.e. written by companies to make customers buy their products.

Chris Moon competes in the
135-mile ultra-marathon race in
Death Valley National Park, US.

9
Against all odds

GOALS

- Make inferences about a writer's opinion
- Talk about future plans, goals and hopes
- Discuss challenges, successes and failures
- Understand contrasts when listening
- Adapt to direct and indirect communication styles
- Write a job application email

1 **Work in pairs. Discuss the questions.**

1 Look at the photo and caption. What makes the person's success special?

2 Which of these things mean success for you? Put them in order from the most to the least important.

> the ability to help others   the chance to travel
> dealing with difficult challenges   enormous wealth
> inner peace and happiness   a lot of friends
> a loving family   a rewarding career

WATCH ▶

2 ▶ 9.1 Watch the video. Which of the things in Exercise 1 matter the most to Robbie and Paola? What else matters to them?

NATIONAL GEOGRAPHIC EXPLORERS

ROBBIE SHONE   PAOLA RODRÍGUEZ

3 Make connections. Write a one-sentence answer to the question *What does success mean for you?*

4 Share your sentence with your classmates. Whose sentences express similar ideas? Whose are similar to Robbie's or Paola's?

9A
Paths to success

LESSON GOALS
• Make inferences about a writer's opinion
• Consider perspectives of other readers
• Talk about a personal success

READING

1 Think of someone you know or have heard about who has succeeded despite facing challenges. What did they achieve? What problems did they have? Tell a partner.

2 Work in pairs. Read the four mini biographies on page 109 and discuss the questions.
   1 Name a key skill or talent each person has.
   2 Name a challenge each person has faced.
   3 Whose story sounds the most inspiring? Why?

3 What do the collocations in bold mean? Use the biographies and a dictionary to help you.
   1 still **faced** serious **challenges**
   2 **experienced personal tragedies**
   3 **refused** to **give up**
   4 challenges that **stand in her way**
   5 started from **modest beginnings**
   6 **donates** millions **to good causes**

4 Read the biographies again. Then close your books. In pairs, summarize what you remember about each person.

5 Look at the Reading skill box. What do the extracts (1–4) suggest about the writer's opinions of the things or people in brackets?

READING SKILL
Making inferences about a writer's opinion

A writer may clearly state their opinion or leave it open to the reader to interpret. Look for how the writer supports their point of view.

• Do particular words and expressions they use suggest a particular opinion?
• What information did they include and leave out?

1 Guilhermina gets stronger by meeting challenges that stand in her way. (Terezinha Guilhermina)
   The writer thinks Terezinha is a great athlete because she has the right attitude.
2 ... he pays his employees well and donates millions to good causes. (Hamdi Ulukaya)
3 However, initially, the Nobel committee did not even nominate her because she was a woman! (the people on the committee)
4 In fact, it was the first non-English-speaking film to win Best Film after almost 100 years of the Academy Awards. (the Academy)

6 Look at the Critical thinking skill box. Then discuss the questions (1–4) in pairs.

CRITICAL THINKING SKILL
Recognizing other perspectives

When we read a text, we are likely to have an immediate reaction to it. However, other readers might react differently. This can depend on where we come from, our beliefs and values, our knowledge of the world, etc. Trying to understand how others might react to a text can help you see the information in a new light and question your initial reaction.

1 What might other businesspeople think about Hamdi's modest start in life or his generosity?
   They might admire him because he did it all himself without family help.
2 What might Polish people think of Maria and her achievements? Would this be any different from someone who is not Polish?
3 What might other visually-impaired people think of Terezinha's achievements?
4 What might those who booed *Okja* at the Cannes Film Festival think of that reaction now that Joon-ho has won an Oscar?

SPEAKING

7 Choose one success in your life, big or small. You can choose from the ideas below or use your own idea. Answer the questions (1–3) to organize your ideas. Then share your story in groups.

> winning a prize   passing a very difficult exam
> getting a job you really wanted

1 Why was the achievement important?
2 Did you face any difficulties? How did you overcome these?
3 How did you feel after achieving your goal?

EXPLORE MORE!

Search online for the people mentioned in the article. What's the most interesting thing you learned about them?

There are many paths that lead to success, but for some their roads are longer than others. Here are four inspiring stories of people who've managed to succeed despite difficulties.

Maria Skłodowska Curie, SCIENTIST

Maria Salomea Skłodowska was born in 1867 in Warsaw, Poland which, at that time, was part of the Russian empire. People were not allowed to study in Polish, and women could not enrol in universities at all. This meant Skłodowska had to study at the Flying University, a secret organization. Despite these difficulties, and having almost no money, she later continued her education in Paris, France.

In 1903 she was awarded the Nobel Prize in Physics. However, initially, the Nobel committee did not even nominate her because she was a woman! Even after winning her second Nobel Prize, she still faced serious challenges and experienced personal tragedies, such as the death of her husband, Pierre, in 1906. Best known by her French name, Marie Curie, she is now one of the most famous and inspiring figures in scientific history.

Bong Joon-ho, FILMMAKER

Bong Joon-ho made history as the first South Korean director to win an Oscar for his film *Parasite*. In fact, it was the first non-English-speaking film to win Best Film after almost one hundred years of the Academy Awards. Even though he seemed calm on the outside when receiving the award, he's actually suffered from anxiety all his life. 'I have severe anxiety … to the point where it would be impossible for me to have a social life. But thanks to filmmaking, I've been able to survive', he told *Vanity Fair*.

He's also struggled as a director. His first film, *Barking Dogs Never Bite*, didn't make much money and his film *Okja* was booed at the Cannes Film Festival! Still, he refused to give up.

Terezinha Guilhermina, ATHLETE

Terezinha Guilhermina, a Brazilian athlete, won gold in the 100m and 200m at the 2012 Paralympic Games in London. She was born with an eye disorder that causes visual impairment, so athletes in her category run with a guide to help them.

Aged 22, Guilhermina realized she wanted to be an athlete but, in order to compete, proper running shoes were necessary – a luxury that she couldn't afford. It was only when her sister gave her a pair that she could join the running club. Guilhermina gets stronger by meeting challenges that stand in her way. 'People that don't have anything can make it,' she says. 'I have never accepted how little I had.'

Hamdi Ulukaya, BUSINESSMAN

Ulukaya's company, Chobani, makes the best-selling Greek-style yoghurt in the US, but he started from modest beginnings. His family were sheep farmers in Turkey. He moved to the US in 1994, where he learned English and, after a number of jobs, eventually started manufacturing yoghurt.

The first two years he made very little money and he says that these were the most challenging years of his life. He has since transformed the business into an international empire. Famous for his generosity, he pays his employees well and donates millions to good causes. In 2016, he shared the ownership of the company with his staff to say thank you. 'There are a lot of important things in business, but people come first.'

9B
Emails to my future self

LESSON GOALS
- Talk about future plans, goals and hopes
- Write about your hopes for the future
- Practise pausing when reading out loud

READING AND GRAMMAR

1 Work in pairs. Tell your partner what you would like to achieve personally and professionally …

1 this year.
2 in a few years' time.
3 by 2050.

2 Read three emails written by people to their future self (A–C). Discuss the questions.

1 What do you imagine the writers are like? (age, personality)
2 Which of these reasons for writing do all the emails have in common?
   a to check they are happy
   b to express hope for the future
   c to give their future self some inspiration

3 Read the emails again and answer the questions. Underline the expressions in each email that helped you answer them.

1 What one big change does each writer expect to have happened?
2 What does each writer expect they'll be doing in the future?

4 Match the sentences you found in Exercise 3 with the functions (a–c). Then read the Grammar box to check.

a an action that will be in progress at a particular time in the future
b an action that will be complete before a particular time in the future
c an action the writer is less certain will happen

GRAMMAR Talking about the future

Use the **future continuous** to predict things in progress at a particular time in the future.
*You **won't** still **be sitting** on that sofa.*

Use the **future perfect** to refer to actions that will be complete before a particular time in the future.
*When you read this, you **will have just graduated**.*

Use **should** and **might** instead of **will** to show you are less certain that something will happen.
*You **should be making** some money.*
*There's a photo you **might be needing** to see.*

Go to page 150 for the Grammar reference.

A

Dear Future Me,

If I know you – and I think I do ;) – when you read this you will have just graduated. Yay! And you should be making some money! But I'm determined to make things perfect, so if I haven't already … go and find Karsten and ask him out!

Old Me
Sent to nine months in the future

B

Dear Kris,

Confused? It's likely you've forgotten you sent this email to yourself, so if you've still got that copy of *War and Peace* on the bookshelf, go take a look – there's a photo in it you might be needing to see about now. Anyway, sincerely hoping that by now you'll have done what I can't right now and apologized to the family for what you did. If not, I'll be disappointed. Take care,

Kris
Sent to five years in the future

C

Hey FutureMe,

If I've stuck to my plan, you won't still be sitting on that sofa and you should have joined the gym! If you haven't, this is the reminder that you need! A voice from the past. Now is the time to get moving.

Remember that you can do anything you put your mind to. I just thought that you needed to hear that today.

Love,

Me
Sent to one year in the future

5 Use the words to form sentences.

1 I / should / finish / university / in two years.
2 I / might / live / another country / next year.
3 My best friend / will / start / her online business / by the end of this year.
4 I / will / travel / around Asia / next summer.

6 Read Paola Rodríguez's email to her future self. What hopes and plans does she mention? Which does she sound the most confident about?

Dear Future Pao,

You are a really determined person, so I have no doubt that you will have done very well at work, so let's not talk about that. What I really want to know is, how was your trip to Europe for your 41st birthday? It's likely that your first stop was London and specifically the London Eye. Is the view as amazing as I picture it? And please tell me that you visited that café in Madrid – I'm determined to have that amazing cup of coffee. Also, there's a fifty-fifty chance that you took a selfie at the Eiffel Tower – yes, the one you swore you weren't going to take because it's such a cliché, but you are bound to get really amazed and take it anyway.

So … what's next? Please tell me that it's a trip to Australia.

As always keep going! Hugs,

Present Pao
Sent to three years in the future

---

7 Underline the phrases in Paola's email that talk about her future. Which ones describe plans? Which describe predictions? Look at the Useful language box to check your answers.

Useful language Talking about the future

Plans
I'm about to … ; I'm determined to …
I'm thinking of/considering +-ing …

Predictions
I'm bound to …
It's likely/unlikely that …
There's a good/fifty-fifty/slight chance …
I doubt that …

PRONUNCIATION

8 🎧 **9.1** Look at the Clear voice box and listen to the example. Then divide Paola's text from Exercise 6 into short pauses (|) and long pauses (‖).

CLEAR VOICE
Pausing

Pauses make what you are saying easier to understand. Short pauses (|) divide sentences into shorter sections, which are usually grammatical chunks. Typically, one word in each section will be stressed. Long pauses (‖) divide longer clauses or whole sentences from each other.

It's important | to set goals | for ourselves, ‖ but we are likely | to forget things sometimes. ‖ It's useful | to remind ourselves | of these goals, ‖ and writing future self emails | could be a good way | to do this.

9 🎧 **9.2** Listen to Paola read her email to check your answers to Exercise 8.

WRITING AND SPEAKING

10 Write an email to your future self. Choose a reason for writing from Exercise 2. Use the Useful language box to help you express your plans and predictions.

11 Work in pairs. Read out your emails to each other. Think about where to pause. Ask your partner follow-up questions.

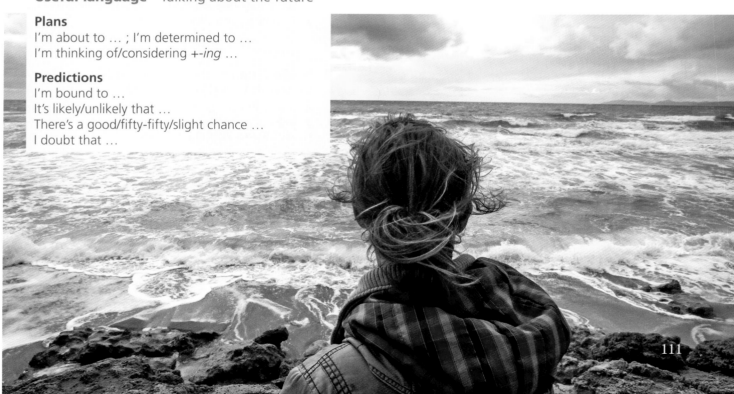

Learning from mistakes

LESSON GOALS
- Understand contrasts when listening
- Discuss challenges, successes and failures
- Learn verb-noun collocations
- Practise pronunciation of /ʃ/, /ʒ/, /tʃ/ and /dʒ/

SPEAKING

1 Do the quiz. Then look at the answers on page 156. How easy do you find turning negative experiences into positive ones?

NEGATIVE TO POSITIVE

How do you deal with negative experiences? We all have good and bad days, but do we all use the bad days to our advantage?

1 You've failed your driving test. Do you ...
- A kick yourself and book more lessons?
- B quit now and accept that driving is just too hard?
- C learn how to cycle instead?

2 You lose a lot of money and time when your small business fails. Do you ...
- A decide being a business owner is not for you, and get a job in a big company instead?
- B promise yourself that you'll never try anything difficult that you could fail at ever again?
- C analyse why it didn't succeed and build a better new business?

3 You're shy and public speaking makes you uncomfortable, but you have to give a presentation. Do you ...
- A spend days worrying and losing sleep over it but do it anyway?
- B find a colleague who will do the presentation for you?
- C ask your friends to help you fight the fear?

LISTENING

NATIONAL GEOGRAPHIC EXPLORER

2 🎧 **9.3** Listen to Robbie Shone telling two anecdotes about incidents in his life. Which anecdote, 1 or 2 ...
- a resulted in Robbie learning something valuable about himself?
- b involved Robbie getting help from friends?
- c was the most difficult for Robbie?
- d ended with Robbie learning a practical lesson?

3 🎧 **9.4** Look at the Listening skill box. Then listen and complete the extracts from the anecdotes.

LISTENING SKILL
Understanding contrasts

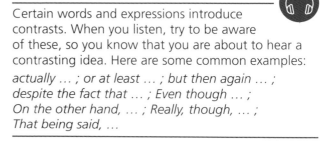

Certain words and expressions introduce contrasts. When you listen, try to be aware of these, so you know that you are about to hear a contrasting idea. Here are some common examples:
actually ... ; or at least ... ; but then again ... ; despite the fact that ... ; Even though ... ; On the other hand, ... ; Really, though, ... ; That being said, ...

1 To get out of the cave we all just simply jumped in the river. _____ that it was quite safe, we still all needed buoyancy aids to help us float.
2 And what you thought was a failure at first, _____ make you better at what you do.

4 🎧 **9.3** Listen to the interview again. Are the sentences true (T) or false (F)?
1 It wasn't easy getting out of the Clearwater cave.
2 Robbie realized what the problem was before he opened the container.
3 Robbie had to return to the UK because his expedition had ended.
4 In the interview, the editor didn't like any of the photos Robbie showed her.
5 After the interview, Robbie got a job painting bridges.
6 Robbie is now glad that he had such a disappointing interview in Washington.

5 Work in pairs. Answer the questions.

1 Which of the experiences Robbie talks about had the biggest effect on him?

2 Do you agree with Robbie that failing at something is a good way to learn? Why?

3 Have you ever experienced a similar setback or problem to Robbie? What happened?

VOCABULARY

6 Complete the sentences with these pairs of words. Which sentences describe successes?

achieved + objectives   made + mess   made + through
overcame + issues   struggling + understand
tackle + problem

1 We need to _____ the main _____ before it gets worse.

2 I'm _____ to _____ this website. It shouldn't be this tricky to shop online!

3 It was a tough time , but we _____ it _____.

4 Oh! I'm not getting anywhere with this tax form and I've _____ such a _____ of it.

5 She eventually _____ her self-confidence _____ and opened her first shop.

6 The project wasn't perfect, but it has _____ its main _____.

Go to page 139 for the Vocabulary reference.

7 Read the Focus on box. Then find verbs in Exercise 6 that collocate with the expressions (1–5).

> **FOCUS ON**   Verb-noun collocations
>
> It's useful to notice common combinations of words, or collocations. Different types of word collocate, e.g. *a tough time* and *tough competition* are **adjective-noun collocations**.
> Another group to learn are **verb-noun collocations**. Recording words in the collocations you find them in can help you remember them.

Go to page 150 for the Focus on reference.

1 _____ your aims / your objectives / very little

2 _____ a mess / it through / a decision

3 _____ obstacles / difficulties / problems

4 _____ to understand / with the problem

5 _____ the crisis / issue / problem

PRONUNCIATION

8 Look at the Clear voice box. Then complete the table with the words (1-10), according to the consonant sounds they have in common. Underline the letters that produce the sound.

CLEAR VOICE
Saying /ʃ/, /ʒ/, /tʃ/ and /dʒ/

For clear pronunciation, it's important that you can say /ʃ/, /ʒ/, /tʃ/ and /dʒ/. Spelling patterns can help you know which sound to say.

/ʃ/ **ss** e.g. mi*ss*ion; **ti** e.g. combina*ti*on; **ch** e.g. ma*ch*ine

/ʒ/ **si** e.g. conclu*si*on; **ge** e.g. bei*ge*; **su** e.g. mea*su*re

/tʃ/ **tu** e.g. fu*tu*re; **ch** e.g. *ch*allenge

/dʒ/ **ge** e.g. pa*ge*; **dge** e.g. bri*dge*; **j** e.g. *j*object

1 ambition
2 professional
3 achieve
4 issue
5 knowledge
6 manage
7 decision
8 objectives
9 project
10 vision

/ʃ/	/ʒ/	/tʃ/	/dʒ/

9 🎧 **9.5** Listen to check your answers to Exercise 8. Then practise saying the words.

SPEAKING

10 Play 'Fortunately, … Unfortunately, …' in groups.

1 Take turns to tell a story, each person saying one sentence at a time.

2 Use one of these sentences to begin or your own idea.

I lost my mobile phone the other day. Fortunately, …

Some new neighbours moved in next door …

My football team won the match yesterday …

3 Sentences must alternate good and bad news.

I got a new job. → Unfortunately the pay wasn't very good. → Fortunately, they gave me a company car. → That being said, it was only a toy car. → However, my colleagues were really nice.

4 Decide together whether each sentence continues the story successfully. Players score a point for each successful new sentence.

5 Players can score an extra point if they successfully include words from today's lesson!

9D
Adapting to direct and indirect styles

LESSON GOALS
- Understand the difference between direct and indirect communication
- Adapt to direct and indirect communication styles
- Ask for clarification

SPEAKING

1 Work in pairs. Look at the cartoon and answer the questions.

1 What's the problem with the language used in each situation?
2 What's the best caption for the cartoon?
  a Be as polite as possible at all times.
  b Understand when to use direct or indirect language.
  c Don't use a hundred words when one is enough.

MY VOICE ▶

2 ▶ 9.2 Watch the video. Which style do you use more often?

3 ▶ 9.2 Watch the video again. Are the sentences true (T) or false (F)?

1 Both direct and indirect communication styles can lead to better relationships.
2 People who are more indirect feel that being efficient when communicating is important.

3 The student talked about the situation rather than directly asking for paper from their classmate.
4 Using the wrong style can create problems.
5 It's important you recognize your and the other person's preferred style.

4 Work in pairs. Read the situations (1–3). Decide if the speaker is being too indirect or direct. What do you think the indirect people are really saying? How could the direct person be perceived?

1 A colleague explains to Marcus a project she wants to propose to the boss. It is very ambitious and will cost the company a lot of money. Marcus: 'Well … it's a very *brave* proposal.'
2 Kareem is trying to finish his essay. It has to be given in tomorrow. His flatmate is practising for a speaking exam.
   Kareem: 'Go upstairs, OK? I'm trying to concentrate here.'
3 Patri is going to a job interview. It's raining hard. Her friend has a car.
   Patri: 'Isn't the weather horrible today! I hope my suit doesn't get wet.'

5 Look at the Communication skill box. In pairs, write a continuation of the conversations from Exercise 4 to show how the directness or indirectness could be dealt with effectively.

'Er, sorry, when you say 'brave', what do you mean?'
'Well, you've got some good ideas, but I think there are some issues with it. Let's talk it through together.'

COMMUNICATION SKILL
Adapting to direct and indirect communication styles

1 When communicating with someone who is being more indirect, use the background information to interpret their information, show curiosity and ask questions for clarification.

2 When communicating with someone who is being more direct, remember they are simply trying to be efficient and clear, not rude. If you need more context, don't be afraid to ask for it.

3 Consider the situation and the person you're speaking to and adapt your communication style as appropriate. Discuss your preferred communication style with the other person.

6 Look at the Useful language box. Answer the questions (1–2).

Useful language Adapting to different communication styles

Asking for clarification
I appreciate your honesty, but could you explain your reasons a bit more?
What exactly do you mean by …?
Why do you say that?
Just to check I understand, do you mean …?

Talking about different styles
I tend to get to the point quickly, so please ask me questions if anything is unclear.
Sometimes I take a while to get to the point, so feel free to ask me to be more direct.

1 Which expressions in the 'Asking for clarification' section could be used when speaking to someone who is: a) communicating directly?; b) communicating indirectly?

2 Which expressions in the 'Talking about different styles' section could be used if you are: a) a direct speaker?; b) an indirect speaker?

SPEAKING

7 Read the messages (1–3) that users of a study centre have sent in an online chat group. Match them with the comments (a–c).

● **STUDY GROUP**

1 **PAT**

TO EVERYONE! Please don't use the study centre on Thursday from 4:30 – 5:30. I need it. (If I don't hear anything from you, I'll assume that's OK.)

2 **JI-SOO**

☺ Let's all work together to keep the centre tidy! ☺ I'm not sure we all are, are we?

3 **BLAS**

Do you like reading mysteries, fantasy and sci fi? There are some great books in English. Talking about the books we love is good English practice too! Why don't we do something like a club? I'd love to know what you think.

a 'He was talking about it the other day in the canteen. I love how excited he is about this idea of his, but I'm not exactly sure what it is!'
b 'She did the same thing last week. I was on the computer and she came in and asked me to leave. I don't think she can just use the room like that whenever she wants!'
c 'That's typical of him. He came in the other day and rushed around putting all the books back on the shelves. He wasn't very pleased!'

8 OWN IT! Imagine you are part of the online chat group in Exercise 7. Make notes for each question.

1 Which of the three situations would make you the most uncomfortable? Why?
2 How would you normally react in a situation like this? Do you think you might react differently, having learned about direct and indirect styles?
3 What message would you send in response? Use the Useful language to help you.

9 Work in pairs. Compare your different responses to each situation. If your responses are different, discuss why that is.

9E
I got the job!

LESSON GOALS
- Explain why you are suitable for a job
- Provide specific examples of your skills and experience
- Write a job application email

SPEAKING

1 Work in pairs. Look at the job adverts and discuss the questions.

1 Which of these jobs would you be interested in? Which would interest you least? Why?
2 Which do you think you might be good at? Why?

Professional sleeper
'El Descanso' hotel in Mexico is looking for a professional sleeper to test the quality of its beds.

Full-time Netflix watcher
Netflix is hiring people to watch content before it becomes publicly available.

Drying paint watcher
We will hire a part-time worker to watch how long it takes for our paint to dry.

Scuba diving pizza delivery person
Jules Undersea Lodge is looking for an experienced scuba diver to deliver pizza to its guests.

READING FOR WRITING

2 Read the hotel receptionist job advert and application email. Answer the questions.

1 Do all requirements for the job seem necessary or fair? Why? / Why not?
2 Does Alexander mention all the other requirements from the job advert in his email?
3 How does Alexander provide evidence for his skills and qualities?

HOTEL RECEPTIONIST

X

Seafront Hotel is looking for a female hotel receptionist to work either part- or full-time.

Requirements:

- minimum two years of experience in a similar position
- excellent communication skills
- ability to solve unexpected problems
- strong organizational skills
- native English speaker and fluent in at least one European language
- minimum Master's degree or certificate in hospitality preferred

APPLY NOW

---

3 Look at the Writing skill box. Which of the sentences (1–4) would be relevant in a job application for the hotel receptionist role?

WRITING SKILL
A job application email

When writing a job application email, it is important to mention all the key requirements listed in the job advert. You should also avoid including information that is not relevant to the position you are applying for. Finally, try to provide evidence and specific examples to prove you really have the necessary skills, experience or qualities.

1 I can communicate fluently in English.
2 I have previously worked as a chef in a restaurant.
3 I have developed my ability to communicate with people from different countries.
4 I am creative and able to solve unexpected problems quickly.

Dear Sir or Madam,

I am writing to apply for the position of hotel receptionist as advertised on your website.

As outlined in my CV, which I have attached, I have over three years' experience working as a hotel receptionist. During my BA degree in hospitality, I worked part-time at the Imperial Hotel in Berlin where I gained valuable experience. Since graduating, I have been working at the Riverside Hotel, Berlin, but I will be relocating to New York next month.

As far as my personality is concerned, I am friendly and approachable. I have always received high ratings in guest satisfaction surveys. Moreover, I am able to organize my daily tasks well to fulfil them on time, which is something my previous employers have positively commented on.

Thanks to my experience in the German hotel industry, I have also learned how to communicate effectively with international guests. While I am not a first language user of English, I am highly proficient in it. Having welcomed many international guests, I have developed a good working knowledge of French and Spanish, in addition to my first language (German).

With regards to my qualifications, I hold a BA degree in hospitality from SRH University Berlin. I am also about to complete a professional development course in international communication.

I would be very interested in joining your team at Seafront. The values your hotel stands for, such as an individual approach to guests and attention to detail, are very much in line with my own professional values. I hope you will consider me for the role.

Yours sincerely,

Alexander Müller

4 Read Alexander's application email again. Underline phrases that mean …
1 got really good experience
2 since finishing university
3 moving to
4 about my personality
5 speak very well with
6 my French and Spanish aren't too bad
7 I'm now almost done with

5 Look at the Useful language box. Then write sentences about …
1 your education.
2 the languages you speak.
3 your work experience and/or personal skills.

Useful language Job application emails

Previous experience
I have enclosed/attached my CV.
I gained valuable experience in …
I work part-/full-time in/as a …

Languages
I am (highly) proficient in …
I have a good working knowledge of …

Education
I hold a degree in …
I completed a course in …
I graduated in …

Introducing a new topic
With regards to …
As far as (my personality) is concerned …

WRITING TASK

6 **WRITE** Write an email of 200-250 words applying for a job. You can choose to apply for …
- the hotel receptionist job from Exercise 2.
- a job advert of your choice from the internet.

7 **CHECK** Use the checklist. I have …
☐ included evidence and examples of skills / experience.
☐ only included information relevant to the job.
☐ used formal language.

8 **REVIEW** Work in pairs. Exchange job adverts and application letters. Decide if you would invite your partner to a job interview and give them feedback.

Go to page 134 for the Reflect and review.

EXPLORE MORE!

Search online for 'top tips for a job interview'. Which tips did you find the most useful?

Children playing in Haryana, India.

10

A world of cultures

GOALS

- Identify and understand figurative language in creative writing
- Learn verb patterns with infinitive and *-ing*
- Talk about your cultural identity
- Understand ellipsis in spoken language
- Learn to deal with assumptions to avoid misunderstandings
- Write a report about cultural attractions

1 **Work in pairs. Discuss the questions.**

1 Look at the photo. What game do you think the children are playing? Did you play a similar game as a child?
2 What other games do you think are played by children all over the world?
3 What other behaviours and customs do you think are universal around the world? Which do you think are different?

WATCH ▶

2 ▶ **10.1** Watch the video. Answer the questions.

NATIONAL GEOGRAPHIC EXPLORERS

ALYEA PIERCE   **LIA NAHOMI KAJIKI**

1 What cultures do Alyea and Lia compare?
2 What similarities do they each notice?

3 **Make connections. What do Alyea and Lia's stories have in common? Do you have any similar stories?**

10A
A thousand rhythms

LESSON GOALS
• Identify and understand figurative language in creative writing
• Evaluate the relationship between a text and its supporting media
• Talk about your favourite music and its role in your identity and culture

SPEAKING

1 🎧 **10.1** Listen to three short pieces of music. Discuss the questions with a partner.
1 Which piece of music did you like best? Why?
2 How did each piece make you feel?
3 How would you describe the music? Use these words and your own ideas.

> cheerful   mournful   rapid   rhythmic
> rich   slow   traditional

READING

2 Look at the title of the article on page 121. Which place do you think is 'the land of a thousand rhythms'? Quickly skim the article to check.

3 Read the article. Then discuss the questions.
1 What was the most interesting thing you learned from the article?
2 Which of the places the writer describes would you like to visit the most? Why?
3 What traditional music is there in your country? How is it similar or different to the music styles the writer describes?

4 Look at the Reading skill box. Then read the article again and find …
1 one simile (paragraph 2)
2 one metaphor (paragraph 4)
3 two examples of personification (paragraph 7 and 8)

READING SKILL
Identifying figurative language in creative writing

Figurative language is frequently found in creative writing, such as stories, poetry, articles and songs. It includes …
• similes – comparing two unrelated things using *as* or *like*: *The look in his eyes was like ice*.
• metaphors – saying one thing *is* another thing (no *as* or *like*): *During rush hour, the motorway is a giant car park*.
• personification – giving human qualities or feelings to something that isn't human: *My alarm clock yells at me every morning*.

5 Work in pairs. Discuss the questions.
1 What does the figurative language you identified in Exercise 4 mean? For example, in what way is San Basilio de Palenque similar to a greenhouse?
2 Why did the writer use this language in the article? What effect does it have on the reader?

6 Look at the Critical thinking skill box. Discuss the questions in the box, thinking about the photos, music and article from this lesson.

CRITICAL THINKING SKILL
Evaluating the relationship between text and supporting media

Understanding a text can sometimes be just one part of the whole story. The text might be accompanied by photos, graphs, maps, video or audio, which can help you understand the text. But they can also influence your opinion of the text or create an emotional reaction. Consider:
• What additional information do the photos or video/audio contain?
• How do these help you understand the text?
• How do they influence your reaction to the text?

SPEAKING

7 Take notes about your favourite types of music and why you enjoy them. Find examples of this music to play to your classmates. Consider these questions:
1 What do you like about these music types? How do they make you feel?
2 What has influenced this music? For example, traditional songs, other musical styles, a specific culture or group of people. Use the internet if you need to find this information.
3 Is this music popular among many people in your country? Is it popular among a specific age group?

8 Share your favourite music in groups of three. Play the music to your classmates.

EXPLORE MORE!

Choose a country you are interested in. Find and listen to three different music styles from there. Which did you like the most? Why?

Afro-Colombian singer La Burgos and her group Las Alegres Ambulancias.

So You Want to Explore the Land of a Thousand Rhythms?

1 For the past few weeks, I have been on a remarkable music exploration. Most people have probably heard of, and hopefully danced to, international hits by artists like Shakira and Carlos Vives. But fewer are familiar with other fascinating folk rhythms of Colombia that have been calculated at an incredible 1,025 different types.

Palenque: Afro-Colombian vibes

5 A visit to San Basilio de Palenque, considered the first free town in the Americas, is like a trip to a greenhouse. You'll be greeted by 10 high temperatures, humidity and dusty streets. Maybe not much to this town after all? [para 2]

Wrong.

The strong and proud Afro-15 Colombian spirit in this town tells the story of human determination and is likely to touch your heart. Four hundred years ago, when ships transporting enslaved 20 people arrived in Cartagena, many people escaped and settled in the remote and hard-to-access *palenques*, or tiny towns, where they would not be found. They'd 25 brought with them from Africa the rhythmic music that I was now hearing everywhere: 15+ drum types played both at mournful funerals and cheerful celebrations. 30 This music is a trip across time and space. [para 4]

Cali: More than just salsa

For those who love Latin American music, Cali – the 35 Salsa capital of the world – needs no introduction. My first thought? I have arrived at the right place!

For the locals, or *caleños*, salsa 40 is a native sound, a musical style to be proud of. The rich and rapid tunes are bound to make you dance all night (and day!) long. But Cali goes beyond 45 salsa sounds.

Each year, rhythms such as *Currulao* or *Chirimia* dance in the air during Petronio Alvarez Music Festival. Artists such as 50 Esteban Copete, grandson of the iconic Colombian composer after whom the festival takes its name, take these traditional local vibes a step further, 55 mixing them with well-known international music styles, such as R&B, Bossa Nova and jazz. [para 7]

Los Llanos: Cowboy music

I finally arrived in *Los Llanos*, or 60 flatlands, where life goes about its business slowly and unchanged over generations. The daily tasks are accompanied by an oral tradition known as *cantos de* 65 *vaqueria*. Cows are milked at dawn and the songs are adapted to rhyme with the name of each cow. Sometimes slow and sad, the songs are frequently improvised. [para 8]

70 Moving my feet to the rhythms, I thought about how *Los Llanos* preserve not only natural beauty, but also the voices and identity of those Colombian cowboys 75 fighting hard to maintain ancestral knowledge and vanishing traditions.

The land of a thousand rhythms is a fascinating example of how the 80 different people who have come to Colombia have brought their music with them, influencing and changing not only the local culture but global culture as well.

GLOSSARY:

ancestral (home/knowledge/traditions) – related to your relatives from a long time ago
improvised (music/performance/dance) – not prepared in advance

121

10B
Dare to express yourself

LESSON GOALS
- Learn verb patterns with infinitive and -ing
- Practise aspiration of voiceless consonants
- Talk about groups and clubs you belong to

READING AND GRAMMAR

1 Look at the illustrations (a–h). What subcultures can you identify? Match each one with its name.

cosplayer gamer geek hippy
influencer rapper steampunk surfer

2 Work in pairs. What subcultures do you know about in your country?

3 Read the article about subcultures. Answer the questions.
1 Why do subcultures develop?
2 What was your favourite fact about subcultures?
3 Which subcultures would be fun to be a part of?

4 Match the beginnings of the sentences (1–4) with the endings (a–d). Then read the article again to check.
1 Subcultures tend …
2 Sometimes the main culture adapts subculture fashion …
3 The internet makes …
4 Cosplayers often spend weeks …

a … designing their costumes.
b … to appeal to people who find it hard to fit in.
c … to make it more appealing to the rest of society.
d … finding people you identify with much easier.

5 Underline the verbs in the article that are followed by infinitives. Circle the verbs followed by a verb in the -ing form. Then read the Grammar box.

GRAMMAR Verb patterns with infinitive and *-ing*

Verbs followed by verb + *-ing*: *can't stand, carry on, enjoy, feel like, give up, keep, make recommend, remember, suggest*
The internet **makes finding** your group much easier.

Verbs followed by *to* + *-ing*: *be/get used to, look forward to*
People **look forward to showing off** their costumes.

Verbs followed by the infinitive with *to*: *afford, arrange, can't wait, dare, deserve, expect, forget, remember*
People can **dare to express** themselves.

Go to page 151 for the Grammar reference.

Why so many subcultures?

Subcultures are groups of people with interests, ways of behaving, etc. that are different to the rest of society. They tend to appeal to people who struggle to find their place in 'normal' society. Within the space of the group, people can dare to express themselves. From the outside it may appear as though members of a group are pretending to be something they are not, but the more likely truth is that subcultures allow people to be who they really are.

Members of a subculture may identify with exciting clothes or unusual music, but often the main culture will adapt these to make them more acceptable. This happened with hip hop and now its influence can be seen in everyday street fashion and pop music.

The internet makes finding your group much easier, but members of subcultures still love getting together. 130,000 cosplayers are expected to show up at the San Diego Comic Con each year, dressed as their favourite cartoon characters and superheroes. People look forward to showing off their costumes and some spend weeks designing them.

Many subcultures develop around a hobby or passion. Surfing and skateboarding are attractive because of the sport as much as the lifestyle and attitude. In a way, there are as many subcultures as there are interests!

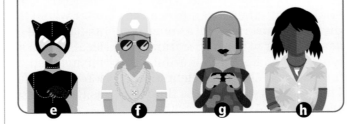

EXPLORE MORE!

Search online for a subculture you've never heard of and watch a video online of members talking about it.

6 🎧 **10.2** Listen to Alyea Pierce talk about a subculture in Trinidad and Tobago. Then complete the sentences with the correct form of the verbs in brackets.

1 As soon as you arrive in Trinidad, you can't help _____ (notice) the humidity.

2 Alyea remembers _____ (see) very diverse people of different ages and races on the streets.

3 Alyea kept _____ (wonder) why some people had two sticks in their back pockets.

4 The local musicians, called pannists, tend _____ (vary) in age.

5 You can expect _____ (recognize) pannists easily because of these metal sticks they carry.

Pannists in the Shell Invaders Steel Orchestra perform in Trinidad and Tobago.

PRONUNCIATION

7 🎧 **10.3** Look at the Clear voice box and listen to the words. With which words (column A or B) does more air leave the mouth in the sounds /p/, /k/ and /t/ in bold? Practise saying the words.

CLEAR VOICE
Aspirating /p/, /k/ and /t/

Aspiration is the quick burst of air that comes out of your mouth when you say certain sounds. It occurs on sounds /p/, /k/ and /t/ in stressed syllables, when they are followed by a vowel, e.g. *tend* /tend/, *occur* /əˈkɜː/ but not *appreciate* /əˈpriːʃieɪt/. Put your hand in front of your mouth and say *pan, cot, tear*; you should feel a burst of air on your hand.

A	B
keep	re**c**ommend
pre**t**end	presen**t**
people	hi**pp**y
cosplay	expe**c**t

SPEAKING

8 Use the words to form questions. Then write two of your own questions using verbs from Exercise 5.

1 which / subcultures / remember / see / when you were young?

2 what / look forward / do / after studies or work?

3 ever / feel like / join / clubs or groups? Which?

4 enjoy / dress up / in costumes?

5 which subcultures / you / struggle / understand? Why?

9 Work in pairs. Ask and answer the questions from Exercise 8.

10 Tell your partner about any groups or clubs you belong to or belonged to in the past. What attracted you to the group?

11 Share the information you learned about your partner with other classmates.

10C
My different cultures

Lia Nahomi Kajiki practising kyūdō, Japanese archery.

LESSON GOALS
- Understand ellipsis in spoken language
- Talk about your cultural identity
- Say /th/ clearly
- Understand when to use *the* when talking about groups of people or things

SPEAKING

1 Look at the infographic. Discuss the questions.

1 How diverse is your city or town compared to the places in the infographic?

2 Which place(s) mentioned in the infographic would you like to visit? Why?

Some of the most diverse places on Earth

Bareilly, India There are over 40 festivals a year, each celebrating the different peoples that live there.

Brussels, Belgium Only about a third of 'Brusselians' are Belgian, so as well as Belgian waffles, you can try cuisine from all around the world.

Dubai, United Arab Emirates Meeting a local in this modern and diverse city can be a challenge when 86% of residents are foreigners.

São Paulo, Brazil Over 2.3 million immigrants from all over the world, including Portugal, Spain and Japan, arrived in São Paulo between 1870 and 2010.

Sydney, Australia With 250 languages spoken on its streets, it's one of the most linguistically diverse places in the world.

LISTENING

NATIONAL GEOGRAPHIC EXPLORER

2 🎧 **10.4** Listen to Lia Nahomi Kajiki talk about her cultural roots. Does she feel Brazilian, Japanese or a bit of both?

3 🎧 **10.5** Listen to three short extracts from the interview. Which words are left out after the word in bold (1–3)? Why did the speaker leave them out? Look at the Listening skill box to check.

1 You're of a mixed Brazilian and Japanese background: which of the **two** do you feel you most fit in with?

2 I think **some don't**, especially my father, who was born in Japan.

3 One **thing** is football, especially during the World Cup!

LISTENING SKILL
Understanding ellipsis

In spoken conversation, not all words are said. This is usually because they were mentioned before and so the sentence can be understood without them. This is called ellipsis. The speaker might leave out …

a noun phrase: *which of the two (backgrounds)*

a verb and object: *I think some don't (feel 75% Brazilian and 25% Japanese).*

part of the question (in your response): *One thing (that brings the nation together) is football.*

4 🎧 **10.4** Listen to the full interview again. Are the sentences true (T) or false (F)?

1 It's easy for Lia to identify with one culture.
2 Lia feels she fits in more with Brazilian culture.
3 The way she expresses her opinion is influenced by her Japanese origins.
4 Lia doesn't share the same values as the other people who practise kyūdō.
5 Lia felt like an outsider when she was at school.
6 Lia's father was raised in Japan.
7 Many people in Brazil are of mixed cultural background.
8 Lia likes that Brazil is so culturally diverse.

VOCABULARY

5 Look at the sentences in Exercise 4 again. Underline the collocations that talk about identity and 'belonging' to a group.

6 Complete the sentences to make them true for you. Then share with a partner.

1 Generally speaking, I think / don't think I fit in well with _____.
2 I share the same values as _____. For example, we _____.
3 There are some aspects of my culture, such as _____, that I don't identify with.
4 One person I know / have heard about who comes from a mixed background is _____.
5 I live / don't live in a culturally diverse place. For example, _____.

Go to page 139 for the Vocabulary reference.

PRONUNCIATION

7 🎧 **10.6** Listen to three different speakers. How does each speaker say the words *think* and *the*?

8 Look at the Clear voice box. Which pronunciation of *th* do you prefer? Why? Practise it with the sentences in Exercises 4 and 6.

CLEAR VOICE
Saying *th*

In standard British and American English, *th* is said with the tongue between your teeth: *think* /θɪŋk/ and *the* /ðə/. But many people say 'th' as /f/ and /v/, or /t/ and /d/. This change will <u>not</u> make your pronunciation less clear. However, avoid mixing different pronunciation.

GRAMMAR

9 Read the text. Can you guess which city from the infographic in Exercise 1 it's about?

> You can try <u>dishes</u> from all around the world there, but the <u>dishes</u> typical of this city are fries with mayonnaise, beef stew and waffles. Interestingly, most people there are <u>foreigners</u>, such as <u>people</u> from France, Romania or Morocco. The <u>locals</u> only make up about one third of the <u>residents</u>.

10 Look at the underlined plural nouns in Exercise 9. When is *the* used? When is *the* not used? Read the Focus on box to check.

FOCUS ON *the* with groups of people and things

With plural nouns, you typically don't need *the*.
You can try <u>dishes</u> from all around the world there.
However, if you're referring to a specific set of things or people, you do need to use *the*.
... but <u>the</u> dishes typical of this city are ...
Use *the* with *majority, some of, many of* and *none of*, e.g. <u>the</u> majority of people, some of <u>the</u> people. Don't use *the* with *most, some, many* or *no*, e.g. *most people*.

When referring to groups of people, always use *the* with an adjective (*the Japanese*), but not with plural nouns (*Brazilians, Australians*).

Go to page 152 for the Focus on reference.

11 Complete the sentences with *the* or *X* when no article is needed.

1 _____ majority of people who live in my city have been here for _____ generations.
2 It's nice how _____ different cultures and languages mix together in New York.
3 Hospitality is typically important to both _____ Brazilians and _____ Japanese.

SPEAKING

12 Work in pairs. Talk about the different cultural influences in your life. Do you think they've influenced who you are? Use these topics and your own ideas.

books you read   films and series you watch
meeting people from other cultures
sports and hobbies   travelling   your family's origins

LESSON GOALS
- Talk about false assumptions
- Consider differences in behaviour and the reasons for them
- Learn to deal with assumptions to avoid misunderstandings

WRITING AND SPEAKING

1 Create a word cloud showing the different groups that you identify with. Use the size of the words to show which groups are the most important to you (biggest = most important).

Use these categories or your own ideas: age, ethnic group, interests, nationality, physical and mental ability, profession, gender.

WOMAN STAR TREK FAN MALAYSIAN
PERSON WITH HEARING LOSS
YOUNG ADULT
ENGINEERING STUDENT

2 Choose one of your groups from Exercise 1. Use one expression from the table to write about a false assumption that other people often make about that group. Then use one expression to challenge this assumption.

False assumptions about people	Challenging the assumption
Many people assume that …	In fact, …
People typically think/ believe that …	Even so, I think it's important to understand that …

Many people assume people with hearing loss can't speak. In fact, that isn't true for most deaf and hard of hearing people. We can all communicate with hearing people, but we might need you to be patient.

3 In groups, share what you have written. Which assumptions about your classmates' groups have you heard before?

4 Work in pairs. Read the three situations (1–3). What assumptions does each person make about the behaviour of the other person? What are other possible reasons for the other person's behaviour?

1 | Vihaan is doing a PhD and visits his supervisor to discuss his research project. Whenever Vihaan begins talking about the project, the supervisor closes her eyes, as if she is asleep. When Vihaan finishes speaking, she opens her eyes and makes comments or asks a question. 'I don't know what's wrong with her. She falls asleep every time I speak. Am I just boring?'

2 | Gautam and Marlies are having dinner together for the first time. At the end of the meal, the waiter puts the bill on the table. Gautam takes the bill and offers to pay for everything. Marlies looks offended and says: 'Why are you paying?! Do you think I can't pay for myself? I have money.'

3 | Louis and his baby daughter are visiting a friend in another country. When they meet people in the street, many stop to admire his daughter and comment on how fat she is. Louis is offended: 'Do they not realize how rude that is?'

MY VOICE ▶

5 ▶ **10.2** Watch the video. Put the five steps for dealing with assumptions in the order they are mentioned. Then take notes to add more information about each step.

a Make connections with the other person's behaviour.

b Consider what assumptions you are making about the other person.

c Be aware of your feelings.

d Analyse the reasons behind the other person's behaviour.

e Adapt your behaviour.

6 🎧 **10.7** Look at the Communication skill box. Then listen to Vihaan and a friend analysing his situation from Exercise 4. Which steps from the box do they follow?

COMMUNICATION SKILL
Dealing with assumptions

When people from different backgrounds communicate, they may make assumptions that get in the way of the communication process. To understand why a misunderstanding may have occurred, try these steps:

Be aware – How am I feeling? What was I expecting?

Don't judge – What assumptions am I making? Could my assumptions be wrong?

Analyse – Why is the other person doing/saying this?

Make connections – Do I relate to the other person's reasons? What behaviour of mine is similar to theirs?

Try to adapt – Can I live with their behaviour now that I understand it better? Is there anything I can do to adapt my behaviour to make the relationship work better?

7 Work in pairs. Imagine you are Marlies and Louis from Exercise 4. Use the steps in the Communication skill box to deal with assumptions they made about the other people in the scenarios.

Step 1: I'm feeling …

Step 2: I'm assuming Gautam …

Step 3: Perhaps Gautam offered to pay because …

SPEAKING AND WRITING

8 **OWN IT!** Look at the list of contexts where differences in viewpoint and misunderstandings can occur. Which ones have you experienced?

- Between people from different generations, e.g. children and parents/grandparents.
  When I was younger, we would never dare talk back to our parents.

- Between people from different countries, e.g. in tourist areas or in international business situations.
  I don't get why they smile so much in a serious situation. It feels really fake.

- Between people from different regions of the same country, e.g. a company where people from different regions work together.
  It's so annoying they never seem to say what they think; where I come from we just speak our minds.

- Between people from different subcultures, e.g. football fans, book lovers, rock fans.
  They're all just so violent and unpleasant; it's scary.

- Between people from different professions, e.g. teachers, plumbers, doctors.
  He lost me after the first sentence – all those medical terms.

9 Work in pairs or on your own. Discuss or make notes about one of your experiences from Exercise 8, explaining what happened and what the misunderstanding was. Then answer the questions.

1 How did you feel in that situation?

2 What assumptions did you make about the other person? Do you think they made any about you?

3 What might have been the real reasons for the behaviour?

4 How could you or the other person have adapted your behaviour to avoid misunderstanding?

10 Share your experiences in groups or work individually and write a short summary of the situation.

Cultural highlights

LESSON GOALS
* Express numbers approximately (e.g. *just under a third*)
* Design and carry out a survey
* Write a report about cultural attractions

SPEAKING

1 Work in pairs. Which aspects of cultural interest would you make sure you experienced on a trip to a new region? Why?

> architecture and historical buildings
> art and entertainment   festivals and events
> markets and shops   museums   music and dance
> sport venues   theatres   theme parks   typical food

READING FOR WRITING

2 Read the report and answer the questions.
  1 Where does the information for the report come from?
  2 Which aspects of cultural interest does it mention?

3 Read the report again. Complete the headings (1–4) with one word.

Recommendations for cultural highlights of the Muscat region

The aim of this report is to recommend places and activities of cultural interest in the Muscat region in Oman. It is based on feedback from local residents, who responded to an online survey.

The top (1) _____

The vast majority of respondents agreed that the most important cultural destination is the Grand Mosque, (a) _____. Over half of those questioned also mentioned the Natural History Museum and the Mutrah Souq market (b) _____. A small number said that the Sultan's Palace is the best place to visit.

Festivals and other (2) _____

Oman has a rich cultural heritage in terms of celebrations and events. As might be expected, the event that most respondents mentioned is the Muscat Festival, (c) _____, although the annual highlight for a large number of people (d) _____ is the cycling race *Tour of Oman*, which goes through Muscat.

Local (3) _____

By far the largest percentage of those surveyed stated that rice and curry should be the defining food of the region, (e) _____. Several people mentioned *Kabsa* – made with rice, meat and spices – as the national dish, though there was disagreement here. There was also little agreement as to which is the best restaurant in the capital although a few chose *Bait Al Luban* to represent the most typical cuisine.

Regional (4) _____

Unsurprisingly, the most popular choice for an entertainment venue was the Royal Opera House, even though the building has only been open for about ten years. Of the works of art on public display in the city, respondents identified the National Museum as the best location for learning about Oman's artistic heritage, (f) _____.

Port Sultan Qaboos waterfront in Muscat, Oman.

4 Choose from the relative clauses (1–6) the one that best fits each space in the report (a–f).

1 whose five towers overlook the city
2 where you can buy souvenirs and gifts
3 which includes beautiful jewellery, traditional costumes and musical instruments
4 which is situated on the Indian Ocean and is influenced by Indian and African cuisine
5 which takes place over a month in January and features fireworks, dancing and crafts
6 who enjoy sport

5 Work in pairs. Answer the questions.

1 In what different ways does the writer of the report refer to the people who took part in the survey? *local residents, …*
2 What different verbs are used to report what the people in the survey said? *agreed, …*

6 Look at the Writing skill box. Which expressions in the box could be used instead of the percentages (1–6)? What other ways of summarizing the survey results can you find in the report?

WRITING SKILL
Expressing numbers approximately

Reports summarize large amounts of information, often statistics, so that readers don't have to read long, boring documents full of numbers. To make them easier to read, they can also describe the statistics with vague language, e.g. 72% = *most*. Here are some other useful expressions.

The vast majority of (the respondents) …
Roughly a third (suggested) …
One in four (people said) …
Just under half of (those questioned) …
A small number of (people) …
Only a tiny percentage …

1	2%	4	34%
2	8%	5	48%
3	25%	6	93%

7 Look at the charts from a class survey. Write five sentences describing the statistics shown, using words and expressions from the Writing skill box.

As might be expected, the vast majority of those questioned preferred going to the cinema.

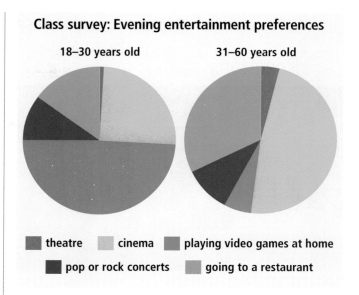

Class survey: Evening entertainment preferences

18–30 years old   31–60 years old

- theatre
- cinema
- playing video games at home
- pop or rock concerts
- going to a restaurant

WRITING TASK

8 Work in pairs. Design a survey to ask other classmates about your city or region. Decide whether you will ask about cultural highlights in general or focus on one aspect of culture (e.g. music, food). Write five questions.

Which of the following attractions would you most recommend tourists visit: the City Museum, the castle, …?

9 Carry out your survey. Divide the work between you and your partner. Speak to as many classmates as possible. Then share your results with your partner.

10 **WRITE** Write a report summarizing the information you have collected. Divide your survey results into sections with headings. Make sure you include an introduction.

11 **CHECK** Use the checklist. I have …

☐ included a report title and several sections with short, clear headings.
☐ written an introduction explaining the purpose of the report.
☐ used a variety of ways of referring to the respondents to avoid repetition.
☐ given a clear idea of the information without boring the reader with statistics.

12 **REVIEW** Read a classmate's report. Give feedback using the checklist in Exercise 11 to help you. Which information in the report did you find the most surprising?

Go to page 134 for the Reflect and review.

Go to page 134 for the Reflect and review.

EXPLORE MORE!

Find out more about a place or event of cultural interest near you. Record a two-minute mini-presentation (audio or video) about it.

Reflect and review

1 Reactions *Pages 10–21*

1 Look at the goals from Unit 1. How confident do you feel about them? (1 = very confident, 4 = not confident at all)

    Identify reasons in an article

    Review and practise asking questions

    Talk about strong emotions

    Infer emotions when listening

    Demonstrate empathy in a conversation

    Write an informal email giving news

2 Work in pairs. Discuss the questions.

  1 Which goal are you the most confident with? Why?

  2 Which goal is the most important for outside of class? Why?

  3 Which goal do you most want to improve on? Why?

3 Choose two ways you can work on the Unit 1 goals. Add one more idea. Then share your ideas with a partner.

- Read more articles in English
- Underline reasons in articles I read
- Ask more questions in conversations
- Try to imagine what a speaker may be feeling as I listen
- Make a section in my notebook with vocabulary for emotions
- Try to use new adjectives and adverbs in my speech
- Practise using phrases to empathize
- Write emails to my friends in English

My idea: _____

2 Language and communication *Pages 22–33*

1 Look at the goals from Unit 2. Tick (✓) the two that are the most important for you to achieve. In your notebook, make notes about why they are important.

    Skim and scan an article to identify the main ideas

    Discuss language learning experience and tips

    Talk about communication using phrasal verbs

    Use discourse markers to understand a podcast

    Understand how first language identity can be used in building relationships

    Write a formal email asking for information

2 Work in pairs. Write a short email to your partner describing your language learning experience on this course so far. Choose two things you want to improve on and ask for advice. Then exchange emails and write a response.

3 Read the ideas for working on the Unit 2 goals. Then look for useful apps or websites you can use to practise.

- Read one article in English every week
- Learn one new phrasal verb every day
- Write an email of enquiry to find out about something you're interested in
- Listen to two podcasts in English every month

3 Unfamiliar places *Pages 34–45*

1. Look at the goals from Unit 3. How important are they for you to achieve? Order them from 1 (very important) to 6 (not a priority).

   - Practise active reading by annotating
   - Use narrative tenses to tell personal stories
   - Talk about journeys
   - Use visual information to help you listen
   - Fix misunderstandings and confirm understanding
   - Write a blog post

2. Write down …
   - phrasal verbs to talk about journeys that you learned in this unit.
   - as many travel-related collocations with *go on* as you can.
   - four recommendations about things to do in your town.

3. Read the ideas for working on the Unit 3 goals. Choose three ideas and write when you want to complete them (this week, before the end of the month, etc.).
   - Read a blog post about somewhere you'd like to visit
   - Subscribe to a blog
   - Tell a friend about a trip you have taken
   - Think about a trip you want to take, and write down what might be difficult about it
   - Listen to an audiobook about a famous journey or voyage
   - Watch an English-language travel programme
   - Write down useful language for fixing misunderstandings in a conversation
   - Write a blog post about a travel experience you have had
   - Write a blog post about a trip you want to take

4 Reconnecting *Pages 46–57*

1. Look at the goals from Unit 4. How confident do you feel about them? Write the letters (a–f) on the scale.

   a Summarize and synthesize information from written and spoken sources
   b Report what people say
   c Discuss personal relationships
   d Understand different accents
   e Understand and adapt to different turn-taking styles
   f Write a story

   Not confident ←————————→ **Very confident**

2. Choose a topic and write a short story.
   - a time when you reconnected with an old friend
   - a moment when you had a misunderstanding
   - a time when you became closer to someone in your family
   - a moment when you lost touch with someone
   - a memorable experience spending time in nature

3. Work in pairs. Discuss the questions.
   1. What strategies can you use when you need to summarize information? Are there any new strategies you would like to practise?
   2. Which accents are the most challenging for you to understand? How can you get better at understanding difficult accents?
   3. Are there any new communication strategies from this unit that you want to use in the future?

Reflect and review

5 Healthy body, healthy mind *Pages 58–69*

1 Look at the goals from Unit 5. How confident do you feel about them? Write the letters (a–f) in the table.

a Identify and understand cause and effect in an article

b Talk about consequences using conditionals

c Discuss mental and physical health

d Listen for key words to understand general meaning

e Adapt language to be easier to understand

f Write a 'for and against' essay

Goals I feel confident about	Goals I need more practice on

2 Choose a topic and make a mind map.

- expressions to talk about cause and effect
- words and expressions to talk about mental and physical health
- strategies to adapt your English to communicate more clearly

3 Look at the table in Exercise 1. Choose two goals you need more practice on. Make a plan for how you will achieve this.

For each goal:

- write two things you will do to work on this goal
- list the resources you will use to help you, e.g. articles, videos, apps
- set yourself a deadline for achieving this, e.g. by next month, by next year

6 Breaking news *Pages 70–81*

1 Look at the goals from Unit 6. How confident do you feel about them? Write the letters (a–f) on the scale.

a Identify unsupported claims in an article

b Report news using passive structures

c Understand catenation in connected speech

d Talk about the news

e Practise influencing others

f Write a news article

Not confident ◄─────────────► **Very confident**

2 Write a list of words related to news and media that you have learned in this unit. Then write questions using the words. When you have finished, ask a partner your questions.

objective ➔ Why is it important to read objective news?

3 Read the ideas for working on the Unit 6 goals. Order the ideas according to how helpful they will be for you. Then write notes about how you will complete your top three goals (specific websites you will use, apps you will download, etc.).

Read at least one news article in English every day

Identify examples of the passive voice when you read

Pay attention to connected speech by watching news programmes

Make a list of situations where you might have to persuade someone. Think about which influencing styles (inspiring, negotiating, convincing) might work well in each situation

Write a news article about an event that has happened in your school, town or city

7 Shared spaces *Pages 82–93*

1 Look at the goals from Unit 7. How easy are they for you to achieve? Order them from 1 (the easiest) to 6 (the most difficult).

    Deal with unknown words in an article

    Use causative verbs to talk about solutions to problems

    Identify figurative language when listening

    Describe places

    Explain a problem without offending others

    Write and respond to social media posts

2 Work in pairs. Discuss the questions.
1 Which goal comes the most easily to you? Why do you think this is?
2 Which goal is the most difficult for you? What steps can you take to work on it?

3 Read the ideas for working on the Unit 7 goals. Choose three ideas and write when you want to complete them (this week, before the end of the month, etc.).

- Try to work out the meaning of unknown words in two online articles.
- Note down the causative verbs you learned in this unit. For each one, write an example sentence that is personal to you to help you remember the correct verb pattern.
- Listen to a podcast in English and write down the figurative language you hear.
- Write a description of a place you have visited using at least five new words from this unit.
- Tell a friend, or write a summary, about useful strategies for dealing with difficult conversations from this unit.
- Write a social media post in English about an issue that is important to you.

8 Incredible technology *Pages 94–105*

1 Look at the goals from Unit 8. Which goals are the most important to you? (1 = very important, 6 = not a priority)

    Recognize synonyms and antonyms in an article

    Speculate about the past using modal verbs

    Talk about gadgets and technology

    Understand prepositions in connected speech

    Understand and discuss online etiquette

    Write a product review

2 What is a piece of technology you couldn't live without? Why? Write a short paragraph, using vocabulary you have learned in the unit. Then share your answer with a partner.

3 Look at the goals in Exercise 1. Choose two goals that you want to work on. Then look at the example and make your own plan for how and when you will achieve your goals.

Goal: Write a product review

Today – Make a list of technology vocabulary, useful multi-word adverbs and phrases for giving your opinion

This week – Prepare a set of flashcards that I can use to practise these words

This month – Review my flashcards at least twice per week and read some product reviews in English

Two months from now – Write a product review using at least 10 of the words

Reflect and review

9 Against all odds *Pages 106–117*

1 Look at the goals from Unit 9. Tick (✓) the two that you are least confident about. Make notes about what you find difficult about them.

- Make inferences about a writer's opinion
- Talk about future plans, goals and hopes
- Discuss challenges, successes and failures
- Understand contrasts when listening
- Adapt to direct and indirect communication styles
- Write a job application email

2 Think about your plans, goals and hopes for the future. Write a list of predictions using the prompts below.

- In one year, I will / won't be …
- In five years, I will / won't have …
- In ten years, I might / should have …

3 Work in pairs. Ask your partner which goals from Unit 9 he/she would most like to work on. Then give your partner some advice about how to achieve the goals. Use the ideas below to help you.

- Each time you read an opinion piece, reflect on the writer's opinion, think about your own reaction to the text and consider how other people might react differently
- Keep a notebook with useful grammar for talking about the future
- Make a mind map with vocabulary related to challenges, successes and failures
- Memorize common expressions that communicate contrasting ideas
- Think about how you could adapt to communicate more effectively with people you know who use a more direct or indirect style
- Read a blog with tips about writing job application emails

10 A world of cultures *Pages 118–129*

1 Look at the goals from Unit 10. How confident do you feel about them? Write the letters (a–f) in the table.

a Identify and understand figurative language in creative writing
b Learn verb patterns with infinitive and *-ing*
c Talk about your cultural identity
d Understand ellipsis in spoken language
e Learn to deal with assumptions to avoid misunderstandings
f Write a report about cultural attractions

Goals I feel confident about	Goals I need more practice on

2 Write a summary of your experience working on this unit. This might include a description of something you feel you did well, something useful or interesting you learned or something that you would like to improve on.

3 Look at the goals from Units 1–10 again. Follow the steps.

1 Choose two goals that you feel more confident about now. What did you do to improve?
2 Choose two goals that you would like to improve on. How could you do this?
3 Share your goals with a partner. Give advice to help them with their goals. Are there any tips or strategies that worked well for you?

Vocabulary reference

UNIT 1

astonished (adj) /əˈstɒnɪʃt/   *I was astonished when I heard the news. It was just so unexpected.*

concerned (adj) /kənˈsɜːnd/   *I'm concerned about tomorrow's exam. I think it's going to be difficult.*

furious (adj) /ˈfjʊəriəs/   *I can't believe you borrowed my car without asking. I'm absolutely furious!*

impatient (adj) /ɪmˈpeɪʃnt/   *What a great programme! I'm so impatient to see the next series.*

motivated (adj) /ˈməʊtɪveɪtɪd/   *Since she's such a good teacher, everyone in the class feels motivated.*

optimistic (adj) /ˌɒptɪˈmɪstɪk/   *I'm optimistic we'll have good weather for our bike ride next Saturday.*

petrified (adj) /ˈpetrɪfaɪd/   *I don't think I would watch that film again. It left me feeling absolutely petrified.*

relieved (adj) /rɪˈliːvd/   *Thank goodness you're OK! I don't think I've ever been so relieved!*

thrilled (adj) /θrɪld/   *We're thrilled to announce that we're getting married!*

1 Choose the correct option to complete the sentences.

1 I hope Anka gets here soon. I'm starting to feel *impatient / thrilled*.

2 She always feels things will work out, maybe because she's quite *astonished / optimistic*.

3 I'm *concerned / motivated* about Paul. I haven't heard from him recently.

4 Jed was *impatient / astonished* when he heard the news. He wasn't expecting it at all.

5 I feel *petrified / relieved* now I've heard from you. I was starting to worry.

6 My children have such great teachers. They make them feel really *furious / motivated*.

7 That ride was so scary. We felt absolutely *petrified / relieved*.

8 Congratulations on your promotion! I'm *concerned / thrilled* for you.

9 Farah looks *optimistic / furious*. I wonder what made her so angry?

2 Write three questions, using adjectives from the word list. Then work in pairs. Ask and answer your questions.

Have you ever read a book that left you completely astonished? What was it about?

UNIT 2

bring up (phr v) /brɪŋ ˈʌp/   *I'm not sure why you brought that up. It was really rude.*

come up (phr v) /kʌm ˈʌp/   *A number of interesting topics came up in the discussion.*

come up with (phr v) /kʌm ˈʌp wɪð/   *If we all work together, I'm sure we can come up with a solution.*

get across (phr v) /get əˈkrɒs/   *Lukas is very confident, so it's easy for him to get his ideas across.*

make up (phr v) /meɪk ˈʌp/   *Every time my sister is late, she makes up a different excuse.*

pick up (phr v) /pɪk ˈʌp/   *Lin is great at languages. She picks them up so easily!*

point out (phr v) /pɔɪnt ˈaʊt/   *I'd like to point out that this isn't the first time it's happened.*

read up on (phr v) /riːd ˈʌp ɒn/   *I spent the weekend reading up on linguistics.*

1 Match the beginnings of the sentences (1–8) with the endings (a–h).

1 I'm sorry to bring this up, but
2 Laura spent six weeks in Rome,
3 Hardly anything interesting came up,
4 I'm having trouble coming up with
5 As soon as the teacher pointed out
6 To prepare for our exam, you should
7 I find it hard to get my ideas across,
8 Whenever Hiba misses a deadline,

a even though we talked for two whole hours.
b read up on phrasal verbs.
c ideas about what to do next weekend.
d she makes up a crazy excuse.
e I'm disappointed you can't come to my party.
f maybe because I'm quite shy.
g our mistake, everything made more sense.
h but she didn't pick up much Italian.

2 Complete the sentences with your own ideas. Then compare with a partner.

1 In our next class, something that might come up is …

2 I wish someone could come up with a solution for …

3 The language I would most like to pick up is …

4 I would like to read up on …

Vocabulary reference

UNIT 3

end up (phr v) /end 'ʌp/   *After a series of wrong turns, I ended up completely lost.*

go on (phr v) /gəʊ 'ɒn/   *Next month, I'm going on a trip to Paris.*

head back (phr) /hed 'bæk/   *It looks like it's going to rain. Maybe we should head back.*

make it (phr) /'meɪk ɪt/   *It's quite late already. Will you make it to school on time?*

reach (v) /riːtʃ/   *Everyone was happy when we reached the top of the mountain.*

set off (phr v) /set 'ɒf/   *What time do you think we should set off?*

steer (v) /stɪə(r)/   *Expert sailors can steer any kind of boat.*

stop over (phr v) /stɒp 'əʊvə(r)/   *It was late when we finished dinner, so I stopped over at my sister's house.*

turn back (phr v) /tɜːn 'bæk/   *I forgot my keys. I'll have to turn back.*

1 **Complete the conversation with the correct form of the words or phrases from the word list.**

Charlie: What time shall we ¹_____ tomorrow?

Victor: Maybe eight o'clock? That way we can ²_____ Bristol before lunch.

Charlie: OK. I hope we don't ³_____ getting lost, like last time.

Victor: I don't think we will. I think it was because Ana wanted to ⁴_____ at that hotel the night before.

Charlie: That trip was a bit stressful. Remember when we had to ⁵_____ when she forgot her phone? It was nearly midnight by the time we ⁶_____ there.

Victor: We should ⁷_____ another trip with Ana sometime though. She's a lot of fun!

2 **Write a short story using the prompt or your own idea. Try to use at least five verbs or phrasal verbs you have learned in this unit.**

With only £100 in my pocket, I wasn't sure how far I would get. I was hoping to reach Paris, or maybe …

UNIT 4

catch up (phr v) /kætʃ 'ʌp/   *We should meet soon. We haven't caught up in a long time.*

get along with (phr v) /get ə'lɒŋ wɪð/   *Paul is very friendly. It's no surprise that he gets along with everyone.*

hit it off (phr) /hɪt ɪt 'ɒf/   *Samer and I have a similar sense of humour. Maybe that's why we hit it off.*

keep in close contact (phr) /kiːp ɪn kləʊs 'kɒntækt/   *My cousins and I keep in very close contact. We speak to each other every day.*

keep in touch with (phr) /kiːp ɪn 'tʌtʃ wɪð/   *Thanks to technology, there are lots of great ways you can keep in touch with friends.*

lose touch with (phr) /luːz 'tʌtʃ wɪð/   *I'm not sure what happened to Lizzy. I lost touch with her a few years ago.*

reconnect (v) /riːkə'nekt/   *I'm so happy that we've reconnected after all this time!*

stick together (phr v) /stɪk tə'geðə(r)/   *It's important that we stick together, especially at a time like this.*

1 **Complete the sentences with the correct form of the words or phrases from the word list.**

1 I've been so happy ever since we _____. Let's not lose touch again!

2 We should get together soon. It's been ages since we _____.

3 I _____ Janet several years ago. I don't know how to contact her.

4 Even though we live in different cities, we _____ contact.

5 I'm not very good at _____, but email does make it easier.

6 At difficult moments, it's important for families to _____.

7 My classmates and I _____ right away. It'll be sad when the course ends.

8 I don't really _____ my brother. We always argue.

2 **Work in pairs. Discuss the questions.**

1 When you catch up with friends, what do you tend to speak about?

2 Do you ever keep in touch with people by writing emails?

3 Why do people sometimes lose touch?

4 In what circumstances is it important to stick together?

5 Which family members do you get along with best?

6 Do you keep in close contact with any old school friends?

UNIT 5

anxiety (n) /æŋˈzaɪəti/   *Losing your job can cause feelings of anxiety.*

at risk (phr) /ət ˈrɪsk/   *Many children are at risk of developing a technology addiction.*

burnout (n) /ˈbɜːnaʊt/   *Towards the end of his career, my father suffered from burnout.*

call in sick (phr) /kɔːl ɪn ˈsɪk/   *Kyle called in sick today.*

come down with (phr v) /kʌm ˈdaʊn wɪð/   *Last week I came down with a terrible cold.*

cope with (phr) /ˈkəʊp wɪð/   *My sister is very good at coping with stress.*

depression (n) /dɪˈpreʃən/   *Nearly three million people suffer from depression every year.*

feel sorry for yourself (phr) /fiːl ˈsɒri fə(r) jə(r)ˈself/   *I decided to stop feeling sorry for myself and try to fix the problem instead.*

get over (phr v) /get ˈəʊvə(r)/   *How long did it take you to get over your injury?*

symptom (n) /ˈsɪmptəm/   *The doctor asked me about my symptoms.*

stay in shape (phr) /steɪ ɪn ˈʃeɪp/   *Jogging is an excellent way to stay in shape.*

take a nap (phr) /teɪk ə ˈnæp/   *I sometimes take a short nap after lunch.*

1 Complete the text with the correct form of the words and phrases from the word list.

Have you ever experienced burnout? You're not alone. These days, more and more people suffer from high levels of ¹_____ and stress. ²_____ these emotions is not an easy task. Contrary to popular belief, most people can't just ³'_____ it'.

Common ⁴_____ of burnout include low motivation and tiredness. ⁵_____ a cold is also quite normal. If you believe you may be ⁶_____ of burnout, try not to ⁷_____ yourself. Instead, make self-care a priority. ⁸_____ if you feel tired, or consider ⁹_____. Regular exercise is also very important, as ¹⁰_____ can give you energy and improve your mood.

2 Read the message. Write a short response, using the word list to help you.

> I was worried when I didn't see you in the office today. I just wanted to check that you were OK. Are you sick? Is there anything I can do to help?

UNIT 6

in-depth (adj) /ɪn ˈdepθ/   *The analysis was very in-depth. The reporter included a lot of relevant details.*

make the headlines (phr) /meɪk ðə ˈhedlaɪnz/   *We don't know why yesterday's fire didn't make the headlines.*

objective (adj) /əbˈdʒektɪv/   *When carrying out serious research, it's better to read objective sources.*

report (v) /rɪˈpɔːt/   *The journalists looked visibly upset as they reported yesterday's events.*

sensational (adj) /senˈseɪʃənl/   *I don't like that newspaper because the articles are too sensational. When I read a newspaper, what I want is facts.*

skim over (phr) /skɪm ˈəʊvə/   *In the mornings, I skim over the headlines as I drink my coffee.*

tabloid (adj) /ˈtæblɔɪd/   *My sister sometimes reads tabloid newspapers because she loves celebrity gossip.*

the press (n) /ðə pres/   *In my opinion, the scandal should have received more coverage in the press.*

top story (n) /tɒp ˈstɔːri/   *I can't believe you don't know about this. It was the top story for most of last year!*

1 Complete the conversation with words from the word list.

Marcos: The news these days is so depressing. Some days I can't even bring myself to ¹_____ the headlines.

Anne: I know what you mean. If the ²_____ isn't some scandal, it's something else equally upsetting, like a disaster of some kind.

Marcos: And do you feel like the coverage that ³_____ gives to a lot of things isn't as ⁴_____ as it used to be? Even the major papers don't go into much detail.

Anne: Yeah, I agree. And not only that, but the way that journalists ⁵_____ things is getting to be more and more biased. They only tell one side of the story. I prefer to read ⁶_____ articles if I can.

Marcos: Yeah, that's definitely a problem. A similar issue is that some news is just too ⁷_____. When I check out the news, I don't want to read about drama. I just want facts, you know?

Anne: Do you ever read the ⁸_____ news? Like, celebrity gossip and stuff?

Marcos: Only articles about my favourite actor!

2 Write a description of a news article you have read recently. Use the word list to help you.

Vocabulary reference

UNIT 7

absolutely stunning (phr) /ˈæbsəluːtli ˈstʌnɪŋ/ *The sunrise was absolutely stunning this morning.*

breathtaking (adj) /ˈbreθteɪkɪŋ/ *At the top of the mountain, the view was simply breathtaking.*

cold and damp (phr) /kəʊld ənd dæmp/ *I hate it when the weather is cold and damp.*

cramped (adj) /kræmpt/ *It was very cramped inside the cave. I couldn't wait to get back outside.*

densely crowded (phr) /ˈdensli ˈkraʊdɪd/ *In summertime, some national parks become densely crowded.*

elegantly decorated (phr) /ˈelɪgəntli ˈdekəreɪtɪd/ *The hotel was elegantly decorated with beautiful artwork.*

light and airy (phr) /laɪt ənd ˈeəri/ *The building was light and airy, with large windows and high ceilings.*

narrow (adj) /ˈnærəʊ/ *The corridor was so narrow that we had to walk one by one.*

sheltered (adj) /ˈʃeltəd/ *We hardly noticed the wind because the beach was sheltered by the cliffs above.*

spacious (adj) /ˈspeɪʃəs/ *The student centre is very spacious. There's lots of room to study or meet friends.*

vast (adj) /vɑːst/ *On our visit to the Amazon rainforest, I was impressed by how incredibly vast it is.*

warm and cosy (phr) /wɔːm ənd ˈkəʊzi/ *The log fire makes the living room really warm and cosy.*

1 Choose the correct options to complete the advert.

> Tired of riding ¹*densely crowded / sheltered* commuter trains? Want to get away from the ²*vast / cold and damp* winter weather? Why not book a short break at the Astoria Hotel?
>
> Surrounded by ³*densely crowded / breathtaking* views, you can spend the day exploring our ⁴*absolutely stunning / narrow* countryside or the town's ⁵*cold and damp / narrow* cobblestone lanes before coming back to our ⁶*cramped / warm and cosy* fireside lounge. All of our rooms are ⁷*sheltered / elegantly decorated* and have a ⁸*narrow / spacious* en suite bathroom.
>
> We're also accepting bookings for events in our ⁹*cramped / light and airy* garden room.

2 Read the message. Write a reply using at least five words from the word list.

> I know you are on holiday, but I really miss you! I thought I would check in and see how you were getting on. How was your trip? And how is the hotel? Have you taken any photos?

UNIT 8

gadget (n) /ˈgædʒɪt/ *My brother's room is full of gadgets. He loves to take them apart and then put them back together again.*

handy (adj) /ˈhændi/ *I find it handy to wear a watch because sometimes my mobile phone is in my bag.*

innovative (adj) /ˈɪnəvətɪv/ *The researchers use quite innovative methods in their investigations.*

outdated (adj) /aʊtˈdeɪtɪd/ *I can't believe you still use a fax machine! They are completely outdated.*

perform (v) /pəˈfɔːm/ *The new technology isn't performing quite as well as we had hoped.*

pocket-sized (adj) /ˈpɒkɪt saɪzd/ *Larger phones are more popular, but I prefer to have one that is pocket-sized.*

recharge (v) /riːˈtʃɑːdʒ/ *I need to recharge my phone before we go out for the evening.*

sophisticated (adj) /səˈfɪstɪkeɪtɪd/ *Modern technology is becoming more and more sophisticated. Just look at what simple phones can do these days!*

user-friendly (adj) /ˈjuːzə ˈfrendli/ *My new PC is so user-friendly. It's much simpler to use than my old one.*

waterproof (adj) /ˈwɔːtəpruːf/ *Most tablets aren't waterproof, so be careful not to get yours wet.*

1 Choose the correct option to complete the sentences.

1 My new laptop has lots of *innovative / outdated* features that I want to try out.
2 Excuse me, would it be alright to *perform / recharge* my phone here?
3 Today, architects use *sophisticated / waterproof* applications to plan their projects.
4 Photo editing apps are really *pocket-sized / handy*. I need to download one.
5 My hard drive is *sophisticated / pocket-sized*. But even though it's small, it has loads of memory.
6 My sister redesigned my website. Now it's much more *outdated / user-friendly*.
7 I accidentally put my phone in the washing machine. I hope it's *handy / waterproof*.
8 My family often gets lost. I'm not sure our GPS always *performs / recharges* properly.
9 I can't believe you still have an mp3 player. What an *innovative / outdated* gadget!

2 Work in pairs. What are your two favourite gadgets or apps? Why?

UNIT 9

achieve objectives (phr) /əˈtʃiːv əbˈdʒektɪvz/ *If you want to achieve your objectives, you have to work at them every day.*

make a mess (phr) /meɪk ə mes/ *It's the first time I've been given so much responsibility. I'm worried I'll make a mess of everything!*

make it through (phr) /meɪk ɪt ˈθruː/ *My colleagues and I have no idea how we'll make it through this week. We have so much to do.*

overcome an issue (phr) /əʊvəˈkʌm ən ˈɪʃuː/ *The company had to overcome a number of issues when they decided to expand.*

struggle to understand (phr) /ˈstrʌgl tuː ˌʌndə(r)ˈstænd/ *It was easy for me to read and write in French, but I struggled to understand when I spoke to people.*

tackle a problem (phr) /ˈtækl ə ˈprɒbləm/ *In order to tackle your problems, it's important to stay positive.*

1 Complete the sentences with the correct form of words from the word list.

1 Come on guys, keep your spirits up! I know we can _____ the presentation!

2 Unless I make a timetable, I find it hard to _____ .

3 I'm _____ to understand this maths problem. Would you be able to help me?

4 My manager is very confident. She says we can _____ any issue.

5 It's better to _____ straight away. It will only get worse otherwise.

6 I made such _____ of that exam. I'm going to have to take it again.

2 Work in pairs. Discuss the questions.

1 What objectives would you like to achieve this year? How will you do this?

2 What is something that you have struggled to understand or learn? Were you able to do it in the end?

3 What should you do in order to stay positive when you're tackling a problem?

4 When you make it through a difficult time, how do you like to celebrate?

UNIT 10

culturally diverse (adj) /ˈkʌltʃərəli daɪˈvɜːs/ *I love living in New York because it's very culturally diverse.*

cultural background (n) /ˈkʌltʃərəl ˈbækgraʊnd/ *My best friend has a mixed cultural background. She is half Spanish and half Vietnamese.*

feel like an outsider (phr) /fiːl laɪk æn aʊtˈsaɪdə/ *It can be upsetting to feel like an outsider, but these experiences can also help us grow.*

fit in (phr v) /fɪt ɪn/ *I am quite different from my brothers and sisters. For some reason I just don't fit in.*

identify with (v) /aɪˈdentɪfaɪ wɪð/ *I'm half French and half Italian, but I identify more with the French.*

influenced by (v) /ˈɪnfluənst baɪ/ *Teenagers tend to be influenced by their peers.*

origins (n) /ˈɒrɪdʒɪnz/ *As an adult, I've begun to take a greater interest in my family history and our origins.*

raised in (v) /reɪzd ɪn/ *I was raised in a big city, but I'd like to bring up my children in the countryside.*

share values (v) /ʃeə ˈvæljuːz/ *My friends and I share the same values, so we rarely have disagreements.*

1 Match the beginnings of the sentences (1–8) with the endings (a–h).

1 My husband and I don't …

2 As a nurse, the people I most identify with …

3 People who live abroad often …

4 Children who are raised in …

5 My choice of profession was definitely …

6 In our globalized world, more and more …

7 My partner and I both have …

8 Many teenagers go through …

a feel like outsiders in their new communities at first.

b mixed cultural backgrounds.

c influenced by my parents' opinions.

d are other medical professionals.

e a stage where they feel as though they don't fit in.

f share the same values as most of our neighbours.

g people are growing up in culturally diverse places.

h the countryside often have a lot of freedom.

2 Complete the sentences with your own ideas. Then compare with a partner.

1 Someone I was really influenced by is …

2 If you don't fit in, you might …

3 My family were raised in …

4 One advantage of living in a culturally diverse place is …

5 It's important to know about your origins because …

Grammar reference

1B Grammar: Forming questions

Most questions are formed with auxiliary verb + subject + main verb. In the present and past simple, where there is no auxiliary verb, add *do/does* or *did*.

> **Do** you **want** a coffee?
> **Can** you **help** me with my homework?

It's also possible to use a question word with this structure.

> **What do** you **want** for lunch?

Negative questions

You usually use negative questions when you expect your listener to agree, or in order to express surprise or annoyance.

To form a negative question, use auxiliary verb + *not* + subject + main verb.

> **Isn't** this food amazing? (expecting to agree)
> **Didn't** you **like** the book? (surprise)

It's also possible to use a question word with this structure.

> **Why don't** you **want** to come with me?

Short questions

Use short questions to express surprise or interest, or to encourage the other speaker to continue.

To form a short question, use auxiliary verb (+ *not*) + subject.

> A: Paula complained about quite a few things in today's meeting.
> B: **Did she**? Like what?

> A: Jad hasn't been to any lectures this week.
> B: **Hasn't he**? Why not?

Subject questions

You use subject questions to find out more information about a subject, e.g. a person or thing that is performing an action.

To form a subject question, use *Who / What* + verb + object. Do not use an auxiliary verb with subject questions because *who* or *what* is the subject of the question.

> **Who** went with you?
> **What** helps you study?

Indirect questions

You use indirect questions when you want to be more polite.

To form an indirect question, use subject + verb within part of a longer sentence. Unlike other types of questions, there is no inversion of subject and verb.

> Could you tell me where **the bus stop is**?
> (NOT ~~Could you tell me where is the bus stop?~~)

You often use indirect questions with a set phrase, e.g. *Could you tell me … ? Do you happen to know … ? Would you mind letting me know … ? Do you have any idea … ?*

You can also form indirect questions as statements, using a set phrase, e.g. *I'd like to know … What I am asking is …* The structure is also subject + verb. You can use *if* or *whether* after the set phrase.

> **I'd like to know if tomorrow is** a holiday.

Question tags

Question tags are short phrases that you add to the end of a statement.

Use them to:

- check information. When you do this, you use a rising intonation in the tag question.
- ask the listener to agree. When you do this, you use a falling intonation.

Form tag questions with auxiliary verb + pronoun. If the statement is positive, add a negative question tag and if the statement is negative, add a positive question tag. If the statement includes a proper noun, replace it with a pronoun in the question tag.

> We are going for dinner on Friday, **aren't we**?
> You don't study at the university, **do you**?
> Nada isn't coming later, **is she**?

1 Find and correct the mistakes in the questions.
1. Could you tell me when does the meeting start?
2. She was very surprised, was she?
3. Haven't gone we there before?
4. I'd like to know where is the bank?
5. A: I think my sister looks a bit tired.
   B: You do?
6. Who did came with you to the restaurant?

2 Complete the conversations with these words. There is one option you do not need.

are you	did you	does it	have you
how much is	why didn't	will take	wouldn't you
would you mind			

A

Harry: I thought that exhibition was fantastic.
 [1]_____ enjoy it?

Lucinda: I did, yes. But [2]_____ say it was a bit expensive?

Harry: Hmm … perhaps. I think our ticket lets us in to some other events, though.

Lucinda: [3]_____?

B

Omar: [4]_____ listened to the new Radio 5 podcast?

Lidia: No, I don't think so.

Omar: It has some great tips about meditation.

Lidia: How interesting. You're not normally interested in that, [5]_____?

C

Passenger: Excuse me. 6_____ the fare to Green Park?

Bus driver: It's £3.20.

Passenger: And 7_____ letting me know how long the journey 8_____?

Bus driver: We should be there in about 25 minutes, sir.

1C Focus on: Adverbs of degree

Adverbs of degree go before an adjective to change its strength. Compare:

I am happy. 😊😊
*I am **very** happy.* 😊😊😊
*Gary felt **a bit** frustrated.* 😠
*Gary felt **really** frustrated.* 😠😠😠😠

Some adverbs of degree make adjectives stronger, and some adverbs make them weaker.

Adverbs that make a word stronger		Adverbs that make a word weaker	
absolutely completely extremely really	totally tremendously very	a bit a little fairly pretty	relatively slightly somewhat

The word *quite* can make words stronger or weaker.

*I made it **quite** clear that I don't want to talk about it any more.* (stronger = absolutely/completely clear)

*Our teacher is **quite** sure the exam is on Thursday, but she is going to double check.* (weaker = fairly sure, but not completely sure)

1 Choose the correct adverb of degree to complete the sentences.

1 I'm *absolutely / fairly* certain. There is no doubt in my mind.

2 Luke is *extremely / a bit* tired because he skipped his afternoon nap.

3 I can't concentrate on my work because I'm *really / slightly* hungry. I have to get something to eat!

4 It was a *relatively / tremendously* good film. I think everyone should see it.

5 Julia was *a little / totally* amazed by the spectacular mountain scenery.

6 Amir felt *very / somewhat* stressed that his bus arrived five minutes late, but he knew he'd still get to work on time.

2 Read the sentences. Decide whether *quite* makes the adjective stronger or weaker.

1 You're quite right. I should never have doubted you.

2 Leticia must have been quite upset. I had never seen her cry before.

3 Our dog is quite energetic, but nothing compared to how she used to be.

UNIT 2

2B Grammar: Present tenses

Present simple

Use the present simple to describe present habits, actions that happen regularly and facts or things that are always true.

*I **wake up** at seven o'clock every day.*
*I **don't watch** films very often.*
Do you take the number 5 train to work?

Present continuous

Use the present continuous to describe things that are happening in the present moment (right now) or things that are happening around the present moment (not exactly now).

I'm walking around the museum just now.
*You **aren't cooking** dinner.*
*Is John **working** today?*

Present perfect simple

Use the present perfect simple to describe the present results of past actions when the time is not specified. You often use it to describe life experiences, changes that have happened over a period of time and accomplishments.

To form the present perfect simple, use *have/has* + past participle.

*Sally **has finished** her project.*

You can also use it with state verbs (e.g. *have, be, know, love*) to describe a situation that began in the past but is still true in the present.

*I **have** always **wanted** to take piano lessons.*

Use it when you want to specify how many times an action has happened.

*My boss **has had** three cups of coffee today.*

Present perfect continuous

Use the present perfect continuous to describe actions that began in the past, are still in progress and are likely to continue in the future.

To form the present perfect continuous, use *have/has* + *been* + verb + *-ing*.

*Maya **has been learning** Japanese since she was at school.*
*We'**ve been going** to that restaurant for years.*

The present perfect continuous emphasizes the length of time that has passed since the action started (the action may or may not be finished), while the present perfect simple emphasizes the completion of the action.

*We **have been studying** for hours!*

You don't usually use state verbs (*have, be, know*, etc.) in the present perfect continuous.

Grammar reference

1 Choose the correct option to complete the sentences.

1 In general, my sister *picks up / is picking up* languages easily.

2 We *are reading up / have been reading up* on the Renaissance recently.

3 *I have been / I'm studying* French at the moment. I have a big exam next week.

4 Thank you, but I don't want any coffee. I *have had / have been having* two cups already.

5 They *don't come up / haven't come up* with an idea yet.

6 I don't think *we've made / we make* many mistakes, but let's double check.

2 Complete the diary entry with the correct form of the verbs in brackets.

It ¹_____ (be) two weeks since I arrived in New York for my language course. I ²_____ (enjoy) life in the city a lot. I have a small room in a student residence. Every day, I ³_____ (have) breakfast with my classmates at a local café. In the afternoon we explore the city. I ⁴_____ (visit) the Empire State Building and the Statue of Liberty. I ⁵_____ (miss) home quite a lot since I got here. But at the same time, I ⁶_____ (have) lots of things to keep me busy. I ⁷_____ (study) for my exam at the moment and ⁸_____ (spend) a lot of time practising writing in English.

2C Focus on: Separable and inseparable phrasal verbs

Most phrasal verbs are **separable**: the object can come before or after the preposition.

> Please can you **turn off the lights** before you leave?
> Sorry, I forgot to **turn the lights off**.

However, if the object is a pronoun, it must come <u>before</u> the preposition.

> I remembered to **turn them off**.
> NOT ~~I remembered to turn off them.~~

Some phrasal verbs are **inseparable**: the object always comes <u>after</u> the preposition, even if the object is a pronoun.

> We'll have to **come up with** a solution.
> NOT ~~We'll have to come up a solution with.~~

Phrasal verbs can be put into the following categories:

Two-part verbs (separable)	Two-part verbs (inseparable)	Three-part verbs (inseparable)
bring up	take after	come up with
look up	look after	get away with
make up	get over	look up to
pick up	look for	put up with
point out	go over	read up on

Verbs in the first category are always separable when the object is a pronoun.

> I'll **pick you up** at five.
> NOT ~~I'll pick up you at five.~~

They tend not to be separable when the object is a longer word or noun phrase.

> I **picked up** quite a lot of Japanese when I visited Tokyo last year.
> NOT ~~I picked quite a lot of Japanese up when I visited Tokyo last year.~~

When the object is a short word or phrase, separating the verb is optional.

> Did you **pick up** any French in Paris?
> Did you **pick** any French **up** in Paris?

A small number of phrasal verbs must always be separated, e.g. *get across* and *call back*.

> Marika didn't **call** Peter **back**. ~~NOT Marika didn't call back Peter.~~

Three-part verbs (verbs with two particles) are always inseparable.

> I need to **read up on** phrasal verbs. ~~NOT I need to read up phrasal verbs on.~~

1 Choose the correct option (a or b) to complete the sentences.

1 I really appreciate you …
   a pointing that out.
   b pointing out that.

2 It's a good idea to use a dictionary to …
   a look the spelling and definitions of new words up.
   b look up the spelling and definitions of new words.

3 I sometimes find it difficult to …
   a get across my point.
   b get my point across.

4 I don't have anyone to …
   a look the children after this evening.
   b look after the children this evening.

5 If you don't know the answer, just …
   a make it up.
   b make up it.

6 John really …
   a looks up to his dad.
   b looks up his dad to.

UNIT 3

3B Grammar: Narrative tenses

Past simple

Use the past simple to describe consecutive events that started and finished in the past, or the main events of a story.

*I **had** a great time in Paris. I **visited** the Louvre and **went** to the Eiffel Tower. I **bought** a lot of souvenirs.*

You often use it to describe important events in someone's life.

*Leonardo da Vinci **was born** in 1452. He **became** famous for his art and creative inventions.*

Past continuous

Use the past continuous to describe background events, or to give the background to the main story.

To form the past continuous, use *was/were* + verb + *-ing*.

*Susannah **was feeling** happy as she made her way to the bus stop, as it had been a great day.*

You also use it to describe longer actions or events that were in progress when something else occurred.

*I **was looking** for a place to have lunch, when suddenly I realized that my phone had disappeared.*

Past perfect simple

Use the past perfect simple to describe events or actions that happened before the main event.

To form the past perfect simple, use *had* + past participle.

*She **had visited** the city before.*

You can use it to emphasize that events or actions have been completed.

*We **had** already **decided** to go on a trip, but we weren't sure which country we wanted to visit.*

Past perfect continuous

Use the past perfect continuous to describe longer events or actions that were in progress in the past, either before or up to the main event.

To form the past perfect continuous, use *had been* + verb + *-ing*

*We**'d been expecting** the train journey to be long, but we didn't know it would be so uncomfortable.*

You can use it to emphasize the duration of an activity.

*They **had been working** all night long.*

1 Choose the correct options to complete the text.

Ever since I was a child, I [1]*was dreaming / had dreamed* of visiting Granada. I [2]*wanted / was wanting* to explore the narrow winding streets of the Albaicín, just as my mother [3]*had done / was doing* when she was in her twenties. After my plane [4]*landed / had been landing* in Madrid, I [5]*had / was having* to take a five-hour bus ride through the dusty Spanish countryside. The trip [6]*has been made / was made* longer by frequent stops in small villages that [7]*had been lying / lay* hidden amongst miles of olive groves for centuries.

Eventually, we [8]*had reached / reached* my destination. As my bus [9]*had been pulling / was pulling* into the city, I caught a glimpse of the sun setting over the Sierra Nevada. I [10]*had arrived / was arriving*.

2 Complete the sentences with the correct narrative tense.

1 We _____ (walk) to the train station when we _____ (come across) an old antiques market.

2 More than two hundred people _____ (stop by) the visitor centre yesterday. Perhaps one of them _____ (find) Divya's mobile phone.

3 Beatrice _____ (look forward to) her trip for months, so she _____ (feel) very upset when the airline cancelled her flight.

4 After I _____ (become) interested in archaeology, I _____ (decide) to visit Pompeii.

3C Focus on: Travel collocations with *go on*

You form many travel collocations by combining *go on* with words or expressions to do with travel.

Some describe different types of journey:

go on a cruise
go on a bus tour
go on a voyage

Some describe different types of holiday:

go on a package holiday
go on a city break
go on a safari
go on a guided tour
go on a ski holiday
go on a backpacking trip

Some describe travel for specific purposes:

go on a business trip
go on a language exchange
go on a scientific expedition

1 Complete the sentences with the correct form of the expressions from the list above.

1 If I had the chance to _____, I'm not sure I would take it. I'd feel frightened to be so close to so many wild animals.

2 Lucy doesn't usually _____, because she prefers to be more independent when she travels.

3 We're _____ next month. We know it'll be hard, but we're excited about improving our Portuguese.

4 A team of researchers is _____ to Antarctica. The trip has taken months of hard work and planning.

5 Next month, I'm _____ to Singapore. I'm quite nervous, as I'm new to the company.

6 My aunt _____ around the Mediterranean. She stopped in Mallorca, Sicily and many other islands.

Grammar reference

UNIT 4

4B Grammar: Reported speech and reporting verbs

Reporting verbs describe what someone else said or did. When you use reporting verbs, verb forms and reference words (pronouns, time and place expressions, etc.) tend to change.

Hannah: 'I'm going to help you tomorrow.' ➜ *Hannah said that **she** was going to help **me** the **next day**.*

Many reporting verbs follow a specific pattern.

verb + *to* + infinitive	agree, offer, promise, threaten They **agreed to help.**
verb + object + *to* + infinitive	advise, ask, convince, invite, order, remind, warn I **advised him to study** hard.
verb + *-ing* form	recommend, remember, suggest She **recommended arriving** early.
verb + preposition + *-ing* form	admit, apologize, confess, insist He **apologized for hurting** her feelings.
verb + object + preposition + *-ing* form	accuse, blame, praise She **accused me of lying.**

In negative sentences, use the negative infinitive or *-ing* form.

> She **accused me of not telling** the truth.
> They **agreed not to get** in the way.

Some verbs, e.g. *accept, complain* and *explain* follow the structure verb + *that* + clause.

> Vincent **explained that** he didn't know where the hotel was.

Some verbs in the table above can also follow this structure, e.g. *admit, agree* and *promise.*

> He **admitted that** he forgot to buy the tickets.

1 Rewrite the sentences using the correct reported speech pattern.

1 Adam: 'I'm going to come tomorrow.'
   Adam said that
   _____.

2 Ben: 'My sister was feeling tired.'
   Ben mentioned that
   _____.

3 Zack: 'I've been feeling ill.'
   Zack complained that
   _____.

4 Silvia: 'We should go for dinner next week.'
   Silvia suggested that _____.

2 Complete the sentences with the correct form of the verbs in brackets.

1 Dania agreed _____ (help) me with the project.

2 My aunt blamed me _____ (break) the vase.

3 She accused me _____ (forget) her birthday.

4 My wife and I offered _____ (come) early.

5 David admitted _____ (make) a mistake.

6 We apologized _____ (be) late.

7 She reminded me _____ (arrive) on time.

8 My boss recommended _____ (ask) lots of questions.

4C Focus on: Transitive and intransitive phrasal verbs

Transitive verbs require an object. Intransitive verbs do not require an object.

Many phrasal verbs can be both transitive and intransitive. You can add *with* to many intransitive phrasal verbs to make them transitive. Compare the following examples:

> My family and I **get along**.

This sentence does not have an object. *Get along* is being used intransitively.

> I **get along with** my family.

In this sentence, *my family* is the object. *Get along* is being used transitively.

1 Underline the phrasal verbs in the sentences. Then write T if the verbs are being used transitively or I if they are being used intransitively.

1 Technology makes it much easier for friends to keep in touch. _____

2 I had a great time catching up with my sister last weekend. _____

2 Rewrite the sentences so that the phrasal verb is transitive.

1 We should catch up sometime.
   I'd love to catch up with you sometime.

2 Do you and Lei keep in touch?
   Do you _____ ?

3 My best friend and I hit it off right away.
   I _____ .

4 I felt very sad when my cousin and I lost touch.
   When I _____ .

5 My cousins and I keep in close contact.
   I _____ .

UNIT 5

5B Grammar: Conditionals

Zero conditional

Use the zero conditional to describe facts, or things that are generally true.

The form is *If / When* + present simple, … present simple. You can also use the present continuous or present perfect.

> *If you **heat** water to 100°C, it **boils**.*
> *When plants **don't get** enough water, they **die**.*
> *If you **are** constantly **feeling** tired, you **are** probably **not sleeping** enough.*
> *If you **haven't seen** the Eiffel Tower, you **haven't seen** the most famous landmark in Paris!*

You can change the order of the clauses so the main clause comes first. When the *if* clause comes first, you must use a comma to separate the two clauses. When the main clause comes first, you don't use a comma.

> *I **have** an allergic reaction **if** I **eat** peanuts.*

First conditional

Use the first conditional to describe possible future situations.

The form is *If* + present simple, … *will / won't* + infinitive.

You can also use the present continuous or present perfect in the *if* clause. You can use other future forms in the main clause, e.g. *going to*, future perfect or future continuous.

You can change the order of the clauses so the main clause comes first.

> *If **it's** sunny, we'**ll go** to the park.*
> *You **won't be** able to sleep **if** you **have** another coffee.*
> *If you'**re** still **studying**, I'**m going to go** to the party without you.*
> *If you **haven't finished** the assignment by tomorrow, you'**re going** to regret it.*

Most first conditional sentences use *if*, but you can sometimes use other words, e.g. *unless, as long as* and *provided that*. You use *unless* to say *if not*.

> ***Unless** the meeting **is** cancelled, we **won't be** able to come to the lunch.*

(= If the meeting isn't cancelled, we won't be able to come to the lunch.)

> ***As long as** I **have** enough money, I'**ll buy** some new clothes.*
> ***Provided that** we **leave** right now, I'm sure **we won't** miss the train.*

Second conditional

Use the second conditional to describe the consequences of an unreal or imaginary situation in the present or future.

The form is *If* + past simple or past continuous, … *would / wouldn't* + infinitive.

You can change the order of the clauses so the main clause comes first.

> *If I **had** more money, I **would buy** a nicer phone.*
> *They **would understand if** they **were** in my situation.*
> *If you **were coming down with** a cold, you **would be** coughing and sneezing.*

In second conditional sentences, you can use *might / might not* and *could / couldn't* instead of *would / wouldn't*.

> *She **could get** higher marks **if** she **tried** harder.*

Third conditional

Use the third conditional to describe the consequences of an unreal or imaginary situation in the past. Common consequences include wishes and regrets.

The form is *If* + past perfect or past perfect continuous, … *would / wouldn't have* + past participle.

You can change the order of the clauses so the main clause comes first.

> *If I **had woken up** earlier, I **would have arrived** on time.*
> *You **wouldn't have got** a low mark **if** you **had studied** more.*
> *Ahmed **would have come** to dinner if he **hadn't been playing** basketball.*

In third conditional sentences, you can use *might / might not have* and *could / couldn't have* instead of *would / wouldn't have*.

> *I **might not have been** upset **if** you **had talked** to me first.*

1 Decide whether the sentences are zero, first, second or third conditional. Write 0, 1, 2 or 3.

1 If you have time later, will you give me a call?

2 If you feel ill, you shouldn't go to work.

3 If Lauren had a fever, she would take some ibuprofen.

4 You would have more energy if you exercised more.

5 If I hadn't been so tired, I would have come with you.

6 You'll miss your train if you don't hurry up.

2 Complete the conversation with the correct form of the verbs in brackets.

Andrew: Are you coming to the cinema later?

Bella: I don't think so. If I ¹_____ (have) more time I ²_____ (come). But I'm a bit stressed about my new project at work.

Andrew: Is there anything I can do to help?

Bella: Maybe … you know a bit about web design, right?

Andrew: I enrolled on a course last year. If I ³_____ (manage) to finish, I'm sure I ⁴_____ (learn) quite a lot. But I dropped out halfway through.

Bella: That's a shame.

Andrew: If you tell your boss you need a bit more time, I'm sure you ⁵_____ (feel) better.

Bella: Yeah, that's a good idea. If I ⁶_____ (take) a break, that ⁷_____ (help) too.

Grammar reference

5C   Focus on: *I wish …* and *If only …*

You can use *I wish …* and *If only …* to describe things that you want to be true.

Use *I wish / If only* + past simple to talk about a situation in the present or future.

I wish I was going on holiday this year.
If only I could remember his name.

Use *I wish / If only* + past perfect to talk about a situation in the past that you want to be different.

I wish I had stayed at home today.
If only she hadn't sprained her ankle.

You can use *were* rather than *was* with *I, he, she* or *it* to sound more formal.

I wish I were feeling better.

1 Match the beginnings of the sentences (1–6) with the endings (a–f).

1 I hate being ill. I wish …
2 I was hoping to go to the park. If only …
3 Our basketball tournament is next week. If only …
4 Wei is absolutely exhausted. She wishes …
5 Daniel feels a bit unwell. If only …
6 We have an important meeting. I wish …

a she could have a nap.
b he could stay at home.
c the weather was nicer.
d you hadn't called in sick.
e I hadn't broken my ankle.
f I didn't have this dreadful cold.

2 Complete the sentences with the correct form of the verb in brackets.

1 Jackie wishes she _____ (have) more free time.
2 I wish I _____ (know) how to play the piano.
3 If only you _____ (go) to sleep earlier last night.
4 I wish I _____ (not have) to take the train.
5 If only Isaac _____ (not forget) his phone.
6 Robin wishes he _____ (train) more. He might have won the race.

UNIT 6

6B   Grammar: Passive structures

Use the passive to place emphasis on the action that is being performed, rather than on the person or thing that is performing the action. You can also use it when the person or thing that did the action is unknown, unimportant or obvious. It is commonly used in news reports.

If you want to mention the person or thing performing the action, you can introduce it with the preposition *by*.

Form the passive with *be* + past participle. However, the form of *be* changes according to the verb tense being used.

Present simple	Many decisions **are made** every day.
Present continuous	Important steps **are being taken.**
Present perfect	Three men **have been** arrested.
Future with *will*	Several key ideas **will be presented.**
Future with *going to*	The best proposals **are going to be discussed.**
Past simple	A lot of questions **were brought up.**
Past continuous	The president **was being questioned.**
Past perfect	Many ideas **had been put** forward.

There are also infinitive (with and without *to*) and *-ing* forms of the passive.

*She didn't expect **to be praised** so much.*
*My article might **be published!***
*I enjoy **being photographed.***

Passive reporting verbs
You can use passive verbs to report beliefs, opinions and rumours, especially in news reports. Verbs that are commonly used include *think, say, report, understand, believe, hope* and *recommend*.

It + be + past participle + (that) + clause	**It is hoped that** the situation will soon improve. **It is said** we may never know the answer.

You can report events in the passive using a subject instead of *it*. You don't usually use the verbs *recommend* and *hope* in this pattern.

To report a past action in the present perfect or past simple with this pattern, use a perfect infinitive (infinitive with *have* + past participle).

To report an action in the future or in progress now with this pattern, use a continuous infinitive (*be* + *-ing*).

subject + *be* + past participle + *to* + infinitive	*The person responsible* **is thought to be** *in France.* *The fire* **is believed to have begun** *sometime last night.* *Real Madrid are said* **to be looking** *for a new manager.*

1 Complete the sentences with these phrases.

are being	been spent	is believed to
is going	understood to	will be presented

1 Jenny Wiles _____ be one of the best athletes of her generation.
2 The awards _____ at Hippodrome Centre on 22nd September.
3 A lot of money has _____ on this year's publicity campaign.
4 Generally speaking, bankers are _____ earn high salaries.
5 The government's decision _____ to be announced this afternoon.
6 Some questions _____ raised about the company's approach.

2 Look at the first sentence in each pair. Complete the second sentence so that it has the same meaning.

1 We discussed a number of important issues at the meeting.
   At the meeting, _____.
2 Many people hoped that the problem would be resolved.
   _____ would be resolved.
3 People believe that Jaime Vega is the best person to lead the company.
   _____ to lead the company.
4 An author has written an important book on the subject.
   An important book _____.
5 The recommendation is to arrive at 5 p.m.
   _____ we arrive at 5 p.m.
6 Someone is going to answer all of our questions soon.
   All of our questions _____ soon.

6C   Focus on: *the … the …*

Use *the … the …* to describe the relationship between two things. It shows the effect that one thing has on another. You can use it with verbs, nouns, adjectives and adverbs.

Notice that each sentence has two clauses with *the* and each clause can use *the* in a different structure.

the + comparative adjective / adverb + subject + verb	**The older my students are**, *the more they know.* **The more clearly you explain** *this, the better I'll understand.*
the + *more / less* + subject + verb	**The less I sleep**, *the worse I feel.*
the + *more / less / fewer* + noun + subject + verb	**The more friends I have**, *the happier I am.*

1 Complete the sentences with these words.

the better	the more	the more loudly
the older	the sooner	

1 _____ you go to sleep, the more energy you'll have tomorrow.
2 The more homework my children get, _____ they learn.
3 The less time I spend on social media, _____ I tend to feel.
4 _____ Roberto sings, the angrier his neighbours become.
5 _____ Janet gets, the more her parents worry about her.

2 Find and correct the mistakes in the sentences.

1 The less I study, the more free time have for my hobbies.
2 The fewest pets people have, the cheaper it is for them.
3 The more quickly we drive, soon we'll get to the airport.
4 The time you can spend relaxing on holiday, the better you will feel.
5 The darker my bedroom is, the more easy I get to sleep.

Grammar reference

7B Grammar: Causative verbs

Use causative verbs to indicate the different ways that the actions of someone or something can be affected.

Verb + object + *to* + infinitive

With this pattern, use *allow* and *permit* to describe allowing someone to do something or giving permission, *enable* to describe how something is made possible, *encourage* to describe motivating someone to do something, and *force* for obligation (when you <u>must</u> do something).

*The airline **permitted us to fly** with two pieces of luggage.*
*They **require us to arrive** at 5 p.m.*

Verb + object + infinitive (without *to*)

With this pattern, use *help* to describe giving assistance to allow something to happen, *let* to describe allowing something to happen or giving permission and *make* for obligation (when you <u>must</u> do something).

*My mum **is letting me go** to the cinema tonight.*

Verb + object + (*from*) + *-ing*

With this pattern, use *prevent, save* and *stop* to describe stopping something from happening.

*My work might **prevent me from attending** this weekend's event.*

1 Choose the correct option to complete the sentences.
1 I'm sorry, but I can't *allow / let* you to say that kind of thing.
2 We *advised / made* clients to think carefully about their business strategy.
3 My students *are encouraging / are helping* me see many things differently.
4 Proper rest *forces / prevents* people from getting ill.
5 I'm afraid we *can't let / can't permit* you board the train without a ticket.
6 Going to pick up supplies now *will enable / will save* us from having to go later.

2 Complete the paragraph with the correct form of the verbs in brackets.

A few years ago, I decided to begin cycling to work. This change to my lifestyle has made me [1]_____ (become) a healthier and happier person. It's enabled me [2]_____ (include) exercise as part of my daily routine and has helped me [3]_____ (save) money. It requires me [4]_____ (leave) home a little earlier. However, it stops me [5]_____ (feel) stressed about finding a seat on the metro and prevents me [6]_____ (worry) about missing my train. Recently, I've encouraged a few friends [7]_____ (begin) cycling to work as well. Of course, I'd never force anyone [8]_____ (give up) public transport in favour of a bike, but I'd advise anyone who is looking for a lifestyle change [9]_____ (try out) cycling!

7D Focus on: Useful structures for complaining

so + adjective or *such (a)* + adjective + noun

Use these structures to put emphasis on something that has annoyed or upset you.

*It's **so annoying** when you do that!*
*I had **such a** bad day – you just wouldn't believe it.*
*We had **such** terrible weather on our holiday.*

Present continuous with *always*

Use this structure to communicate that something happens all the time.

*You**'re always interrupting** me when I talk!*
*She**'s always turning up** late.*

I wish / If only + past simple or *I wish / If only* + *would* + infinitive

Use these structures to say that you want something to be different or true.

*I wish I **didn't have to come in** early.*
***If only** you **would listen** to me once in a while!*

1 Match the beginnings of the sentences (1–6) with the endings (a–f).
1 I thought the meal last night was so …
2 I don't like to fight, but John is always …
3 That was so embarrassing. If only …
4 Last night, Miguel was in such …
5 He's a bit lazy. I wish he …
6 I don't believe you. You're always …

a you would try to be a bit more polite next time.
b a bad mood that he refused to speak to me.
c making up lies and excuses.
d expensive! I don't think we'll eat there again.
e took on a bit more responsibility sometimes.
f starting arguments about the silliest things.

2 Put the words in order to make sentences. For each sentence, one word will not be used.
1 find / such / frustrating / I / so / long queues
2 she / only / harder / would / if / work / will
3 bad / too / Henry / in / such / is / a / mood
4 the / I / weather / is / wish / better / was
5 always / my / telling / boss / such / me / is / off

UNIT 8

8B   Grammar: Speculating about the past

To talk about possibility and certainty in the past, use modal verbs together with *have* + past participle.

Use *must have* + past participle to say that it is very probable or certain that something happened.

> *My laptop doesn't seem to be working. I **must have** accidentally **downloaded** a virus.*

Use *may have / might have / could have* + past participle to say it is possible that something happened. Similarly, use *may not have / might not have* + past participle to say it is possible that something didn't happen.

> *Jenny isn't at her desk. She **might have gone** to lunch.*
> *Alicia **might not have read** the email because she's not normally late.*

Use *can't have / couldn't have* + past participle to say you are almost sure that something didn't happen, or that it is impossible that something happened.

> *It **can't have been** easy to live without the internet.*
> *Carlos **couldn't have forgotten**. I reminded him yesterday!*

Use *should have / shouldn't have* + past participle to talk about mistakes or express criticism or regret.

> *I **should have woken up** earlier this morning.*
> *You **shouldn't have spent** so much money.*

1 Choose the correct meaning (a or b) for each sentence.

1   Thousands of workers must have been needed to construct the temple.
    a   Thousands of workers were probably necessary to build the temple.
    b   Thousands of workers participated in the construction of the temple.

2   It can't have been easy to be a nineteenth-century scientist.
    a   Perhaps it wasn't easy to work as a scientist in the nineteenth century.
    b   There is no way it was easy to work as a nineteenth-century scientist.

3   The developers shouldn't have forgotten to double-check their work.
    a   Not double-checking their work was the wrong thing to do.
    b   The developers didn't forget to double-check their work.

4   This tool might have been used for cutting vegetables.
    a   It's possible this tool was used for cutting vegetables.
    b   This tool was definitely used for cutting vegetables.

2 Complete the sentences with the correct modal verb. Sometimes more than one answer is possible.

1   Inventing the first computer _____ have been difficult. I wouldn't know where to begin!

2   This pottery _____ have originated in Chile, but I'm not sure. Maybe an archaeologist would know.

3   We _____ have worked harder, to get better results. For our next project, let's dedicate a bit more time.

4   Vaccines are so complicated. The researchers _____ have found it very easy to develop this one.

5   She's not answering her phone, so she _____ have left the office already.

6   You _____ have done that. It wasn't very safe.

8C   Focus on: Forming nouns, verbs and adjectives

The list below shows nouns, verbs and adjectives that you form with common suffixes. Studying these patterns is a useful way to expand your vocabulary because you can learn new words by exploring the word families of words you already know.

> *Annie **persuaded (v)** me to come to the cinema. She is a very **persuasive (adj)** person.*
> *The speaker gave a very **motivational (adj)** speech. It gave me the **motivation (n)** I needed to try something new.*

Nouns

-ion: *create → creation, innovate → innovation, invent → invention, accuse → accusation*

-ment: *enjoy → enjoyment, achieve → achievement*

-ity: *possible → possibility, responsible → responsibility*

-e/ance: *depend → independence, perform → performance*

-ness: *weak → weakness, happy → happiness*

Adjectives

-al: *tradition → traditional, universe → universal, critic → critical*

-ical: *economy → economical, history → historical*

-able: *afford → affordable, enjoy → enjoyable, memory → memorable, recharge → rechargeable*

-ous: *mystery → mysterious, anxiety → anxious*

-ive: *attract → attractive, create → creative, invent → inventive*

Verbs

-ate: *graduation → graduate, motive → motivate*

-ize: *critic → criticize, empathy → empathize, memory → memorize, apology → apologize*

-ify: *simple → simplify*

-en: *weak → weaken, strength → strengthen*

Grammar reference

1 Choose the correct option to complete the sentences.

1 I'm sorry, but that is a complete *impossible /
impossibility*.

2 Winning first prize at the science fair was far from her
only *accomplishment / accomplish*.

3 I think you're being far too *critic / critical*.

4 The governor has issued a *statement / state* about her
plans for next year.

5 Our holiday last year was incredibly *memory /
memorable*.

2 Complete the announcement with the correct form of
the words in brackets.

***Develop a* 1_____ *(create) mobile phone
app and win $5,000!***

Are you into programming? Do you believe in the
endless 2_____ (possible) of technology? If
so, this 3_____ (compete) may be for you.
We are seeking interesting phone apps that meet the
following criteria:

• 4_____ (origin) concept with an
  5_____ (attract) design

• Useful and 6_____ (afford) for students

• Easily 7_____ (download) over our
  networks

8_____ (add) information can be found
at the IT Department. All 9_____ (submit)
must be received by 31st October.

UNIT 9

9B Grammar: Talking about the future

Future continuous (subject + *will* + *be* + *-ing*)

Use the future continuous to describe or make predictions
about events or actions that will be in progress at a particular
time in the future. You can also use it to ask questions about
plans at a particular time in the future.

*This time next week, **they'll be skiing** in the Pyrenees.
We **won't be going away** this summer.
Will you **be starting** university in September?*

Future perfect (subject + *will* + *have* + past participle)

Use the future perfect to refer to actions that will be completed
by a particular time in the future. You can often use it with a
time expression such as *in two weeks, in two weeks' time* or *by
that time*.

*In a week's time, Teriha **will have arrived** back home.
Unfortunately, I **won't have finished** my book until
  next year.
Will you **have reached** the restaurant by that time?*

Should and might to talk about the future

Use *should* and *might* instead of *will* to show that you are less
certain about something. *Should* expresses a higher degree of
certainty than *might*.

*The plane **should be taking off** in the next half hour.
I **might have moved** into my new apartment by then.*

1 Complete the sentences with these phrases.

'll be   might have   should   will have   won't
---

1 By December, it's almost certain that Paolo
  _____ finished his second novel.

2 On Saturday, I _____ tidying up the house.
  It's a total mess.

3 By 2023, I _____ have finished my degree.

4 We _____ be travelling this summer because
  we have too much work to do.

5 We _____ discovered a cure by the end of
  the decade, but it's not certain.

2 Complete the email with the correct future form of the
verbs in brackets. Sometimes more than one answer is
possible.

Dear students,

We're sure you are looking forward to your first term at
university. By this time next week, you 1_____
(arrive) and, hopefully, 2_____ (chat) with new
friends as you unpack. You 3_____ (think of)
some questions. So, the purpose of this email is to clarify a
few last-minute details.

On Saturday, a member of staff will meet you at
Harrington Gate to show you to your accommodation. You
4_____ (receive) an email with information
about transport options already. If you have not received this
message by Friday, please contact us.

On Sunday morning, during breakfast at Avery Hall,
administrators 5_____ (explain) the timetable
for our induction week. As preparation, we've requested
that you submit a short statement describing your hobbies
and interests. Ideally, you 6_____ (submit) this
statement by Thursday.

9C Focus on: Verb-noun collocations

A collocation is a group of words that often go together. It is
important to use the correct collocation because mistakes with
collocations can make your speech sound unnatural. Here are
some collocations for five common verbs.

achieve	your aims your objectives a goal very little
make	a mess of something it through a decision a choice
overcome	difficulties obstacles problems objections
struggle	to understand something for survival with the problem
tackle	a crisis an issue a problem

1 Match the beginnings of the sentences (1–6) with the endings (a–f).

1 If you're struggling …
2 Even if you make …
3 Most people tackle …
4 In order to achieve …
5 Some kinds of difficulties …
6 I couldn't have made …

a problems at some point in their life.
b cannot be overcome, no matter how hard you try.
c a mess of something, you shouldn't give up.
d it through without the help of my friends and family.
e your objectives, you should make a plan and stick to it.
f to understand something, ask someone for help.

2 Complete the sentences using the correct form of the verbs. One verb will be used twice.

achieve   make   overcome   struggle   tackle

1 The main objective I want to _____ this year is learning to drive.
2 It's easier to _____ obstacles with the help of supportive friends.
3 Last month was tough, but we somehow _____ it through.
4 Many species around the world are _____ for survival.
5 The crisis we are _____ is unlike any other I've known.
6 If you _____ a mess of something, you should admit it.

UNIT 10

10B   Grammar: Verb patterns with infinitive and -ing

When one verb follows another, the form of the second verb depends on the first verb.

Verbs followed by verb + -ing

Use this pattern with certain verbs and phrases including *enjoy, feel like, can't stand, carry on, give up, hate, keep, love, recommend* and *suggest*. You also use it with *remember* (in the sense of thinking about the past).

*As I child, I used to **enjoy swimming**.*
*We **can't stand hiking** in rainy weather.*

Verbs followed by to + -ing

You usually use an infinitive after *to*. However, in certain cases you use *-ing*. This is because the *-ing* form of the verb acts like a noun. Use this structure with the verbs *be used to, get used to* and *look forward to*.

*I**'m not used to living** in such a hot country.*
*She's **looking forward to travelling** abroad.*

Verbs followed by infinitive with to

Use this pattern with certain verbs and phrases, including *afford, arrange, can't wait, dare, deserve* and *expect*. You also use it with *remember* (in the sense of thinking about something you need to do).

*I can't **afford to buy** a new car.*
*Let's **arrange to have** dinner next week.*

Verbs followed by infinitive without to

This pattern is typical of causative verbs such as *let* and *make* (see Unit 7). You also use this pattern after modal verbs.

*We **make our children tidy** their rooms.*

1 Complete the sentences with the correct form of the verbs in brackets.

1 We really enjoyed _____ (listen) to the music at last night's festival.
2 This year, I can't afford _____ (go) anywhere on holiday.
3 Are you looking forward to _____ (attend) the conference?
4 I'm finding it hard to get used to _____ (wake up) early.
5 I'm always happy when my flatmate remembers _____ (clean) the bathroom.
6 We've arranged _____ (spend) Saturday morning with my cousins.
7 Can you help _____ (tidy up) the flat, please?

Grammar reference

2 Find and correct the mistakes in the sentences.

1 What do you feel like to do this evening?
2 I think the students deserve winning a prize.
3 We are looking forward to go scuba diving.
4 We remember to travel to the Caribbean as children.
5 My younger sister always makes me to laugh.

10C Focus on: *the* with groups of people and things

To describe groups of people and things, use *the* in the following contexts:

- to describe a specific set of things and people.
  *At this hotel, **the staff** are so hardworking.*

- before the word *majority*, and after the words *some of*, *many of* and *none of*.
  *The festival was attended by **the majority** of the town's residents.*
  ***Many of the** students are bilingual.*

- when referring to groups of people using the adjective form of the nationality.
  ***The French** are known for their food.*

You don't need *the* in these contexts:

- to describe plural nouns when you are speaking in general.
  ***Spices** are an important part of many cuisines.*

- with the words *most, some, many* and *no*.
  ***Many** cultures have festivals in the springtime.*
  ***Some** countries have several national languages.*

- when referring to groups of people using the plural noun form of the nationality.
  ***Canadians** often enjoy watching ice hockey.*

1 Choose the correct option to complete the sentences.

1 *The most / Most* bilingual people find speaking more than one language incredibly useful.
2 Perhaps due to their diet, *the Japanese / Japanese* have a long life expectancy.
3 The internet has made it easier for *the many / many* subcultures to develop and grow.
4 *The tapas / Tapas* are small savoury dishes that are served as a snack.
5 At last night's show, *the dancers / dancers* gave an excellent performance.
6 Independence Day is celebrated by *the Colombians / Colombians* on 20th July.

2 Read the paragraph. Find and correct eight mistakes related to *the*.

Living in a diverse community is very important to me, perhaps because I've lived in the many multicultural cities throughout my life. My parents were the diplomats and as a result we travelled all over the world. I loved majority of the places we lived, although I found the climate in some of warmer countries hard to adapt to. On the other hand, in every country I met the incredible people and got to experience the culture in a unique way. Now, as an adult, I live in the East End of London. For me, the East End is a perfect fit because it reminds me of my travels. I love hearing dozens of the different languages as I walk through streets, and doing the shopping at family-owned corner shops is just the best. I buy my vegetables at an Indian grocery shop and owners are teaching me short phrases in their language.

Irregular verbs

INFINITIVE	PAST SIMPLE	PAST PARTICIPLE
be	was / were	been
beat	beat	beaten
become	became	become
begin	began	begun
bite	bit	bitten
blow	blew	blown
break	broke	broken
bring	brought	brought
build	built	built
burn	burned / burnt	burned / burnt
buy	bought	bought
catch	caught	caught
choose	chose	chosen
come	came	come
cost	cost	cost
cut	cut	cut
deal	dealt	dealt
dig	dug	dug
do	did	done
dream	dreamed / dreamt	dreamed / dreamt
drink	drank	drunk
drive	drove	driven
eat	ate	eaten
fall	fell	fallen
feel	felt	felt
fight	fought	fought

INFINITIVE	PAST SIMPLE	PAST PARTICIPLE
find	found	found
fly	flew	flown
forget	forgot	forgotten
forgive	forgave	forgiven
freeze	froze	frozen
get	got	got
give	gave	given
go	went	gone
grow	grew	grown
have	had	had
hear	heard	heard
hide	hid	hidden
hit	hit	hit
hold	held	held
hurt	hurt	hurt
keep	kept	kept
know	knew	known
lay	laid	laid
lead	led	led
leave	left	left
learn	learned / learnt	learned / learnt
lend	lent	lent
let	let	let
lie	lay	lain
lose	lost	lost
make	made	made

Irregular verbs

INFINITIVE	PAST SIMPLE	PAST PARTICIPLE
mean	meant	meant
meet	met	met
pay	paid	paid
put	put	put
read	read	read
ride	rode	ridden
ring	rang	rung
rise	rose	risen
run	ran	run
say	said	said
see	saw	seen
sell	sold	sold
send	sent	sent
set	set	set
shake	shook	shaken
shine	shone	shone
shoot	shot	shot
show	showed	shown
shut	shut	shut
sing	sang	sung
sit	sat	sat
sleep	slept	slept
smell	smelled / smelt	smelled / smelt
speak	spoke	spoken
spell	spelled / spelt	spelled / spelt

INFINITIVE	PAST SIMPLE	PAST PARTICIPLE
spend	spent	spent
spoil	spoiled / spoilt	spoiled / spoilt
spread	spread	spread
stand	stood	stood
steal	stole	stolen
stick	stuck	stuck
swear	swore	sworn
swim	swam	swum
take	took	taken
teach	taught	taught
tell	told	told
think	thought	thought
throw	threw	thrown
understand	understood	understood
wake	woke	woken
wear	wore	worn
win	won	won
write	wrote	written

Extra speaking tasks

PAGE 48, 4A, EXERCISE 8

SITUATION 1
Student A

You have recently moved to this neighbourhood. You'd like to learn about ways of enjoying nature in the local area.

Student B

You enjoy being outdoors. Recommend to Student A what they can do in the local area to stay close to nature.

SITUATION 2
Student A

You would like to do something outside with Student B, who isn't very keen. Persuade them.

Student B

You don't really like outdoor activities. You prefer staying indoors reading a book or watching a film. Student A will try to persuade you to spend time outside with them this weekend.

PAGE 51, 4B, EXERCISE 10

Student A

You and B are brothers/sisters. When your parents died, they left the family bakery to you both to share the profits equally. You think B is lazy and takes advantage of your work, so you have decided that you should receive most of the profits. You are so angry with B that you don't speak to her/him at all. Your friend C wants to help you and B end the arguments and reach an agreement. Tell C what the problems are. Use reporting verbs when possible.

My sister/brother promised to do more work, but she/he never does.

Student B

You and A are brothers/sisters. When your parents died, they left the family bakery to you both to share the profits equally. You think A is very bossy. She/he also makes you do extra work, while she/he sits in the office and does nothing. You are so angry with A that you don't speak to her/him at all. Your friend C wants to help you and A end the arguments and reach an agreement. Tell C what the problems are. Use reporting verbs when possible.

My sister/brother accuses me of being lazy, but actually it's her/him that doesn't do any work.

Student C

You are a good friend of A and B. They are brothers/sisters. They inherited the family bakery and were supposed to share the profits equally. However, they have been arguing about many things and don't talk to each other at all, so you've decided to help them. Listen to A and B to find out why they are unhappy. Report what each one says to the other and try to help them reach an agreement that they are both happy with.

Your brother/sister says you promised to help out more. Maybe you could take turns to run the bakery at the weekend?

PAGE 55, 4D, EXERCISE 9

1   Choose one of these topics to discuss.

Interesting places you've been to
Keeping in touch with friends
Is having a foreign accent OK?
The best way to keep in touch with friends long distance

2   Your teacher will assign you one of the three turn-taking styles (rugby, bowling, basketball) to use during the discussion. Don't tell your partners which you have.

3   Have a conversation about the topic, using your assigned turn-taking style.

4   After three minutes, stop the conversation and discuss the questions:
    • Which turn-taking style did each person have?
    • How do you know this?

5   Choose a different topic and have another conversation. Keep the same turn-taking style you were assigned. This time, however, adapt your style during the conversation in order to ensure fair participation.

6   After three minutes, stop the conversation and discuss the questions:
    • How did each person adapt their communication style?
    • What went well?
    • What could you do better next time?

Extra speaking tasks

PAGE 67, 5D, EXERCISE 11

Student A

You're the doctor. Speak as fast as you can. Choose at least three of the words in the box to use in a conversation with the patient. Check the meaning of any new words before you begin.

acute pain	do an X-ray
anxiety	elaborate on
appropriate treatment	mental health
come down with (a cold/	physical wellbeing
the flu)	symptoms
cope with	

Student B

You're the patient. You have a lower level of English. Think of a problem you have. The doctor will speak very fast and might use words you will find difficult to understand.

Student C

You're the nurse. Help the patient communicate with the doctor by adapting the language. The doctor might use some of the words in the box. Think how you could explain them to the patient so that they understand. Check the meaning of any new words before you begin.

acute pain	do an X-ray
anxiety	elaborate on
appropriate treatment	mental health
come down with (a cold/	physical wellbeing
the flu)	symptoms
cope with	

PAGE 102, 8D, EXERCISE 3

1-15 Points

You're quite strict about your online etiquette. You try to maintain some level of formality and pay attention to how you communicate online.

16-25 Points

You're somewhere in the middle. You might sometimes break a few online etiquette rules, but you also follow quite a few.

26-40 Points

You're very relaxed about your online etiquette. You think online communication should be informal and prefer not to follow formal rules.

PAGE 112, 9C, EXERCISE 1

Mostly As

You make life difficult for yourself sometimes but try not to give up. Try to remember that things may not be as bad as they seem.

Mostly Bs

Taking the easy option isn't always the best option in the long run. If you face the problem, you may discover a new talent or opportunity!

Mostly Cs

You are good at taking advantage of bad situations. You know how to turn negatives into positives.

Audioscripts

UNIT 1

🎧 1.2

F = Fatima, T = Tomoya

F: Tomoya, you studied psychology, didn't you?

T: Yes. Why?

F: Well, do you think people's feelings are expressed in the same way by everyone?

T: What do you mean?

F: Erm, I guess I'd like to know whether a smile means the same thing all over the world.

T: That's a great question! What do you think, Fatima?

F: Yes, I guess. I mean, I think whoever I met, even if we were from opposite sides of the world and spoke different languages, one thing we'd understand about each other would be our smiles.

F: You're right, but that wasn't what many people thought before.

T: Wasn't it?

F: No. The general idea many years ago was that showing emotions was learned behaviour, so you might learn one facial expression for an emotion in one society, but another one in another society.

F: Huh! That reminds me of the differences in how emoticons look in different cultures. You've noticed, haven't you?

T: You're right! It's always surprised me that in Europe the emoticons are from left to right: first eyes, then sometimes nose and then the mouth.

F: Really? Don't you do it in the same way in Japan?

T: No! Ours are upright, just like your face is.

F: Do you think it means that how we express emotions is different from culture to culture?

T: Kind of. For example, you might find that people smile less in some places, or smile for different social reasons. Some cultures smile in embarrassing situations, or just to be friendly and polite to strangers.

F: I do that!

T: Who do you smile at?

F: Sometimes I smile at people I pass on the street, even if I don't know them.

T: OK, well in some countries they might think that's strange!

F: Haha! Thanks a lot!

🎧 1.3

A: Do you know what the difference is between emoticons and emojis?

B: Yes, emoticons are symbols used to represent faces and emojis are actual pictures.

A: Oh, OK!

B: You know you have to be careful with emojis, don't you? What you see when you send it isn't necessarily what the other person sees.

A: Isn't it?!

B: No! A friend of mine texted his wife 'Do you know how beautiful you are?' and sent the Spanish dancer emoji. Except the emoji on her phone was a fat yellow dancing blob!

A: Oh no! Who designs these emojis – the phone companies? By the way, why did you send me a surprised face when I told you I got the tickets for the match yesterday?

B: What? Didn't I send you a smiley? Oops!

🎧 1.6

/ɪ/	/iː/	/eɪ/	/aɪ/
exhausted	weak	afraid	excited
thrilled	relieved	impatient	delighted
optimistic	pleased		
astonished			

🎧 1.7

Francisco: When I got struck by lightning several years ago, I went through a real rollercoaster of emotions. It took me a few seconds to realize what had happened to me. As I lay on the ground, not being able to hear anything after the explosion, I saw all the woodchips falling like snow on me, from all the beams in the roof above me that had been split in half. That's when I realized I had been hit by lightning, but I still could not believe my bad luck. Then, I tried to breathe and I couldn't. I had to hit my chest a few times before I could take a breath. It was an emotional few seconds. Then I realized that, except for my right arm, I could not move or even feel the rest of my body. Was I paralysed? As people around me began screaming, I tried to say a few words to let them know I was actually not dead. The next few hours were also very extreme. We were in a remote area and we had to drive around the village looking for help, a doctor, someone. It took four hours for us to connect with an actual ambulance that had to come from a nearby town. Just before the ambulance arrived I started feeling tingling in my legs, and shortly after I began being able to move them. I felt enormous joy at that point. I was not paralysed! After a brief visit, the doctor told me I was going to be fine! I still wasn't so sure that was true, but I was relieved and happy I could walk again anyway.

Tsiory: In 2017, I was invited to give a talk on the stage of the National Geographic Grosvenor Auditorium in Washington DC. It was my first time there. It's always hard to give a speech in English, as I always feel my English is bad. I wrote my speech no less than fifty times and repeated it in front of the

Audioscripts

mirror. Backstage, millions of questions crossed my mind. What if I mumble in front of the audience? What if no words came out of my mouth? And even stupid questions like: what if I miss the steps and I fall in front of all those people?

My turn arrives to be on stage. The stage was bright but the audience was in the dark which made me feel more comfortable. I felt a cold stream running down my back. When the light turned to red, my mouth opened and words came out! I had repeated those words a hundred times and I was holding my notes, so I thought 'Everything is going to be alright'. When the clock said 3 seconds left, I was very confident. I realized that something had changed in me. I had overcome one of my biggest fears: talking to an audience and what an audience! I will have to do more speeches like this, but I just have to remember that I did it once and I can do it again.

🎧 1.8

G = Gurpreet, L = Laurent, W = Waiter

W: Would you like to order anything yet?

G: Sorry, I'm still waiting for my friend. He shouldn't be much longer.

W: That's no problem. I'll pop back when they get here.

G: Come on. Why is it always me waiting?

L: Hi there! Sorry I'm a bit late. The metro.

G: A bit? I've been waiting for thirty minutes!

L: Have you? I'm really sorry. I got stuck at work and the metro was really slow.

G: The metro is always slow at this time. I came on the metro as well, you know.

L: Listen, it's only a few minutes. It won't happen again. Come on, let's order.

G: Look, this isn't the first time, is it? You're always doing this to me!

L: And I've told you before, it isn't always easy to get out of work on time - things come up at the last minute.

G: Hmm. I'm really annoyed right now.

L: What can I say? I'm doing my best here. Come on. Let's order.

G: I'm not sure I'm hungry right now.

W: Erm, do you need a couple more minutes?

Gurpreet

I'm so fed up! This happens every time we meet for dinner, or whatever. He's always late, and I always feel so stupid - I hate sitting on my own in the restaurant. I don't understand why, if you're meant to meet someone at 7 o'clock and it takes twenty minutes to get there, why you don't leave at 20 to 7! It's so rude!

Laurent

He takes it so badly. I mean, I was really surprised at how angry he got. I was only a few minutes late. Plus when you arrange 7 o'clock for something, who actually gets there at 7? If this isn't the first time, maybe he could arrive late too if he expects me to be late anyway. I'm really busy at work at the moment, so I was actually working until 7 tonight.

UNIT 2

🎧 2.1

Arianna: I've studied English for a long time. I started in primary school and have been using it ever since. It's been immensely helpful for me in terms of the opportunities that it has opened up. And right now, it's really the main language that I use in my life. More so than Italian, my first language. To the point that when I think to myself, I do it in English. I dream in English!

I also speak French and I've been using it since I was 11. I often speak it with some French-speaking friends I met when I was an Erasmus student in Paris. Their native language is actually German, and because I'm currently trying to learn German, I should probably be practising it with them. But our language has always been French, so we speak in French. Right?

I've also been studying Spanish for several years, starting in high school. Mainly afternoon and evening classes. Unfortunately, I've never had the chance to live in a Spanish-speaking country. However, Spanish is the closest to my mother tongue, so it hasn't been that difficult to learn.

The last language I've been trying to pick up is German. And it's because my job is in Germany. But I have to admit that I'm struggling with that. Like really, really bad. I'm taking classes at the moment, so hopefully I will improve soon.

🎧 2.2

1 I've studied English for a long time.
2 I also speak French and I've been using it since I was 11.
3 I often speak it with some French-speaking friends.
4 Our language has always been French, so we speak in French.
5 Unfortunately, I've never had the chance to live in a Spanish-speaking country.
6 It hasn't been that difficult to learn.
7 The last language I've been trying to pick up is German.
8 I'm taking classes at the moment, so hopefully I will improve soon.

Arianna: I think speaking to people is the best, but I also find it the most stressful. I also watch shows regularly. I can't say this has helped me very much in English because, you know, at the time when I was learning, that wasn't a thing. There was no Netflix, right? But for French, watching shows has definitely helped. And now, more and more, I'm trying to watch things in their original language.

One thing I found that helps me the most is not so much as to speak the new language as much as possible, but to cut out the other languages I know. If you still have the option to speak your own language or another one that you know better, I feel like that's too much of an easy fallback. For example, the first thing I do when I move to a different place is change the language on my laptop and on my phone.

Today, we are going to chat about the global spread of English. It's a topic that has been brought up a few times recently in your comments on social media.

As some of you may know, there are nearly two billion people that speak English. Interestingly, more than eighty per cent of them do not speak it as their mother tongue. In contrast, a similar number of people also speak Chinese, but more than eighty per cent of them speak it as their first language.

Clearly, this means that when you're using English, you're four times as likely to be speaking with people for whom English is a second or third language, rather than someone who speaks it as their first language. Even in places like New York or London, you are very likely to speak English with people for whom it is a second, third or fourth language. On the other hand, when speaking Chinese, Spanish or Arabic, you're most likely to do it with first language users.

This brings me to my next point. I don't know about you, but it's certainly not how I used to think about English when I was learning it. For instance, I believed that English was only spoken in the UK, North America and Australia. We learned a lot about British and American culture. But interestingly, English is an official language in over sixty countries, including India, Kenya, Barbados and Kiribati. I also thought it was really important to speak like 'native speakers'.

It was only when I started travelling and working that I realized that, actually, most people I interact with don't speak English as their first language. And, in fact, some of those difficult British or American idioms I was proud I'd learned weren't helping me get my message across. I started to be fascinated by what it actually takes to become a successful communicator in the global English-speaking community.

When I read up a bit more on it, I found out that, funnily enough, according to many experts, a foreign accent isn't usually a problem. And I used to worry about it so much. Surprisingly, researchers point out that first language users might often be the most difficult to understand in international contexts.

Obviously, this had a huge impact on my identity as an English user. While in the past I very much worried about picking up the 'wrong' accent, I now feel much more comfortable just speaking like I do, rather than trying to imitate someone else.

So I personally feel that English belongs to all of us who use it. Basically, whether you're from Ho Chi Minh City, New York, Warsaw, São Paolo or Nairobi doesn't matter.

What do you think?

One

The speakers are attending capoeira classes. Capoeira is a martial art from Brazil, a combination of fighting and dance.

A: … So, Sibel, I can tell you are enjoying the course. You are so good already!

B: Thank you. Yes, I'm learning so much. Aren't you?

A: Absolutely! Andreza is a very good teacher. Is capoeira practised much in Turkey?

B: I've never seen it, but it's probably around in the big cities. It <u>is</u> loads of fun!

A: Yes, but I am exhausted though!

B: So am I! It's been a very long morning. I'm looking forward to sitting down for lunch.

A: I don't know about you, but I am starving!

B: Ha ha! In my language, we would say: I'm as hungry as a wolf.

A: 'Hungry as a wolf'! Wolf is the wild dog?

B: Yes! Don't you say 'hungry like a wolf'?

A: No, but I know what you mean. The equivalent for us is 'I could eat my arm'!

B: 'I could eat my arm'?! Ha ha! I love it! Well, I could definitely eat my arm right now …

A: Ha ha

Two

Hassan and José Luis are colleagues who work in an office in Buenos Aires in Argentina. Hassan, from the UAE, has recently arrived in Argentina.

C: … But there must be things you miss about your country?

Audioscripts

D: Sure, but it's more people that I miss than places or food or whatever. I miss my friends of course. I miss a game of football in the park in the evening with them.

C: I didn't know you played football in the UAE!

D: Yeah! It's really big!

C: What's your national team like? I've never heard about them.

D: Ha! We're not very good, but we're getting better.

C: Hey! You should come with me next Friday. My friends and I play at the sports centre.

D: I'd love that. Thanks! Hey! Did you see the match last night?

C: Yes! Wasn't it amazing? 4-2 in the end, but I really thought Boca were going to win.

D: I know. The last ten minutes were so exciting.

C: Yeah, and that golazo from Vila, I mean, it was exceptional!

D: In Spanish you say *golazo* for a beautiful goal?

C: Yeah, exactly. Do you have a word for that in Arabic?

D: Erm, that's so annoying! I think there is, but I can't quite get it! In Arabic or in English. Golazo. I'm going to use it. What a golazo by Vila!

∩ 2.8

1 Is capoeira practised much in Turkey?
2 In my language, we would say: 'I'm as hungry as a wolf.'
3 The equivalent for us is: 'I could eat my arm.'
4 Do you have a word for that in Arabic?
5 I can't quite get it!

UNIT 3

∩ 3.1

Andrej: So, this happened eight years ago, in Hurghada on the Egyptian coast. I was travelling as a part of my undergraduate studies. I'd been studying sharks, skates and rays and exploring places where young sharks might be born along the coast.

On the first day, I was walking from the hotel when I saw a small souvenir shop selling papyrus – the paper that ancient Egyptians used to use. The moment I said 'Hello', the salesman asked me if I wanted to see some 'magic' papyrus - one that glows in the dark. Of course, I said 'yes' straight away. But at that moment, all of a sudden, three other guys appeared out of nowhere. They were carrying lots of old newspaper which they started to stick to the windows.

At that moment, I started to wonder what was going on! They had almost completely closed the windows and there was hardly any light in the room, and those three guys were blocking the front door. The salesman had brought out what looked like a wooden object. He put the object on the table, and started to unroll it. It was a huge roll of papyrus and it was

shining in the dark. In English, he said: 'Look, papyrus that glows in the dark!'

Then they invited me to stay for dinner! And for a couple of hours, we communicated slowly, as they didn't know much English. And for the next two weeks I visited them for some Egyptian tea or dinner. Today, eight years since that event, I am still in touch with Zizu and Nigm, the salesman and the shop owner. I'm looking forward to going back again to see the papyrus that glows in the dark.

∩ 3.3

If you were asked to name a famous navigator – or ocean explorer – you might say Magellan, Zheng or Cook. You probably wouldn't think of, arguably, the most successful navigators in history: the ancient Polynesians.

Without a doubt, the Polynesian trips across the Pacific were the most incredible voyages, as these people settled in hundreds of islands over millions of square kilometres. Around three thousand years ago, Neolithic people with the simplest of canoes and no navigation equipment set off and eventually ended up on some of the remotest islands on the planet, hundreds, sometimes thousands, of kilometres from anywhere else. People have compared their achievements to those of the Americans landing on the moon.

Who were they? People had been living on the islands around Papua New Guinea, as far west as the Solomon Islands, for as long as thirty thousand years. These were sailors used to island hopping, making stopovers before moving on to the next island, rarely sailing out of sight of land. But around 1200 BCE, a people we now call the Lapita set off on a journey east. This meant losing sight of land for days at a time. Some settled down in the Santa Cruz Islands, but others carried on, heading for new undiscovered islands further and further east. They sailed against the wind, so if they missed their destination it was easy to turn back and come home. This way, they made it as far as Tonga, four thousand kilometres from Papua New Guinea.

They stayed on these islands for some time, part of a developing culture we know as Polynesia. But something prompted the Polynesians to climb on board their boats again, reaching the Cook Islands in about 500 CE. Then, the Polynesians set off on their most incredible voyages, north to Hawaii, east to Rapa Nui and south west to New Zealand. The distances involved are truly amazing. They even reached South America somewhere around what is now Ecuador, an incredible nine thousand kilometres from the Cook Islands.

The trick was to travel light. Their canoes were the fastest ocean-going vessels in the world, so they didn't need to carry so much water or food for the voyage because they were able to make great distances in a short period of time. However, they took things they would need in the new lands: fishing hooks and other useful tools, animals such as chickens and the plants they would need to farm. The sweet potato is originally from South America, but is an important vegetable in Polynesian cooking. We know that Polynesians ate it before the Europeans arrived, and their word for it, *kumara,* is from an Ecuadorean language. In South America, they introduced the chicken to the people there and brought back with them the sweet potato.

So what was the secret of their success? How did a tiny civilization explore such a huge area of the Earth's surface? Like all sailors, they knew the position of the stars, of course, but they had other knowledge, such as how to interpret and use wind and wave direction. This complex skill, called 'wayfinding', was essential to the Lapita and Polynesians. Nearer their destination, they could use other signs in nature: the direction of bird flight, or the presence of leaves in the water, to find even the smallest of islands.

🎧 **3.4**

1

A: So you can make it to games night next Saturday then?

B: Definitely, it sounds like lots of fun. You need to tell me how to get to your house, though.

A: Of course. OK, so if you're coming by bus from the centre, you take the same bus as if you were heading for the airport, OK?

B: But that's direct to the airport.

A: No, not that one. The number 7 is the local bus and it stops near my place.

B: OK, and I catch that at the bus station …

A: Right. So just get on your normal bus and you'll end up at Kim Ma Station.

B: No, that takes me to Long Bien station, I think.

A: Oh, no. That's true. I'm getting mixed up. The Kim Ma is the one you need. So where are you setting off from? I thought you lived near the Night Market.

B: No, I'm near the Cho Hom.

A: Oh, I see. Right, so you need to change buses at the university.

B: Linh, wait! But if I'm going to the university, I might as well catch the number 13. I think you've got it the wrong way round.

A: Probably! Listen, I think we need to start again from scratch.

2

C: I don't know where we can stay for the money we've got. Everywhere is so expensive.

D: It's funny you say that because just the other day someone was telling me about these hostels, well, they're not really hostels at all, because you get your own room, like, er, you know, like … have you seen those weird places in airports that are sort of Japanese style, do you know what I mean?

C: Er, I'm not sure I follow.

D: Anyway, it's not important, just to say that these things are similar, quite small but they're cheap. Although, now I come

to think of it, if we're only there for a couple of days, do we really want to be on the outskirts, because I believe they're normally not centrally located, so we'd have to find our own way in. Hmm.

C: I didn't really understand much of that. These 'hostels', do you think we should ask about them or not?

D: Of course! That's what I'm saying!

3

E: I'm spending a few days in Poland next week – in Kraków. Have you got any recommendations for lunch?

F: You should go to a milk bar. It's where the locals go. Cheap and homemade.

E: Right. I was thinking more about food.

F: This is food. They're restaurants.

E: OK, but I don't really like milk. Is it more of a breakfast place, then?

F: Eh? What are you talking about? Listen, I don't know what you think milk bars are, but you've definitely got the wrong idea!

E: What are they then?

🎧 **3.5**

B: Linh, wait! But if I'm going to the university, I might as well catch the number 13. I think you've got it the wrong way round.

A: Probably! Listen, I think we need to start again from scratch. I'll have a think and get back to you in a minute, OK?

B: Ha ha. Good idea.

…

B: Hey!

A: Hi. OK, so it's really straightforward. Do you have a pen?

B: Yup.

A: So if we're starting from Cho Hom market, you can catch the number 23 bus that will take you all the way to Kim Ma bus station.

B: Right! That makes sense. I've never been on that bus, but I know where it stops at the market.

A: OK, then, once you're at Kim Ma, ask for the number 7 bus. You need to get off at the park - Youth Park. That's about a ten-minute journey.

B: Is it obvious where I have to get off?

A: Just get off after you see the children's park on the left and a big supermarket on the right.

B: Park on the left and supermarket on the right. Got it.

A: After that, if you walk through the park you'll see my street on the other side. Dien Bien Phu Street. I'm number 160 - Apartment 3.

B: … Apartment 3.

A: Right. Do you want to repeat that all back to me?

B: Sure. OK. So, Cho Hom market. Number 23 bus to the station. Ask for the number 7 bus …

Audioscripts

UNIT 4

🎧 4.1

Carolina: I love nature and I try to be close to it whenever I get the opportunity. I like planning long weekend trips to the sea for surfing or diving. I also enjoy hiking in the woods and listening to the birds in the trees.

I believe that staying in touch with nature is essential to maintain a healthy state of mind. Many of us live in big cities, surrounded by cars, buildings, roads and noise. I guess often I forget that before all these buildings and roads, this place was once covered with trees, and instead of all the noise would be the sounds of the birds. Personally, when I go to the ocean or to the forest, I feel more at peace and aware of my surroundings.

While doing my research, I worked in one of the most remote places in Colombia. The Choco region is a very tropical jungle next to the ocean. There, I interviewed lots of people in fishing communities and got the opportunity to hear about their stories and experiences. One fisherman once mentioned that his family wanted him to move to the city, far away from the place he knows and loves and he said 'it might seem that I don't have much here, but I have everything I need and I love this place. Also, the city's too chaotic! I like the peace of the sea and the jungle.' I will never forget that conversation.

🎧 4.4

I = Interviewer, F = Federico Fanti

I: So, do you still keep in touch with old school friends, Federico?

F: Yeah, there are a few of my friends I've never lost touch with. And we've always been there for one another.

I: And you still see them?

F: Yeah, I still get together with a couple of them from time to time. I mean, it helps working still in the same city I grew up in.

I: That's Bologna in Italy?

F: Yeah. And there's people I hadn't heard from for years, but we've reconnected. It's not as difficult to do that anymore, since Facebook and all of that. I am not a big fan of social media, so I use them to connect, but then I love to pick up the phone or use video calls to keep in touch. Many of my friends live on different continents, so I try to chat to them about once a month.

I: And what about work? I know you travel a lot for work. You must have made a lot of friendships along the way.

F: Absolutely! It's a part of the job I really love, meeting and working with new people, reconnecting with friends around the world. And when we're on a dig, it's essential to get along with everyone, you know, because you can be together for days or weeks at a time. Sometimes you have to work at relationships, you know scientists aren't always the easiest people! You don't want to fall out with anyone because you depend on them, and they depend on you.

Since I travel a lot, I might lose touch with the people I meet on different trips. They may not use social media or pick up a phone, a farmer in the middle of nowhere, for example, but I know if I stepped into their front yard and knocked on the door, they'd probably start a barbecue! There are some people I get along very well with. It could be two years before I see or speak to them again, or it could be ten years, but we always go straight back to friendship again. It's very nice.

I: Yeah, it must be nice going back to places you've been to before where you've made good friends. Is there anyone you've met in your work who you'd like to see more often?

F: Yeah, my best friend was born in Tokyo, Japan, and moved to Canada to become a dinosaur expert when he was young. We met by chance in Alberta, Canada, the first time I was there to complete my undergraduate studies. I was 22 and he was 17. When I was younger, I spent a lot of time in Alberta and we became really good friends. Then you get older and it's hard to be together – the last time we met in person was about two years ago! But we invite each other to dinosaur expeditions, we write research papers together and much more. We're not happy to live so far apart, but we know we can always count on each other.

🎧 4.5

1

A: It's been ages since I last saw you, so tell me what you're up to these …

B: Yeah, I'm curious as well, what's new?

C: Oh not much, you know, still got the same job …

B: That job in IT if I remember …

A: It's a pretty good one, isn't it? Aren't you in charge of …?

B: You're the boss!

C: Ha ha, something like that …

A: Actually, that reminds me …

B: Oh, I know what you're going to say, it reminds you of …

A: … reminds me of Gabriela. Isn't she also working …

C: Who's Gabriela?

2

D: So, are you still a book worm like you used to be when we were in school?

E: Yes. I still really like reading books.

D: I've never really got into reading to be honest. I only read them because we had to.

E: Yes, I remember. And not always, actually.

D: Yes, you're right.

E: Remember that time when you tried to copy the answers from me on a test? And the teacher caught you!

D: Of course! It's funny now, but it wasn't funny then. She told my parents and I got into big trouble!

3

F: Hey! It's so good to see the two of you!

G: You too! Look, Bee!

H: Hi Georgia!

F: Hey! Can you hear me OK?

H: Yeah, we can hear you just fine.

G: I love your earrings, Georgia.

F: Oh, thank you. They were a present from Ngozi. So tell me, how was your day?

H: It was really good. We learned some very interesting things at university.

F: Yeah, like what?

G: You'll love this! Tell her what you told me!

H: It's really amazing. So …

🎧 4.6

A: It's been ages since I last saw you, so tell me what you're up to these …

B: Yeah, I'm curious as well, what's new?

C: Oh not much, you know, still got the same job …

B: That job in IT if I remember …

A: It's a pretty good one, isn't it? Aren't you in charge of …?

B: You're the boss!

C: Ha ha, something like that …

A: Actually, that reminds me …

B: Oh, I know what you're going to say, it reminds you of …

A: … reminds me of Gabriela. Isn't she also working …

C: Sorry, can I just finish what I was saying?

A: Oh, yeah, sure, of course.

B: Absolutely. Sorry, we've talked too much already.

A: So, tell us more about your work.

C: Thanks! So anyway, as I was saying, I've still got the same job, but now I am working …

UNIT 5

🎧 5.2

1 She'd have been fine if she'd managed to sleep on the train.

2 We'd have slept a lot more comfortably last night if the bed had been a bit bigger.

🎧 5.3

I = Interviewer, A = Alec Jacobson, M = Maria Fadiman

I: So Alec, what do you do to stay in shape?

A: I run, road cycle, mountain bike and do some rock climbing and skiing. There's a lot of pressure for people to go to a gym but I think just find whatever it is you like to do and do that. I don't like running for running's sake, but I like to run in the mountains a lot, where I don't see anybody else for hours. If only a running machine is available that doesn't make me as happy.

I: I know you're out on the road a lot and you're very busy. How do you manage not to burn out when you're working?

A: Well, a big challenge is having a limited amount of time. And so I feel like I should be out taking photos or interviewing all the time. It's really easy to get into the habit of working too much and not sleeping enough. But I'm learning to recognize when to push and when to stop. I just wish I was able to sleep when I'm on the road, but I've never been able to take naps in cars or planes or whatever. Years ago, I did a class for journalists. And one of the tips was: if you're not healthy, you can't tell the story. So if you don't get sleep, the next day you can't get the story you need to tell. It's not like you can call in sick, you know?

I: How do you cope with being away from home for long periods?

M: When I'm in a place where I don't speak the language, there are times when everything is just so different, I feel like I can't express myself. And it's so frustrating when I just want to be able to say what I want to say. And I want to understand everyone else. And I'm trying so hard to do the right thing and to be respectful and not mess up. And it's just so exhausting … I'm basically suffering from stress. And so a way that I learned to cope with this was through writing.

I: Really? How does writing help?

M: When I'm writing, I can see it from the outside for just a moment so I can stop feeling sorry for myself. And it also lets me say exactly what I want to say. Sometimes I just want to shout 'Leave me alone!' which I would never say out loud, but I can write it in big, angry capitals. And that way I get it out of my system. And by talking about it in letters to my family, it also helps me understand where I am better and that lets me just kind of relax a little bit.

I: And is there anything else that you do to reduce the anxiety?

M: People have suggested I meditate, and I have tried it, but it's hard for me. But yoga is something I've added into my life. And that is huge for me. I walk out of there with my mind in a calm space. That is not usually how I am, my mind just jumps around. If only I'd discovered it before!

Audioscripts

D = doctor, P = patient

D: How can I help you?

P: Ehm, I have this pain in my foot.

D: OK, I was wondering if you could perhaps be slightly more precise than that.

P: …

D: Could you maybe elaborate a little bit more as to specifically what kind of pain you're experiencing? Is the pain acute or more of an ache?

P: You mean how the pain feels?

D: Yes, exactly, if you could be a bit more specific, that would be great. Is it very acute for example?

P: Ehm, I'm not sure to be honest …

D: Well, you'll need to definitely flesh out the details here for me if I'm to help you. If not the type of pain, do you mind perhaps pinpointing for me precisely whereabouts in your foot you're feeling the pain?

P: Ehm …

🎧 5.5

1 It's my back!
2 Is that your food?
3 He hit it with his hat.
4 Do you have it saved?
5 Take a seat.

🎧 5.6

D = doctor, P = patient, N = nurse

D: So good that you're here, Zhang. I've been trying to explain to the patient that I need her to elaborate on the type of pain she's feeling, but we don't seem to be getting anywhere …

N: Would you like me to help?

D: Yes, please.

N: Hello, can you tell the doctor what pain you feel in your foot?

P: Oh, OK, sure. Ehm, it's strong when I walk.

D: Can you ask her if it's an acute pain?

N: Is it a very sudden, quick pain?

P: I think it is very quick. When I put my foot down, I can feel it suddenly. And then it quickly goes.

N: If I remember right from my Spanish classes, the pain is *agudo*, right?

P: Sí, it's *agudo*!

D: OK, so it's an acute pain. Can you ask her to pinpoint whereabouts in the foot precisely she experiences the pain?

N: The doctor wants to know where in your foot you have the pain.

P: It's right here, at the bottom, close to my toes.

D: OK, we might need to get it X-rayed ASAP to get a better idea of what's going on.

N: We will need to take a picture of your foot now. We want to know what the problem is.

P: Sure.

UNIT 6

🎧 6.1

The plan to become carbon neutral within two years was revealed today by the Costa Rican government. This decision was praised by environmentalists around the world as it is hoped it will lead other nations to take similar action. The plan is thought to be an important step in the global fight against climate change. If successful, Costa Rica would become the first carbon neutral country in the world.

After a decade as the world's biggest-selling film, *Avatar* has lost its record. It has been beaten by the superhero blockbuster *Avengers: Endgame* which is said to have made 2.79 billion dollars from cinema ticket sales. That's one hundred thousand dollars more than *Avatar*. This is quite an incredible achievement considering that, back in 1996, Marvel was believed to be close to bankruptcy.

In sports, Eliud Kipchoge has made history after achieving what had been thought to be impossible – running a marathon in under two hours. However, it has been suggested that the shoes he was wearing gave him an unfair advantage. The shoes were designed to allow long-distance runners to run up to four per cent faster, but it is understood that the World Athletics committee might ban their use in the Olympics.

🎧 6.2

Crowds gathered to welcome Peter Tabichi as he returned from Dubai, where he had been chosen for the best teacher in the world award. The prize is thought to be one of the most important in the world. It is awarded for exceptional teaching achievements. Mr Tabichi was congratulated by the judges on his passion and for inspiring girls to study science. His students' scores are said to have improved dramatically since he started working at the school, and some have won international awards. Mr Tabichi is also admired for his charity. He gives away almost all of his salary every year to help children from poorer families. He is reported to be planning to also donate the one-million-dollar prize he received.

🎧 6.4

1 I get a lot of my news from social media.
2 The five-minute news bulletins give me an idea of what today's top stories are.
3 For example, I often read online newspapers and magazines

🎧 6.5

1 get a lot of
2 an idea of
3 read online

Int = Interviewer, I = Imogen Napper, A = Afroz Shah

Int: Where do you typically get your news from?

I: I get a lot of my news from social media, like Twitter. This is normally what I see when I wake up and go on my phone. But I also listen to podcasts to learn about stories and news more in depth. When I'm driving in the car, or working from home, I always have the radio on. The five-minute news bulletins give me an idea of what today's top stories are. And I watch the television to get foreign news, but I only watch this if I know something significant is happening.

A: I mainly get my news from the internet. But the sources vary a lot. For example, I often read online newspapers and magazines, such as New York Times, Kashmir Observer or Scientific America. I will often skim over the headlines first, before choosing the story that interests me. I definitely prefer news sources that provide more in-depth articles. There are many news reporting sources which I completely avoid, such as tabloid press, because of a lack of honesty, and often exaggerations that are filled with lies. I don't want to name such sources but there are many around!

Int: Have you ever stopped following the news?

I: Sometimes it just seems like a certain news story is on the front page of every newspaper and the headline of every news channel for weeks! You automatically start to ignore it because it isn't new anymore. Because you are so bored of it, you stop reading news stories in depth, you just skim over them. I even remember a radio host once saying 'I bet you are all bored to hear more about this news story again, but here are the latest updates.'

Int: What problems do you see with how the news is reported?

A: Because news has been largely commercialized these days, there is too much focus on certain types of news. In order to make the headlines, the news often has to be very sensational. I feel it's not about objective news reporting anymore but about clickbait articles with attention grabbing pictures. It is entirely on the readers to separate real from fake news.

Int: Has your work ever been reported by the media?

I: Since starting my PhD in 2015, there has been a huge amount of interest with plastic pollution in the ocean. This interest has grown and grown and resulted in some of my research making the headlines in the UK. I was really excited but also really nervous. I didn't want to say the wrong thing!

A: Yes, my work on earthquakes has been published by various media outlets. At first, I was slightly worried that the media might try to make the research sound more sensational. But I was really happy because the way it was reported was accurate and objective.

A: OK, so from what I can hear there are two possible cities, right? Fez or Marrakesh? What are we thinking at the moment? Fuad?

B: I say we go to Marrakesh. I think we'd struggle to find a better option.

C: I'm with you on that. I've read that it's been voted one of the top five cities to visit.

A: It <u>is</u> brilliant, but as I've already been there, would you be willing to consider another city instead?

B: You haven't been there for ten years! I'm sure lots has changed since then …

C: … Well, I've also heard from friends that Fez is supposed to be fantastic.

A: I'd be up for that. It might be a good compromise. What do you think?

B: Just think how much you'd regret missing the chance to see Marrakesh! Just picture this: the Bahia Palace with its beautiful decorations and peaceful gardens, the Jemaa el-Fna market; I know how much you love historical architecture. I'm just so excited about it all!

A: I can see where you're coming from and I understand this is a big thing when you've had Marrakesh on your mind for so long, so how about this: we go to Fez, but Albert and I will let you decide which places to visit for the first two days?

C: Er, yeah, I'd be happy with that, I think … Hey, I just looked at flights to Fez – they're half the price of those to Marrakesh!

B: What?! That can't be right. Let me see that. Are you sure that's the cheapest flight you can find? …

UNIT 7

A = Abby McBride, R = Robbie Shone

A: I don't spend much time in cities because they always make me feel crowded. I think it's a big challenge to have such a small amount of space for a large number of people.

R: I don't own a car. I use the train and buses when I'm here in Innsbruck. The public transport links are great. There are also a lot of road and rail tunnels through the mountains. This saves us from having to make long journeys around the mountains.

A: My living situation varies a lot. I don't own my own house, so there is usually some sort of space limitation that forces me to make adjustments. For example, if I'm staying with a friend for a few days, I might live out of my backpack. When I'm sharing a home with other people, the lack of personal space encourages me to spend time outdoors by myself.

Audioscripts

R: At home, I share my space with Gina, my fiancée, and our two cats, Zirby and Sakai. Fortunately, Gina and I have similar tastes and requirements. Her office is at the university, so that lets me use the home office. In the kitchen, we have a really neat corner cupboard that turns around, which permits us to store all our pots and pans without taking up much space.

A: Travelling so much prevents me from having too many possessions. I enjoyed living out of a car – a station wagon – for a year in New Zealand, because it enabled me to keep everything I needed with me all the time! Since I usually live out of a backpack, a car is more than enough space to keep things.

⌒ 7.2

advise	enable	permit	require
allow	encourage	prevent	

⌒ 7.3

I = Interviewer, R = Robbie Shone

I: Robbie Shone is an expert in 'extreme underground exploration'. He's been to some of the most out-of-the-way places on the planet, including the world's longest and deepest caves. As a photographer, it's his job to tell the story through pictures. Robbie hello, and thanks for talking to us today.

R: A pleasure.

I: Robbie, hopefully you can paint a picture for us of what it's like to visit these extraordinary sites. Just thinking about them frightens the life out of me.

R: Ha! It's not everybody's thing!

I: Do you ever get claustrophobia?

R: Not exactly, but I've been very frightened. My job takes me to some of the most challenging caves in the world. It's never a walk in the park! Sometimes when you're in a narrow passage or there's water around, it can get a bit hairy.

I: Have you had any <u>really</u> scary moments?

R: A couple of years ago we were in Abkhazia, Georgia on an expedition to explore an incredibly deep cave system called 'Veryovkina'. It's the deepest known cave in the world. It's at least two kilometres underground.

It took four days to get to the bottom where we camped. Then on day 10 or 11 we heard what sounded like a huge train coming down through the cave. Suddenly a huge wall of water fell from the black hole in the roof above us. It was deafening. Luckily, the water just missed us but the waterfall was right in the path of our way out. We waited to see how it would develop. After a few hours, everything changed as the water started rising fast. We had no time, so we quickly put our equipment on and one by one began climbing the ropes. It was hard to breathe as we were right in the middle of the waterfall. When the last person left the camp, it was already under water. That was very scary.

I: Have you been back there?

R: I have actually, the following year. Like they say, you've got to get back on the horse. The main reason was to complete the assignment and photograph the upper half of the cave. But also to get over the fear.

I: Don't you ever feel the need for your creature comforts, something a little cosier for a change?

R: When I'm away I don't tend to think about creature comforts because it's a distraction, but towards the end of an expedition, when the end is in sight, I start to think about home. I think about having a nice Italian coffee with my cat sat on my lap. I think about the beautiful view of the mountains from the balcony. I think about some good food and my comfortable bed.

I: And when you're not caving, do you ever feel the need to just get away from it all?

R: Well, it can be a bit strange going from living with nature on an expedition to being back on the busy streets in cities where everyone is rushing past you. On the journey home, I like to sit near the window so that I can look out and forget that I'm on a busy plane or a train. But my village only has a population of about 2,500 people, so home and its surroundings, the mountains, are my escape from my busy life.

⌒ 7.4

1

Brrr! I can't wait to get inside, out of this cold, damp weather and back to my cosy flat.

2

The charming narrow streets of the old town are densely crowded with tourists. It's a good idea to get here early to beat the crowds.

3

A: Where did you sleep?

B: On the first night we slept in the car …

A: Urgh!

B: Yeah! Which was a bit cramped, so we bought a four-man tent, which was more spacious.

A: Rather you than me!

4

C: Look! The view from the top is absolutely stunning!

D: Wow!

C: But it's so windy! Let's find a sheltered spot to eat our sandwiches.

D: Good idea.

5

Suddenly, the passage opened out into a bigger space. Their torches revealed a vast cave. The sight was breathtaking.

6

The rooms are elegantly decorated, with large windows that give them a light and airy feel.

A: So, I've heard you've got a new flatmate? How's he?
B: Oh, don't even get me started …
A: Now I really want to know!
B: He's just so messy. You wouldn't believe it!
A: But you're not too organized around the house either …
B: I know, but this is a different level, I'm telling you. For example, he's always leaving dirty dishes in the sink for days!
A: Ugh, that's disgusting!
B: I know! I wish he would wash them at least once a day.
A: Yeah, I mean, it only takes like five minutes, doesn't it?
B: Exactly! He's also such a party animal. I mean, I don't mind a house party every now and again, but it's a bit too much now. If only he had people over once a week, but it's like three or four nights a week!
A: Wow, that is a bit too much!
B: I know, right?
A: So what are you going to do?
B: I'm not sure to be honest. What would you do?
A: Hmmm, I'm not sure, but I might …

🎧 7.7

1 Could I make a suggestion? Why don't we write a 'to do' list together?
2 I understand that you want to relax in the evening, but so do I.
3 I'm sure you won't mind me asking this, but do you have some headphones you could use?
4 It's just that if you were able to avoid messaging me when I'm at work, I could reply sooner.

UNIT 8

🎧 8.1

N = Nora Shawk, F = Francisco Estada-Belli
N: I'm obsessed with sci fi as a genre. I used to be fascinated by it as a kid. I love that science fiction opens up your imagination. It makes you think and question certain realities. And it helps us try to understand ourselves as human beings more thoroughly.

F: I like the science fiction that is based on real science. I really enjoyed the film *The Martian*. I like the way the main character used his science background to solve challenges that at first seemed impossible to overcome, to survive all by himself on a distant planet and without communication.

N: I think sci-fi films mix reality with a little bit of imagination about science and technology. For example, *Back to the*

Future focuses on real life events but uses time travel. I loved that movie because of the time travel aspect of it. I was always fascinated by going backwards and forwards into different times. We don't have time travel technology yet, but it might be a possibility in the future, you never know!

F: I don't enjoy pseudo-archaeology, you know when it's not real at all, and when they invent all these strange theories about who built the pyramids and stuff like that. It affects my work as an archaeologist because, you know, people start believing these weird theories, so it kind of puts the scientific work we do in danger.

🎧 8.2

Nora: Papyrus was the ancient form of paper, made from the papyrus plant. Sometimes, if we're lucky, we find tightly rolled sheets of papyrus in scrolls – this was one of the earliest forms of a book! We know they used papyrus for writing but they also used it for making sandals to wear, baskets to keep things in and even rope to be used as a tool. Who knows what else they used it for? Papyrus is amazing because of what's written on it as well. They tell us amazing stories about Ancient Egypt.

Hieroglyphics are fascinating. They look like shapes. For centuries no one knew how to read them – that information was lost. I'm sure it was very exciting when the first people learned how to read them again. But we actually don't know what they sounded like in real life! This ancient Egyptian language does not have any vowels. You can't imagine a language without vowels, so there were definitely vowel sounds, they just didn't write them.

We find many clay pots all over sites in Egypt. They were used to hold many things and are the equivalent of our plastic nowadays. We also find many bread moulds which they used to bake bread, so it's possible they made bread in a similar way to how we make it today. There's no doubt pottery was very important to ancient Egyptians because they often had their best types of ceramic buried with them in their tombs!

🎧 8.3

1 The Egyptians may have used papyrus for many other things we don't know about.
2 It must have been very exciting to read hieroglyphics for the first time in centuries.
3 They can't have spoken without vowel sounds even though they only wrote the consonants.
4 They may have made bread in a similar way to how we make it today.
5 This type of pottery must have been very important to ancient Egyptians.

Audioscripts

🎧 8.4

1 He must have said something.
2 They can't have gone.
3 You shouldn't have done that!
4 It may have just been me.

🎧 8.5

Francisco: I'm an archaeologist. I study the Maya civilization - the people who lived in what is now southern Mexico, Guatemala and further south in Central America. I specialize in 'remote sensing', which is about being able to find things from high up, in planes and satellites. This uses a number of devices to find ancient remains - buildings and other structures - that might be on the surface or buried under the ground.

One new advanced technology, called LIDAR, is a measuring tool that allows you to map very accurately what is hiding below all those trees in the jungle. We use LIDAR to discover huge cities, roads, a whole landscape showing how people had once lived. Can you imagine ever doing this on foot? So LIDAR is really innovative and it has advanced the field enormously already. However, it's not very user-friendly; you need a lot of training because it's so sophisticated. Plus, it's very expensive.

There are a number of other gadgets that I use regularly in my line of work. But the one I really couldn't work without, because it's so handy, is my smartphone. I use my smartphone pretty much as a pocket-sized collection of gadgets that I had to carry separately before: G.P.S., compass, flashlight, camera and notepad.

But on the flip side, it's not waterproof, and there are a lot of places where it might get wet and damaged. The other problem is that it is always available and sometimes I forget to stop working even to eat!

🎧 8.6

1 We've had them for a number of years now.
2 MyCarYourCar is revolutionizing the way we travel from town to town.
3 That way they share the cost of the petrol.

🎧 8.7

H = host, M = Marsha, Y = Yuki, J = Jens

H: Today, we're talking about sharing apps. We've had them for a number of years now, and they've completely transformed the way we do business. I'm joined by Marsha Brewer, spokesperson for MyCarYourCar. Marsha, how does the app work?

M: Well, MyCarYourCar is revolutionizing the way we travel from town to town. It's handy and user-friendly. If you're travelling, you could catch an expensive train or a slow bus. With MyCarYourCar you can get the speed of driving for less than the cost of a bus. We put drivers going on a particular journey together with passengers who want to go on the same journey. That way they share the cost of the petrol and keep each other company at the same time.

H: OK, great! Let's open up the phone lines and find out what <u>you</u> have to say. Let's hear from Yuki.

Y: Hi. I think this sounds like a good idea, but I'd be worried about the people I travel with.

H: So you've never used a carpooling service?

Y: No, but when I was younger in Japan I once hitchhiked across the country with a friend. But I wouldn't hitch on my own, and I guess carpooling is like hitching. I don't think I would feel relaxed getting into a stranger's car. And not just because I'm a woman, but also just the idea of spending hours in a car with someone you don't like.

M: Except in the case of hitching you have no control over who your driver is, whereas with MyCarYourCar you can choose your driver. It's a common feeling you're expressing Yuki, but with MyCarYourCar you can read about and talk to the driver before you book. Most importantly, you can see what previous passengers thought about them. This ratings system makes sure the driver is trustworthy. And for women there's Women's Club - only female drivers and passengers.

Y: Well that's reassuring, definitely. But I'm still not sure if I could trust the ratings. It must be possible to get a good rating by behaving well for a few journeys, but that doesn't mean you will always be well-behaved.

H: True. Thanks very much for your call, Yuki. Now let's speak to Jens.

J: Hello, I use MyCarYourCar a lot as a passenger, and I am very keen on it. For me, it's just so easy and I enjoy the interaction with my fellow passengers. And it's good for the planet, reducing the number of cars on the road. It feels good to be part of the solution, you know.

H: Is that true I wonder? What about taking the train? Isn't that cleaner than travelling by road?

J: I read that if you're sharing cars, so instead of one person there are three or four people, and with cars being more efficient, more of them electric, and so on, then I don't think there's much difference.

M: That's true and, to be honest, we don't need to justify it by comparing it with trains. What about driving on your own, or flying for that matter? There's no doubt MyCarYourCar is a green choice.

H: OK, and I think we'll take a break …

UNIT 9

🎧 9.3

Robbie Shone, cave photographer, describes two failures in his career that taught him valuable lessons, not just about his work but also about life in general.

1

In 2009, I was on an expedition exploring the caves in Mulu National Park, Borneo. I had been practising cave photography for about nine years by this point. During one trip, we were exploring a huge river cave called Clearwater. The cave has many entrances but we came out of the main one where the river gushes out. To get out of the cave we all just simply jumped in the river. Despite the fact that it was quite safe, we still all needed buoyancy aids to help us float. I carry my camera equipment in a waterproof container so decided to use that as my buoyancy aid. The trip down the river was so much fun! At the end, we all climbed out of the water happy and excited.

However, when I picked up my camera case, it was unusually heavy. In my heart I knew what the problem was, though I really didn't want to believe it. I knelt down and opened the case and a flood of water gushed out. I picked up my camera but it was destroyed. I felt so bad. I had a lump in my throat. My expedition was over, or at least I thought it was. The expedition members all helped though. We made some phone calls and managed to get a new camera brought out from the UK. I was so thankful for having such good friends. Actually, I went on to take some of the best photos of my career at that point. The lesson to be learned – always travel with a second camera!

2

I think there's one incident which is huge for me. Even though it was painful, it really did help kick-start my career.

I was in Washington to show a National Geographic editor my work. I showed her a book of cave photos that I'd had printed especially. It was quite expensive for me at the time, but I thought the presentation was really important. However, the editor wasn't impressed at all. There was only one she liked and that was the last one.

I came away from the interview in tears. The feeling I had afterwards, I really thought my life was over. I had been working as a professional abseiler, painting bridges and insulating roofs in supermarkets. Whilst at work, I lived in a van. One week I only ate pepper sandwiches to save money. My parents wanted me to 'get a proper job'. But after that meeting, I felt like it had all been a complete waste of time.

But then, you come round and that's an incredible feeling when you convince yourself no, I'm not going to quit. So I went away and practised. I was told to work with other photographers and learn from them. And what you thought was a failure at first can actually make you better at what you do. And you're so much stronger because you're driven, it's the fire inside, it's huge. I certainly benefited so much by what happened on that day.

🎧 9.4

1 To get out of the cave we all just simply jumped in the river. Despite the fact that it was quite safe, we still all needed buoyancy aids to help us float.
2 And what you thought was a failure at first can actually make you better at what you do.

🎧 9.5

/ʃ/ ambition, professional, issue

/ʒ/ decision, vision

/tʃ/ achieve

/dʒ/ knowledge, manage, objectives, project

UNIT 10

🎧 10.2

Alyea: I remember visiting Trinidad and Tobago for the first time. It was the month of August, which is hurricane season in the Caribbean. The first thing you'll notice is the humidity. And then you'll notice the heat. As my uncle gave us a tour of the country, we saw young people, older people, people of all races and religions, but there was one particular type of people that stood out most to me. As we were walking through the streets of Port of Spain, I kept seeing young people with two sticks in their back pockets. Quite curious about these people and the sticks, I turned to my uncle, and he said, 'They are called pannists. And those are their steel pan sticks. You usually always know a steel pan player because they get used to carrying those sticks everywhere with them.' So a pannist uses the metal sticks and pans like drums and drummer sticks to create music. Typically, steel pan musicians tend to range in age. In a traditional, Caribbean band you can find a player as young as in their early teens and as old as 85. As a past musician myself, I always appreciate the fact that when you meet a pannist, visit their home, or even travel in their car, you will find some reminder of their instrument. From the music playing out of their speakers, the variety of sticks depending on what kind of sound they want the pan to make, the pan itself, the stand, or even just the case, pan is a way of life.

Audioscripts

I = interviewer, L = Lia Nahomi Kajiki

I: Hi Lia, I want to start by talking about your cultural roots. You're of a mixed Brazilian and Japanese background: which of the two do you feel you most fit in with?

L: Sometimes I'm not sure which. It can be very difficult to identify with one. Although I feel much more familiarity with Brazilian culture, sometimes I'm not sure how I fit in. I'm a bit lost in this mix of things, because I also feel that I sometimes behave much more like a Japanese or, you know, have a way of thinking that's more Japanese. I'd say I share some of the same typical values as the Japanese. So, yeah, I think that I'm now like 70, maybe 75, per cent Brazilian and 25 per cent Japanese.

I: That's fascinating! What about the rest of your family? Do you think they feel similar to you? 75 per cent Brazilian and 25 per cent Japanese?

L: I think some don't, especially my father, who was born in Japan. I think he feels more the opposite to me because he grew up talking in Japanese with his family. So even though he was raised in Brazil and went to Brazilian schools, he felt a little bit like an outsider being Japanese in a Brazilian school. Now he sees himself as Brazilian, but he always watches Japanese TV channels and he's always following the news about Japan. So I think sometimes he doesn't feel like he fits in.

I: You also mentioned you sometimes 'behave like a Japanese'. What does behaving like a Japanese mean to you?

L: I feel the way I express my opinion in public has been influenced by my Japanese origins. Japanese are usually very cautious in how they express themselves, and the whole culture reflects it – the language, poetry style, painting styles, etc. When I have to express my opinion, I only do it when I feel I will contribute to the conversation.

I: You also practise kyūdō, which is Japanese archery, right?

L: Yes. I feel it makes me feel reconnected with my Japanese origins and I feel the practice changes my perspective on the world and myself. I also love kyūdō because the people who practise it share the same values and goals in this martial art and in their lives: the 'shin-zen-bi', which means truth-goodness-beauty.

I: Coming back to your 75 per cent of culture, what does it mean for you to be Brazilian? What makes you feel like a Brazilian?

L: This is a very difficult question! Brazil is very diverse culturally. People in Brazil come from very mixed backgrounds because of our history of colonization and immigration. The South has a lot of European influence in their food, architecture, music. On the other hand, the North still keeps its indigenous roots, while the Northeast its African roots. I feel this is really beautiful and that we should celebrate this diversity.

I: Absolutely! But tell me, what brings such a diverse nation together?

L: One thing is football, especially during the World Cup! For me, to be a Brazilian is also to know how to enjoy life. And we all share a sense of hospitality, even with strangers and foreigners.

1

I: Hi Lia, I want to start by talking about your cultural roots. You're of a mixed Brazilian and Japanese background: which of the two do you feel you most fit in with?

2

I: That's fascinating! What about the rest of your family? Do you think they feel similar to you? 75 per cent Brazilian and 25 per cent Japanese?

L: I think some don't, especially my father, who was born in Japan.

3

I: Absolutely! But tell me, what brings such a diverse nation together?

L: One thing is football, especially during the World Cup!

A = Amanda, V = Vihaan

A: How was the meeting with the supervisor? Same?

V: Yeah! She just closes her eyes as soon as I start talking! It's really weird! I'm worried that she doesn't like me, or I'm just boring her stupid!

A: You're not boring, Vihaan. And there's no way she doesn't like you. Everyone likes you!

V: That's really nice of you! But, I don't know, I was expecting her to show a bit more interest in my work.

A: You said before that she does make comments … ?

V: That's the weird thing. She asks questions and I do find what she says useful. So maybe she isn't bored! Maybe I'm just assuming that, but I could be wrong.

A: Right. I mean, being bored isn't the only reason she'd close her eyes.

V: I guess. Perhaps she needs to close her eyes for some reason to concentrate on what I'm saying better?

A: Well, you do talk very fast.

V: Do I? I do, don't I? Oh my goodness, maybe that's why! My dad closes his eyes sometimes when I'm talking to him.

A: Ha ha! I do it when I'm concentrating on music.

V: Actually, I block my ears when I'm reading in a noisy place, and this is similar, I guess.

A: I've seen you do that! Well, there you go. It's probably just her way of listening properly. Making sure she gets every word.

V: Yeah, maybe you're right. Next time I won't worry so much. Maybe I should slow down a bit, too.

A: That might help.

Acknowledgements

The Voices publishing team would like to thank all of the explorers for their time and participation on this course – and for their amazing stories and photos.

The team would also like to thank the following teachers, who provided detailed and invaluable feedback on this course.

Asia

SS. Abdurrosyid, University of Muhammadiyah Tangerang, Banten; Hằng Ánh, Hanoi University of Science Technology, Hanoi; Yoko Atsumi, Seirei Christopher University, Hamamatsu; Dr. Nida Boonma, Assumption University, Bangkok; Portia Chang, SEE Education, New Taipei City; Brian Cullen, Nagoya Institute of Technology, Nagoya; David Daniel, Houhai English, Beijing; Professor Doan, Hanoi University, Hanoi; Kim Huong Duong, HCMC University of Technology, Ho Chi Minh; Natalie Ann Gregory, University of Kota Kinabalu, Sabah; Shawn Greynolds, AUA Language Center, Bangkok; Thi Minh Ly Hoang, University of Economics – Technology for Industries, Hanoi; Mike Honywood, Shinshu University, Nagano; Jessie Huang, National Central University, Taoyuan City; Edward Jones, Nagoya International School, Nagoya; Ajarn Kiangkai, Sirnakarintrawirote University, Bangkok; Zhou Lei, New Oriental Education & Technology Group, Beijing; Louis Liu, METEN, Guangzhou; Jeng-Jia (Caroline) Luo Tunghai University, Taichung City; Thi Ly Luong, Huflit University, Ho Chi Minh City; Michael McCollister, Feng Chia University, Taichung; Robert McLaughlin, Tokoha University, Shizuoka; Hal Miller, Houhai English, Beijing; Jason Moser, Kanto Gakuin University, Yokohama; Hudson Murrell, Baiko Gakuin University, Shimonoseki; Takayuki Nagamine, Nagoya University of Foreign Studies, Nagoya; Sanuch Natalang, Thammasart University, Bangkok; Nguyen Bá Học, Hanoi University of Public Health, Hanoi; Nguyen Cong Tri, Ho Chi Minh City University of Technology, Ho Chi Minh; Nguyen Ngoc Vu, Hoa Sen University, Ho Chi Minh City; Professor Nguyen, Hanoi University, Hanoi; Dr Nguyen, Hao Sen University, Ho Chi Minh City; Nguyễn Quang Vịnh, Hanoi University, Hanoi; Wilaichitra Nilsawaddi, Phranakhon Rajabhat University, Bangkok; Suchada Nimmanit, Rangsit University, Bangkok; Ms. Cao Thien Ai Nuong, Hoa Sen University, Ho Chi Minh City; Donald Patterson, Seirei Christopher University, Shizuoka; Douglas Perkins, Musashino University Junior and Senior High School, Tokyo; Phan The Hung, Van Lang University, Ho Chi Minh City; Fathimah Razman, Northern University, Sintok, Kedah; Bruce Riseley, Holmesglen (Language Centre of University Of Muhammadiyah Tangerang for General English), Jakarta; Anthony Robins, Aichi University of Education, Aichi; Greg Rouault, Hiroshima Shudo University, Hiroshima; Dr Sawaluk, Sirnakarintrawirote University, Bangkok; Dr Supattra, Rangsit University, Lak Hok; Dr Thananchai, Dhurakijbundit University, Bangkok; Thao Le Phuong, Open University, Ho Chi Minh; Thap Doanh Thuong, Thu Dau Mot University, Thu Dau Mot; Kinsella Valies, University of Shizuoka, Shizuoka; Gerrit Van der Westhuizen, Houhai English, Beijing; Dr Viraijitta, Rajjabhat Pranakorn University, Bangkok; Dr Viraijittra, Phranakhon Rajabhat University, Bangkok; Vo Dinh Phuoc, University of Economics, Ho Chi Minh City; Dr Nussara Wajsom, Assumption University, Bangkok; Scott A.Walters, Woosong University, Daejon; Yungkai Weng, PingoSpace & Elite Learning, Beijing; Ray Wu, Wall Street English, Hong Kong.

Europe, Middle East and Africa (EMEA)

Saju Abraham, Sohar University, Sohar; Huda Murad Al Balushi, International Maritime College , Sohar; Salah Al Hanshi, Modern College of Business and Science, Muscat; Victor Alarcón, EOI Badalona, Barcelona; Yana Alaveranova, International House, Kiev; Alexandra Alexandrova, Almaty; Blanca Alvarez, EOI San Sebastian de los Reyes, Madrid; Emma Antolin, EOI San Sebastian de los Reyes, Madrid; Manuela Ayna, Liceo Primo Levi, Bollate, Milan; Elizabeth Beck, British Council, Milan; Charlotte Bentham, Adveti, Sharjah; Carol Butters, Edinburgh College, Edinburgh; Patrizia Cassin, International House, Milan; Elisabet Comelles, EIM - Universitat de Barcelona, Barcelona; Sara De Angeles, Istituto Superiore Giorgi, Milan; Carla Dell'Acqua, Liceo Primo Levi, Bollate, Milan; John Dench, BEET Language Centre, Bournemouth; Angela di Staso, Liceo Banfi, Vimercate, Milan; Sarah Donno, Edinburgh College, Edinburgh, UK; Eugenia Dume, EOI San Sebastian de los Reyes, Madrid; Rory Fergus Duncan; BKC-IH Moscow, Moscow; Ms Evelyn Kandalaft El Moualem, AMIDEAST, Beirut; Raul Pope Farguell, BKC-IH Moscow, Moscow; Chris Farrell, CES, Dublin; Dr Aleksandra, Filipowicz, Warsaw University of Technology, Warsaw; Diana Golovan, Linguist LLC, Kiev, Ukraine; Jaap Gouman, Pieter Zandt, Kampen; Maryam Kamal, British Council, Doha; Galina Kaptug, Moonlight, Minsk; Ms Rebecca Nabil Keedi, College des Peres Antonines, Hadath; Dr. Michael King, Community College of Qatar, Doha; Gabriela Kleckova, University of West Bohemia, Pilsen; Mrs Marija Klečkovska, Pope John Paul II gymnasium, Vilnius; Kate Knight, International Language School, Milan; Natalia Kolina, Moscow; David Koster, P.A.R.K., Brno; Suzanne Littlewood, Zayed University, Dubai; Natalia Lopez, EOI Terrassa, Barcelona; Maria Lopez-Abeijon, EOI Las Rozas, Madrid; Pauline Loriggio, International House London, London; Gabriella Luise, International Language School Milan, Milan; Klara Malowiecka, Lang Ltc, Warsaw; Fernando Martin, EOI Valdemoro, Madrid; Robert Martinez, La Cunza, Gipuzkoa; Mario Martinez, EOI Las Rozas, Madrid; Marina Melnichuk, Financial University, Moscow; Martina Menova, PĚVÁČEK vzdělávací centrum, Prague; Marlene Merkt, Kantonsschule Zurich Nord, Zurich; Iva Meštrović, Učilište Jantar, Zagreb; Silvia Milian, EOI El Prat, Barcelona; Jack Montelatici, British School Milan, Milan; Muntsa Moral, Centre de Formació de Persones Adultes Pere Calders, Barcelona; Julian Oakley, Wimbledon School of English, London; Virginia Pardo, EOI Badalona, Barcelona; William Phillips, Aga Khan Educational Service; Joe Planas, Centre de Formació de Persones Adultes Pere Calders, Barcelona; Carmen Prieto, EOI Carabanchel, Madrid; Sonya Punch, International House, Milan; Magdalena Rasmus,

Acknowledgements

Cavendish School, Bournemouth; Laura Rodríguez, EOI El Prat, Barcelona; Victoria Samaniego, EOI Pozuelo, Madrid; Beatriz Sanchez, EOI San Sebastian de los Reyes, Madrid; Gigi Saurer, Migros-Genossenschafts-Bund, Zurich; Jonathan Smilow, BKC-IH, Moscow; Prem Sourek, Anderson House, Bergamo; Svitlana Surgai, British Council, Kyiv; Peter Szabo, Libra Books, Budapest; Richard Twigg, International House, Milan; Evgeny Usachev, Moscow International Academy, Moscow; Eric van Luijt, Tilburg University Language Centre, Tilburg; Tanya Varchuk, Fluent English School, Ukraine; Yulia Vershinina, YES Center, Moscow; Małgorzata Witczak, Warsaw University of Technology, Warsaw; Susanna Wright, Stafford House London, London; Chin-Yunn Yang, Padagogische Maturitaetsschule Kreuzlingen, Kreuzlingen; Maria Zarudnaya, Plekhanov Russian University of Economics, Moscow; Michelle Zelenay, KV Winterthur, Winterthur.

Latin America

Jorge Aguilar, Universidad Autónoma de Sinaloa, Culiacán; Carlos Bernardo Anaya, UNIVA Zamora, Zamora; Sergio Balam, Academia Municipal de Inglés, Mérida; Josélia Batista, CCL Centro de Línguas, Fortaleza; Aida Borja, ITESM GDL, Guadalajara; Diego Bruekers Deschamp, Ingles Express, Belo Horizonte; Alejandra Cabrera, Universidad Politécnica de Yucatán, Mérida; Luis Cabrera Rocha, ENNAULT – UNAM, Mexico City; Bruna Caltabiano, Caltabiano Idiomas, São Paulo; Hortensia Camacho, FES Iztacala – UNAM, Mexico City; Gustavo Cruz Torres, Instituto Cultural México – Norteamericano, Guadalajara; Maria Jose D'Alessandro Nogueira, FCM Foundation School, Belo Horizonte; Gabriela da Cunha Barbosa Saldanha, FCM Foundation School, Belo Horizonte; Maria Da Graça Gallina Flack, Challenge School, Porto Alegre; Pedro Venicio da Silva Guerra, U-Talk Idiomas, São Bernardo do Campo; Julice Daijo, JD Language Consultant, Rua Oscar Freire; Olívia de Cássia Scorsafava, U-Talk Idiomas, São Bernardo do Campo; Marcia Del Corona, UNISINOS, Porto Alegre; Carlos Alberto Díaz Najera, Colegio Salesiano Anáhuac Revolución, Guadalajara; Antônio César Ferraz Gomes, 4 Flags, São Bernardo do Campo; Brenda Pérez Ferrer, Universidad Politécnica de Querétaro, Querétaro; Sheila Flores, Cetys Universidad, Mexicali; Ángela Gamboa, Universidad Metropolitana, Mérida; Alejandro Garcia, Colegio Ciencias y Letras, Tepic; Carlos Gomora, CILC, Toluca; Kamila Gonçalves, Challenge School, Porto Alegre; Herivelton Gonçalves, Prime English, Vitória; Idalia Gonzales, Británico, Lima; Marisol Gutiérrez Olaiz, LAMAR Universidad, Guadalajara; Arturo Hernandez, ITESM GDL, Guadalajara; Gabriel Cortés Hernandez, BP- Intitute, Morelia; Daniel Vázquez Hernández, Preparatoria 2, Mérida; Erica Jiménez, Centro Escolar, Tepeyac; Leticia Juárez, FES Acatlán – UNAM, Mexico City; Teresa Martínez, Universidad Iberoamericana, Tijuana; Elsa María del Carmen Mejía Franco, CELE Mex, Toluca; José Alejandro Mejía Tello, CELE Mex, Toluca; Óscar León Mendoza Jimenéz, Angloamericano Idiomas, Mexico City; Karla Mera Ubando, Instituto Cultural, Mexico City; Elena Mioto, UNIVA, Guadalajara; Ana Carolina Moreira Paulino, SENAC, Porto Alegre; Paula Mota, 4 Flags, São Bernardo do Campo; Adila Beatriz Naud de Moura, UNISINOS, Porto Alegre; Monica Navarro Morales, Instituto Cultural, Mexico City; Wilma F Neves, Caltabiano Idiomas, São Paulo; Marcelo Noronha, Caltabiano Idiomas, São Paulo; Enrique Ossio, ITESM Morelia, Morelia; Filipe Pereira Bezerra, U-Talk Idiomas, São Bernardo do Campo; Florencia Pesce, Centro Universitario de Idiomas, Buenos Aires, Argentina; Kamila Pimenta, CCBEU, São Bernardo do Campo; Leopoldo Pinzón Escobar, Universidad Santo Tomás, Bogotá; Mary Ruth Popov Hibas, Ingles Express, Belo Horizonte; Alejandra Prado Barrera, UVM, Mexico City; Letícia Puccinelli Redondo, U-Talk Idiomas, São Bernardo do Campo; Leni Puppin, Centro de Línguas de UFES, Vitória; Maria Fernanda Quijano, Universidad Tec Milenio, Culiacan; Jorge Quintal, Colegio Rogers, Mérida; Sabrina Ramos Gomes, FCM Foundation School, Belo Horizonte; Mariana Roberto Billia, 4 Flags, São Bernardo do Campo; Monalisa Sala de Sá 4 Flags, São Bernardo do Campo; Yamel Sánchez Vízcarra, CELE Mex, Toluca; Vagner Serafim, CCBEU, São Bernardo do Campo; Claudia Serna, UNISER, Mexicali; Alejandro Serna, CCL, Morelia; Simone Teruko Nakamura, U-Talk Idiomas, São Bernardo do Campo; Desirée Carla Troyack, FCM Foundation School, Belo Horizonte; Sandra Vargas Boecher Prates, Centro de Línguas da UFES, Vitória; Carlos Villareal, Facultad de Ingenierías Universidad Autónoma de Querétaro, Querétaro; Rosa Zarco Mondragón, Instituto Cultural, Mexico City.

US and Canada

Rachel Bricker, Arizona State University, Tempe; Jonathan Bronson, Approach International Student Center, Boston; Elaine Brookfield, EC Boston, Boston; Linda Hasenfus, Approach International Language Center, Boston; Andrew Haynes, ELS Boston, Boston; Cheryl House, ILSC, Toronto; Rachel Kadish, FLS International, Boston; Mackenzie Kerby, ELS Language Centers, Boston; Rob McCourt FLS Boston; Haviva Parnes, EC English Language Centres, Boston; Shayla Reid, Approach International Student Center, Boston.

172

Credits

Illustration: All illustrations are owned by © Cengage.

Cover: © Jim Richardson; **3** David McNew/Getty Images News/Getty Images; **4** (tl1) Yoan Valat/European Pressphoto Agency/Newscom, (tl2) © Gabriele Galimberti, (cl) © Peter Amend, (bl1) Stringer/AFP/Getty Images, (bl2) VCG/Getty Images; **6** (tl1) NASA, (tl2) Olga Kolos/Alamy Stock Photo, (cl) David Ramos/Getty Images News/Getty Images, (bl1) David McNew/Getty Images News/Getty Images, (bl2) pixelfusion3d/E+/Getty Images; **8** (tl) © Edin Whitehead, (tr) © Fernando Caamano, KipperTie, (cl1) Courtesy of Afroz Ahmad Shah, (cr1) © Arianna Soldati, (cl2) © Alec Jacobson, (cr2) © Carolina Chong Montenegro, (bl) Courtesy of Alyea Pierce, (br) Courtesy of Ellie de Castro; **8-9** (spread) Robert Harding Picture Library/National Geographic Image Collection; **9** (tl) Courtesy of Federico Fanti, (tr) Courtesy of Maria Fadiman, (cl1) Courtesy of Francisco Estrada-Belli, (cr1) © Nora Shawki, (cl2) © Eleanor Burfitt, (cr2) © Paola Rodriguez-Troncoso, (bl) © Caio Felipe Santos da Silva, (br) Courtesy of Robbie Shone, (bc) © Tsiory Andrianavalona; **10-11** (spread) Yoan Valat/European Pressphoto Agency/Newscom; **11** (br1) © Tsiory Andrianavalona, (br2) Courtesy of Francisco Estrada-Belli; **13** Benjamin John/Alamy Stock Photo; **15** Source: Google LLC; **16** Andrew Caballero-Reynolds/AFP/Getty Images; **18** Dinodia Photos/Alamy Stock Photo; **20** (tl) DCPhoto/Alamy Stock Photo, (bl) Masterfile; **22-23** (spread) © Gabriele Galimberti; **23** (br1) Courtesy of Maria Fadiman, (br2) © Arianna Soldati; **25** (tl) Christian Ziegler/National Geographic Image Collection, (tc1) George Grall/National Geographic Image Collection, (tc2) zhaojiankang/iStock/Getty Images, (tr) Jon Hilmarsson/Moment/Getty Images, (b) Boscorelli/Alamy Stock Photo, (bl) Atsuo Fujimaru/Minden Pictures; **26** Courtesy of Arianna Soldati; **27** Sam Edwards/OJO images/Getty Images; **28** robertharding/Alamy Stock Photo; **30** Tom Werner/DigitalVision/Getty Images; **32** Anastasia Lembrik/Shutterstock.com; **34-35** (spread) © Peter Amend; **35** (br1) © Fernando Caamano, KipperTie, (br2) Courtesy of Ellie de Castro; **37** © Susan Seubert; **38** Courtesy of Andrej Gajić; **40** (t) AB Forces News Collection/Alamy Stock Photo, (bl1) Andrey_Kuzmin/Shutterstock.com, (bl2) LongQuattro/Shutterstock.com; **43** Elizaveta Galitckaia/Alamy Stock Photo; **44** MarBom/iStock/Getty Images; **46-47** (spread) Stringer/AFP/Getty Images; **47** (br1) Courtesy of Federico Fanti, (br2) © Carolina Chong Montenegro; **49** 501room/iStock Editorial/Getty Images; **50** Michael Hanson/Stock/National Geographic Image Collection; **52** Courtesy of Federico Fanti; **54** Lucy Lambriex/DigitalVision/Getty Images; **55** (tl) Bojanovic/Shutterstock.com, (tc) jo1/Shutterstock.com, (tr) chwl/Shutterstock.com; **56** skynesher/E+/Getty Images; **58-59** (spread) VCG/Getty Images; **59** (br1) Courtesy of Maria Fadiman, (br2) © Alec Jacobson; **61** (tr) photomaster/Shutterstock.com, (bl) © Mark Henderson; **64** (tl) Lynn Johnson/National Geographic Image Collection, (tr) Jonathan Torgovnik/Getty Images News/Getty Images, (cl) Kieran Dodds/Panos Pictures/Redux, (cr) andresr/E+/Getty Images; **66** Tom Werner/DigitalVision/Getty Images; **68** © Gijsbert van der Wal; **70-71** (spread) NASA; **71** (br1) Courtesy of Afroz Ahmad Shah, (br2) © Eleanor Burfitt; **73** (tl) © Jason

Michael McCann/Twitter: @Jeggit, (tr1) Source: First Media, (tr2) Still from Dali Lives © Salvador Dalí Museum, Inc., St. Petersburg, FL, 2020; **74** Herbert Neubauer/AFP/Getty Images; **76** (bc1) (bc2) tanuha2001/Shutterstock.com; **78** Ivy Close Images/Alamy Stock Photo; **80** IRA Block/National Geographic Image Collection; **82-83** (spread) Olga Kolos/Alamy Stock Photo; **83** (br1) © Edin Whitehead, (br2) Courtesy of Robbie Shone; **85** (tl) phichak/Shutterstock.com, (tr) © Paola S. Branco, (b) Peter R. Houlihan/National Geographic Image Collection; **86** SSphotography/Moment Unreleased/Getty Images; **87** (bl) ISA Harsin/SIPA/Newscom, (bc1) AU Photos/Alamy Stock Photo, (bc2) Horacio Garcia Martin/Shutterstock.com, (br) © CJ Worx; **88** Robbie Shone/National Geographic Image Collection; **90** mediaphotos/E+/Getty Images; **92** (bc1) Colorlife/Shutterstock.com, (bc2) safroni safroni/Shutterstock.com, (bc3) Colorlife/Shutterstock.com, (bc4) Eliyev1/Shutterstock.com; **93** (tl1) Andrey_Popov/Shutterstock.com, (tl2) © Bournemouth News and Picture Service, (cl1) (cl2) Andrey_Popov/Shutterstock.com, (bl) dpa picture alliance/Alamy Stock Photo; **94-95** (spread) David Ramos/Getty Images News/Getty Images; **95** (br1) © Nora Shawki, (br2) Courtesy of Francisco Estrada-Belli; **97** (tr) AF archive/Alamy Stock Photo, (b) Atlaspix/Alamy Stock Photo; **98** (bgd) Vadim Sadovski/Shutterstock.com, (c1) Werner Forman/Universal Images Group/Getty Images, (c2) Everett Collection Historical/Alamy Stock Photo, (bc1) ART Collection/Alamy Stock Photo, (bc2) Dinodia Photos/Alamy Stock Photo; **99** (cr) Science & Society Picture Library/Getty Images, (br) © National Museum of the American Indian, Smithsonian Institution (21/0796); **100** © Pacunam/Estrada-Belli; **103** (t) Lukas Rs/Shutterstock.com, (b) Westend61/Getty Images; **104** (tl1) Avijit Sadhu/iStock/Getty Images, (tl2) Dmitry9131/Shutterstock.com, (cl1) Celine Nguyen/EyeEm/Getty Images, (cl2) N8Allen/Shutterstock.com; **106-107** (spread) David McNew/Getty Images News/Getty Images; **107** (br1) Courtesy of Robbie Shone, (br2) © Paola Rodriguez-Troncoso; **109** (tc) Laurent Koffel/Gammo-Rapho/Getty Images, (tr) Francois Nel/Getty Images Sport/Getty Images, (bl) Hulton Deutsch/Corbis Historical/Getty Images, (bc) Tristan Fewings/Getty Images Entertainment/Getty Images; **111** Matthieu Paley/National Geographic Image Collection; **112** makeitdouble/Shutterstock.com; **116** Design Pics Inc/National Geographic Image Collection; **118-119** (spread) pixelfusion3d/E+/Getty Images; **119** (br1) Courtesy of Alyea Pierce, (br2) © Caio Felipe Santos da Silva; **121** © Kike Calvo; **123** © Alyea Pierce; **124** (t) © Helder Shin, (cl) Lisa Kolbasa/Shutterstock.com, (c) ShustrikS/Shutterstock.com, (bl) Lisa Kolbasa/Shutterstock.com, (bc) Sugiyarto/Shutterstock.com; **126** PeopleImages/E+/Getty Images; **128** Robert Harding Picture Library/National Geographic Image Collection; **130** (tl) Yoan Valat/European Pressphoto Agency/Newscom, (tr) © Gabriele Galimberti; **131** (tl) © Peter Amend, (tr) Stringer/AFP/Getty Images; **132** (tl) VCG/Getty Images, (tr) NASA; **133** (tl) Olga Kolos/Alamy Stock Photo, (tr) David Ramos/Getty Images News/Getty Images; **134** (tl) David McNew/Getty Images News/Getty Images, (tr) pixelfusion3d/E+/Getty Images.

Music: 120 © Kike Calvo.

Credits